ALLERGY COOKING WITH EASE

The No Wheat, Milk, Eggs, Corn, Soy, Yeast, Sugar, Grain and Gluten Cookbook

Revised Edition

Foreword by Dr. William Crook, author of *The Yeast Connection*

Nicolette M. Dumke

ALLERGY COOKING WITH EASE:
THE NO WHEAT, MILK, EGGS, CORN, SOY, YEAST, SUGAR, GRAIN AND GLUTEN COOKBOOK
REVISED EDITION

Published by
Adapt Books
Allergy Adapt, Inc.
1877 Polk Avenue
Louisville, Colorado 80027
303-666-8253

©2007 by Nicolette M. Dumke
Printed in the United States of America
Cover design by Ed Nies, Mel Typesetting,
1523 S. Pearl St., Suite B, Denver, Colorado 80210, 303-777-5571

Publisher's Cataloging-in-Publication
(Provided by Quality Books, Inc.)

Dumke, Nicolette M.
    Allergy cooking with ease : the no wheat, milk, eggs,
corn, soy, yeast, sugar, grain and gluten cookbook /
Nicolette M. Dumke ; foreword by William Crook. -- Rev.
ed.
    238 p. 24.6 cm.
    Includes bibliographical references and index.
    LCCN 2006907351
    ISBN-13: 978-1-887624-10-7
    ISBN-10: 1-887624-10-4

    1. Food allergy--Diet therapy--Recipes.   I. Title.

RC588.D53D86 2007   616.97'50654
        QBI06-600547

Dedication

To my husband, Mark, who encourages me,

To my sons, Joel and John,
who inspired cooking creativity as little boys
and now are creative cooks themselves,

To my mother, Mary Jiannetti,
who taught me to love cooking,

And to the memory of my father,
Eugene Jiannetti,
who was my best taster.

Disclaimer

The information contained in this book is merely intended to communicate food preparation material and information about possible treatment options which are helpful and educational to the reader. It is not intended to replace medical diagnosis or treatment, but rather to provide information and recipes which may be helpful in implementing a diet prescribed by your doctor. Please consult your physician for medical advice before embarking on any treatment or changing your diet.

The author and publisher declare that to the best of their knowledge all material in this book is accurate; however, although unknown to the author and publisher, some recipes may contain ingredients which may be harmful to some people.

There are no warranties which extend beyond the educational nature of this book, either expressed or implied, including, but not limited to, the implied warranties of merchantability, fitness for a particular purpose, or non-infringement. Therefore, the author and publisher shall have neither liability nor responsibility to any person with respect to any loss or damage alleged to be caused, directly or indirectly, by the information contained in this book.

If you do not wish to be bound by the above, you may return this book to the publisher for a full refund.

Table of Contents

Foreword

During the past 35 years I've helped thousands of patients with food allergies and other types of food sensitivities. I've accomplished this by putting people on one week trial elimination diets. If and when the person's symptoms improved (as they usually did), the eliminated foods were eaten again one food per day and reactions were noted.

Using this program, many of my patients found that they were sensitive to milk, wheat, corn, egg, and other of their favorite foods.

So, they would come back to me and say, "What can I eat and how can I prepare foods for my family?" In responding to these questions over the years, I have used and recommended many different recipes and many books. Yet, I'm always keeping my mind and eyes open in my search to help my patients.

Then, in the summer of 1991, I received the manuscript of Nickie Dumke's *Allergy Cooking with Ease*. I reviewed this book and liked it. Because I don't claim to be a cook, I passed it along to my allergy colleague, Nell Sellers, who has worked with me and prepared recipes for my patients during the past 30 years. Here are Nell's comments:

"*Allergy Cooking with Ease* is a gem of a book. It incorporates all of the key points I've been telling our patients for years! She even includes starting the rotation diet day at dinner so you'll have food for breakfast and lunch the next day. Her book includes something for everybody. She agrees that the diet has to be livable or people won't follow it for long."

Features of this book include:
- Maintaining a positive attitude
- Diversifying and rotating the diet
- Providing readers with treats using ingredients which are least likely to cause problems.

Other tips in this book include stocking up so as to always have permissible foods on hand to lessen the chances of cheating and making big batches of baked foods and storing them in the freezer for later rotation.

A final word: Nickie Dumke's book isn't only a recipe book. It encourages people to enjoy family, friends, work, and recreation. She says in effect, "Be good to yourself. Don't worry if you fall off your diet now and then. You can always pick yourself up and go at it again."

If you or members of your family are troubled by food allergies or sensitivity intolerances, you'll value this book as a treasured friend!

William G. Crook, M.D.
Author of *The Yeast Connection*

Introduction to the Revised Edition

The first edition of *Allergy Cooking with Ease* grew out of keeping my son Joel happy on a restricted diet. He was allergic to wheat and eggs in early childhood, and at age four, we found out that he was also allergic to milk, corn, soy, peanuts, chocolate, and rice. After a period of eliminating all of his problem foods, he was able to eat some of them in rotation, but he still had to strictly avoid wheat and eggs.

When he was in elementary school, I tried to make sure what he took in his lunch looked "normal" and tasted as good as what the other kids had so he would not feel deprived. For school parties and friends' birthday parties, I brought look-alike party foods. I cooked family meals that he could and would enjoy. We put his little brother, John, on a rotation diet that eliminated all major allergens from his first solid foods "just in case." I told my mother what I had been cooking on a near-daily basis, and she advised me to write a cookbook so other mothers did not have to "invent" new recipes like I was doing. At first I said, "Nah!" Eventually I decided to do what she said.

As the years went by, Joel's food allergies got better and mine got worse. I wrote a book for people with extremely severe food allergies. This book (*The Ultimate Food Allergy Cookbook and Survival Guide*) contained medical information, a rotation diet, and recipes that ran the gamut from near-normal to extremely exotic (rare foods). When people called for help with their food allergies, I told them that the newer book contained everything I knew and that if they were only going to purchase one book, that was the one to get. However, *Allergy Cooking with Ease* remained my bestseller.

Hard times fell on the original publisher of *Allergy Cooking with Ease,* and after thirteen years, the book went out of print. However, people still wanted it, so I bought used copies on Amazon.com so I could supply those who called looking for a copy of the book. Eventually, there were no more books to be had. I decided to revise and add to the book and bring it back.

As I have worked on the revision, I have re-discovered what makes this book popular. It is *fun* like an elementary school age child is. It is Joel as he was when it was written and when the recipes were developed for him nearly twenty years ago. It is John as he chewed on the wheat-free teething biscuits in this book. The emphasis is on keeping your moderately allergic loved ones happy on their allergy diets, not on medical issues or the serious side of life. This is an all-purpose family cookbook, without any additional complications. My mother was right. This book is for all the moms and kids on special diets, or for anyone who needs some fun in their life in spite of their allergies.

About This Book

The purpose of this book is to provide a wide variety of recipes to meet a wide variety of dietary and social needs and, whenever possible, to save you time in food preparation.

Because of the range of allergies addressed by the recipes in this book, not all of the recipes will fit your specific dietary needs. There are grain-free recipes for those who are sensitive to all grains and recipes using a large variety of grains for those who rotate several grains. There are cracker, muffin, and baking-soda-raised bread recipes for those who cannot tolerate yeast and yeast bread recipes for those who can. There are recipes sweetened with fruit and fruit juices for those who can tolerate fruit sweeteners, recipes sweetened with stevia for those with yeast problems, and recipes minimally sweetened with sugar for kids, young and old, who can occasionally tolerate some sugar and may feel deprived without it in some social situations. There are main dish recipes made with game meat for those allergic to ordinary meats, vegetarian recipes, and recipes that can be made with the meats usually found in your grocery store. Rather than concentrating on the recipes that you cannot use (possibly the majority of them), be positive and use those that you can use. "Avoid chronic negativity at all costs," as Marge Jones said in the September 1990 *Mastering Food Allergies* newsletter.

Meeting social needs may be as important as meeting dietary needs, especially for children. Therefore, this book contains a pumpkin pie recipe and a grain-free stuffing recipe for Thanksgiving, cookie press cookie recipes for Christmas, cake recipes for birthdays, and a large variety of cookie recipes for school lunches. Hopefully the cookie recipes will prevent children with no dessert in their lunches from swapping the nutritious foods that you spent much time preparing for something they should not eat.

The amount of time that must be spent cooking for an allergy diet can seem overwhelming, so timesaving ingredients and techniques are used in these recipes. The yeast breads are made with quick-rise yeast. Sources of commercial pasta are given as well as recipes for making your own pasta. The recipes include frozen and canned vegetables and fruits. However, when a "shortcut" method could cause allergy problems, other options are also included. For example, canned tomato products can cause problems for individuals who are very sensitive to yeast, so the more time-consuming recipes using fresh tomatoes are also provided. Use the timesaving tricks and devices that you can, and think of the time you spend cooking as an investment in good health for yourself and those you love.

How Then Can We Live?

"How can I live this way?" is a question frequently asked by those with recently diagnosed food allergies. It seems as though your doctor has told you to completely eliminate most of the foods you have normally eaten and to eat the few foods that are left only every fourth or fifth day. As you read package labels in the supermarket, you find that almost everything contains corn, and what doesn't contain corn contains wheat or milk. How can we live and cope with food allergies and in the process achieve good health? Three things are necessary: the right diet, a practical means of implementing the diet and staying on it, and most important of all, the right attitude.

The right diet is one that eliminates all foods that you are allergic to at least for a time until you may possibly develop some tolerance to them. People with allergies to one or a very small number of foods may "get away with" just avoiding their problem foods. However, people with multiple food allergies often have latent or subclinical allergies to dozens of foods. They need a rotary diversified (or rotation) diet which spaces foods at infrequent enough intervals so that they do not develop overt reactions to their "safe" foods.

In order to be on the diet that you need, you must know what foods you are allergic to. The diagnosis of food allergies can be complex. If you are allergic to frequently eaten foods or many foods, you will need professional help to track down which foods are the culprits for you. Discussion of most of the medical aspects of food allergies is beyond the scope of this book, but if you wish to learn more about food allergy testing, treatment, and other medical issues, see *The Ultimate Food Allergy Cookbook and Survival Guide* as described on the last pages of this book.

The right diet will also introduce you to a variety of new foods. We have all eaten a limited number of foods in the past and may at some level think that those foods are all that exist. Therefore, when we find that we can no longer eat them, we feel that we might starve. However, there are many equally delicious foods that most people have never tasted. Along with familiar but less commonly used grains, such as barley, oats, rye, and rice, this book contains recipes using quinoa, amaranth, spelt, kamut, teff, millet, cassava, tapioca, water chestnut, and chestnut flours. Also, there are recipes made with unusual sources of protein, such as game meats, goat, duck and rabbit, goat or sheep cheese, and unusual vegetables, such as Belgian endive and jicama.

The right diet includes the right pattern of eating the foods that you tolerate. Different doctors vary in the strictness of the rules of rotation that they wish their patients to follow, but generally, each food family is eaten only every fourth or fifth day. All of the foods in each food family may be kept on the same day of rotation, or some may be eaten on Monday and some on Wednesday, for example, with a day off from that food family between. (This is called "splitting" a food family). Some doctors instruct their patients to eat a particular food only once on its rotation day. Others allow each food to be eaten several times in the day. This second pattern is very practical because it cuts down on the amount of cooking that must be done; cooking can be done in large enough batches to be eaten for more than one meal throughout the day. You will notice that certain families tend to appear together in the patterns that fit the author's family's rotation schedule, such as grape juice as the sweetener in rye recipes, apple juice in spelt and quinoa recipes, etc. If these patterns do not fit your needs, you may be able to substitute another fruit juice with each type of flour. (See pages 208 to 209 for more about substitutions). If you need information about food families or help with a rotation diet see *The Ultimate Food Allergy Cookbook and Survival Guide* (described on the last pages of this book). This book contains complete food family tables and an easily personalized standard rotation diet that excludes all the major food allergens such as wheat, milk, eggs, corn, soy, yeast, citrus fruits, etc. The book also includes recipes that fit the diet.

Along with the right diet, we need the practical means to implement and stay on the diet. No diet can improve our health if we cannot follow it. In order to stay on a diet we need variety – after all, we're only human! Variety is especially important for children. They may be eating the same combination of foods every fourth or fifth day, but these foods need to be in different enough forms so that they don't get bored. Often, changing a recipe very slightly and calling it by a different name will improve a child's attitude toward certain foods.

The ability to cook also is a factor in implementing an allergy diet. Although you can buy some commercially prepared foods that fit an allergy diet at a health food store, it is unlikely that you can find the variety you need to stay on a rotation diet. You will need to do some cooking. The most desperate people I talk to are non-cooks who have just found out that they must be on a special diet. *Allergy Cooking with Ease* was written with the assumption that the reader was a cook, at least on a basic level. If you are a novice cook and need a little more instruction in "basics" than this book provides, see *Easy Cooking for Special Diets* as described on the last pages of this book. Also, even if you are an experienced cook, allergy cooking differs in some significant ways. See "Allergy Cooking Tips" on page 208 of this book.

Being prepared is also essential to implementing an allergy diet. We need to plan ahead and have the right foods available before we get hungry. Hunger, combined with the lack of the right foods to satisfy it immediately, causes most of the problems encountered in trying to stay on a rotation diet. Prepare large batches of crackers, breads, and muffins using the same sweetener and oil with each flour each time, freeze them, and you will be prepared when that day of rotation comes around again. If your doctor will allow you to eat foods more than once in each rotation day, start your rotation day at dinnertime, prepare a large portion of the main dish, and eat it for breakfast and lunch the next day.

We also need to be prepared for special social occasions. I was recently talking to a person with food allergies who was suffering from a reaction caused by Christmas rum balls that she had eaten. I advised her to be prepared the next time with some Christmas treats that would be allowed on her diet, and told her that I had made myself a batch of special cookies for the holidays. She replied, "Yes, but those have a lot of Fruit Sweet™ in them." That was true, but for me, occasionally eating more fruit sweetener than I normally do is much better than yielding to the temptation to eat rum balls containing sugar, wheat, butter, eggs, corn, and chocolate, as she had. Be prepared for those special occasions with the most satisfying substitute food you can tolerate.

A final factor in implementing the diet is to try to reduce the amount of work done in preparing all of our food from scratch. If we make our diets more work than we have to, we reduce our chances of being able to follow them. As mentioned above, you can save time by preparing large batches of baked products with the same flour, oil and sweetener used together each time and freezing them. Most main dishes also freeze well. Also, try to use ingredients that save time. If your diet will allow it, use canned and frozen fruits, vegetables, and juices. When making yeast breads by hand, use quick-rise yeast, or use a bread machine to make bread. For more about making allergy breads with a bread machine, see *Easy Breadmaking for Special Diets* which is described on the last pages of this book.

In the years since the first edition of *Allergy Cooking with Ease* was written, new answers to the question, "How then can we live with our food allergies?" have emerged. Advances in medical science have made it possible for some people to be essentially "cured" of their food allergies and many other people find that their allergies are greatly improved. Nowadays there is a new emphasis on identifying and treating the root causes of food allergies which can include nutritional imbalances, problems with digestion, and dysbiosis. (Dysbiosis is an imbalance in the intestinal flora which can include the presence of harmful bacteria, yeast, and parasites and/or the absence of helpful bacteria). By correcting these problems which contribute to the problem of food allergies, one's health can be greatly improved. For more information about these subjects, see *The Ultimate Food Allergy Cookbook and Survival Guide* as described on the last pages of this book.

Also, there have been advances in immunotherapy treatment for food and inhalant allergies and chemical sensitivities. These shots are called Low Dose Allergens (LDA) or Enzyme Potentiated Desensitization (EPD). EPD is made in England and has been used there for over 40 years. It was used in the United States as part of an Investigation Review Board study in the 1990's. Then, due to problems with the FDA, it was replaced in the United States with an American-made shot, LDA. EPD and LDA employ cell-mediated immunity to "turn off" allergies to many things. The shots are taken every two months initially and then gradually spaced out to longer intervals. For more information on low dose immunotherapy, see *The Low Dose Immunotherapy Handbook* as described on the last pages of this book. These treatments can be very effective. My son Joel, whose food allergies were the reason I developed most of the recipes in this book, is now a healthy graduate student who eats an unrestricted diet as a result of treatment with EPD and then with LDA.

How then can we live with our food allergies? The most important factor of all in coping with food allergies is the right attitude. We can continually talk and think about what we CANNOT eat and CANNOT do, but this will depress us and everyone around us. Or we can learn to be content with what we CAN eat and actually begin to enjoy our food. When we stick to our diets we may even find that we feel well enough and have enough energy to enjoy other things in life more, such as our families, friends, work, and recreation, and the importance of food in our lives will decrease. We can also seek out a doctor who will treat the root causes of our food allergies and who employs low dose immunotherapy. The right attitude will also help carry us through these medical treatments.

All of us fall off of our diets at times. Do not be too hard on yourself when this happens. Just pick yourself up and start over again. Parents of allergic children may experience times when their children will not eat what they have spent much time preparing. This is just a temporary setback. Freeze the unwanted food until your children forget that they were tired of it, and find another recipe to try.

Finally, when you cook, be adventurous, inventive, and creative. Use this book as a starting point and experiment on your own. Learn as much about cooking with new foods as you can, and consider a cooking class or cookbook worthwhile if you get a single new recipe or idea from it.

Know Your Ingredients

When you begin cooking for a rotational allergy diet you will encounter foods that you may not be familiar with. This chapter is an introduction to some of the characteristics of those foods.

FLOURS

While they are very delicious and nutritious, alternative flours are different than wheat, so do not expect foods made with them to have a taste or texture identical to wheat-containing baked goods. If you are willing to try new things and have a positive attitude, you will enjoy foods made from these flours as you enjoy improved health.

AMARANTH FLOUR: This flour is not related to the true grains. It is in the same botanical order as quinoa, although it is not in the same food family. Because it is not a grain, it is a welcome dietary addition for those allergic to all grains. It makes very tasty baked goods. Purchase it at a store that refrigerates its flour and refrigerate or freeze it at home since it may develop an unpleasantly strong flavor if stored too long at room temperature. An occasional batch of amaranth flour will yield gummy pancakes or bread. Just toast them, and they will still be delicious.

ARROWROOT: A fine white powder that looks like cornstarch, arrowroot is excellent as a thickener and tends to hold baked goods together and make them less crumbly. It may be derived from plants in several food families, but when it is purchased in a store, it is usually impossible to determine which plant it came from. Therefore, at our house, we rotate it on the same day as bananas which are the only commonly eaten food in any of the families that arrowroot may be in.

BARLEY FLOUR: Barley is a very pleasant tasting gluten-containing grain in the same tribe of the grain family as rye, spelt, kamut, wheat, and triticale. Baked goods made with barley flour are excellent, and it is especially good in pie crust.

CAROB: This plant is in the legume family. The flour made from the pods may be used in baking as a substitute for chocolate. Carob flour or powder is naturally sweet, so it does not require as much additional sweetener in recipes as chocolate does. It tends to form hard lumps upon standing, so you may need to press it through a wire mesh strainer with the back of a spoon before using it. Milk-free carob chips are excellent in cookies. Carob bean gum (also called locust bean gum) is derived from the bean of the carob plant and is used in many commercially prepared foods.

CASSAVA MEAL: Also called mandioca flour, this comes from the same plant as tapioca but is very coarse. It is not strongly flavored and makes good crackers that can be broken up and used as croutons in salads. It may be obtained by mail order for a reasonable price (see "Sources of Special Foods," page 217) and therefore is a welcome addition to a diet that must eliminate all grains. See "Tuber Flours" on page 16 for information about cassava flour.

CHESTNUT FLOUR: Naturally sweet and tasty, this flour is also a good alternative to grains for the totally grain-free diet. Baked goods made with chestnut flour alone are very crumbly, so it is best to use chestnut flour with a binding ingredient such as bananas, arrowroot, or tapioca flour. For information about ordering chestnut flour, see "Sources of Special Foods," page 218.

CORN is not used in any of the recipes in this book but is included in this listing to warn you that if you are allergic to corn you should also avoid corn oil, cornstarch, corn syrup, corn sweeteners, dextrose, glucose, some sources of fructose, maltodextrin, and grits in commercially prepared foods.

GARBANZO FLOUR: This flour is in the legume family. It has a very pleasant, slightly sweet taste and is high in protein. It makes excellent tacos and tortillas.

GLUTEN FLOUR and **GRAHAM FLOUR** are both derived from wheat. They are mentioned here so that you may avoid them.

KAMUT FLOUR is a golden yellow flour with very good flavor. Kamut is very closely related to wheat in its biological classification, being in the same genus but a different species. However, many people who are allergic to wheat can eat kamut. Kamut seems to be tolerated by fewer wheat-sensitive individuals than spelt however. Kamut makes good yeast breads and very tasty non-yeast baked goods, although they are likely to be dense. Kamut flour really shines in pancakes which are much lighter textured than some of the other kamut baked products.

MILLET FLOUR: Millet is a pleasant-tasting non-gluten grain flour that is in a tribe of its own in the grain family. Baked goods made with millet flour tend to be very crumbly even when binding ingredients are also used, but it still is an excellent flour to use in baking if you do not mind crumbs.

MILO FLOUR: Milo is a grain that is commonly used to feed cattle, and at times it has been difficult to locate for human consumption. It is in the same tribe of the grain family as the sugar cane plant. It has a pleasant, bland flavor and is excellent used in baking. To order milo flour, see "Sources of Special Foods," page 218.

OAT FLOUR is a pleasant tasting grain flour. It may tend to be heavy in some baked products but is still delicious if one is not too particular about heaviness. An occasional batch of oat flour may be gummy in baked goods. Oats are in a tribe of their own in the grain family.

QUINOA FLOUR is a very versatile non-grain flour which is excellent in baked goods of all kinds. Although not in the same food family, it is in the same botanical order as amaranth. It is in the same food family as beets, spinach, and chard. Quinoa is an excellent source of high-quality protein and calcium.

RICE FLOUR: A bland, pleasant tasting gluten-free grain flour, rice flour tends to be gritty in baked goods. (Some children refused to eat rice-containing baked goods because of the grittiness). It is in a tribe of the grain family with wild rice.

RYE FLOUR is a very versatile grain flour. It contains gluten and behaves much like whole wheat flour in baking. It has a slightly stronger flavor than some of the other grains, but is very tasty. Rye is in the same tribe of the grain family as barley, spelt, kamut, wheat, and triticale.

SEMOLINA FLOUR is derived from the endosperm of wheat. It is often used in Jerusalem artichoke pasta and is mentioned so that you can avoid it if you are allergic to wheat.

SPELT FLOUR: A very versatile grain flour, spelt makes excellent yeast breads because it is higher in gluten than wheat. Spelt is very closely related to wheat in its biological classification, being *Triticum spelta* while wheat is *Triticum aestivum*. (See "The Spelt-Wheat Debate" on page 214 for more about this). In spite of the close relationship, spelt is tolerated by many wheat-sensitive individuals. Muffins and cakes made with spelt flour tend to be a little drier than those made with other grains, and so the recipes may contain slightly more oil. Spelt makes excellent yeast bread.

At the time of the first printing of the original version of this book, the only spelt flour on the market was produced by Purity Foods. All of the recipes in this book were developed using this flour and I still use it exclusively in my spelt baking. Purity Foods flour is milled from a European strain of spelt that is higher in protein than most spelt flours. In the years since this book was first written, several other companies have also begun to produce spelt flour. These other flours do not work well in the recipes in this book. The are unsuitable for yeast breads and if you use them in non-yeast baked goods, you will have to add a little more flour than the recipes call for and expect less satisfactory results. It is worth the time and effort you spend to get Purity Foods flour. Many health food stores carry it (If yours doesn't, ask them to!) or see "Sources of Special Foods," page 218, for ordering information.

TAPIOCA FLOUR: This fine white powder is very similar to arrowroot and may be used interchangeably with it in baking. It behaves slightly differently than arrowroot in thickening, so it is used as a thickener in different amounts than arrowroot in some recipes. Sauces thickened with tapioca tend to be a little more ropy than those thickened with arrowroot. Tapioca comes from the cassava plant.

TEFF FLOUR: Teff is a slightly strong tasting gluten-free grain. Teff flour tends to be a little gritty, but still makes very nice baked products. It is in a tribe of its own in the grain family.

TRITICALE is a grain that is a cross between wheat and rye. It is usually not well tolerated by wheat-sensitive individuals.

TUBER FLOURS: For individuals sensitive to all grains, flours made from a variety of unusual tubers can be very helpful, although they are expensive. White sweet potato, cassava, malanga, and yam flours, along with recipes and instructions for their use, may be obtained by mail order. See "Sources of Special Foods," page 218, for ordering information.

WATER CHESTNUT STARCH is available in Chinese grocery stores and by mail order. (See "Sources of Special Foods," page 218). It is a useful addition to the diets of individuals who must avoid all grains. Water chestnut starch may be used as a thickener and makes excellent wafers. (See the "Coconut Milk Wafers" recipe on page 30).

LEAVENINGS

Leavenings are the ingredients that make baked products rise. They include baking powder, baking soda combined with an acid ingredient, and yeast.

BAKING SODA is a very pure chemical and is usually allowed on every day of the rotation cycle. It must be used in conjunction with an acid ingredient such as fruit juice, unbuffered vitamin C crystals, or cream of tartar to make baked goods rise.

BAKING POWDER is a combination of acid and basic components that produces gas that makes baked goods rise in baking. Most commercial baking powder contains cornstarch. Featherweight™ baking powder contains potato starch instead, but sensitivity to potatoes is not uncommon. Therefore potatoes and potato-containing baking powder should not be used daily. Most of the recipes in this book contain a built-in baking powder made of baking soda and unbuffered vitamin C crystals. Make sure the vitamin C crystals you use are unbuffered so they are able to add the acid component to the baking powder.

YEAST is what makes commercial bread rise and is a potent allergen for many individuals. However, in *The Yeast Connection Cookbook,* Dr. William Crook says that approximately 50% of patients with candidiasis are able to tolerate yeast-containing foods in their diets.[1] Because many allergy patients tolerate yeast, a chapter of yeast breads is included in this book along with tips on baking yeast breads.

OILS

Most liquid vegetable oils behave similarly in cooking and baking and may be used interchangeably. For purposes of health, however, oils differ. A detailed discussion of the health advantages and disadvantages of the various oils is beyond the scope of this book. However, two oils high in essential fatty acids are canola and walnut oil. Canola oil is in the same family as cabbage and is the lowest in saturated fat and the highest in monounsaturated fat of all the oils currently available. Olive oil is also an excellent choice for health benefits.

You should rotate oils and use each kind on the same day as other foods in the same food family. Safflower or sunflower oil may be rotated on the same day as lettuce, soybean or peanut oil on the same day as legumes, rice bran oil on the same day as rice, canola oil on the same day as cabbage, grapeseed oil on the same day as grapes, etc. In addition to these oils, there are enough other oils available such as avocado, sesame, olive, almond, walnut, etc. to fill almost any rotation pattern.

Coconut oil is the one commonly available oil which behaves differently in cooking than other oils. It is high in saturated fat and therefore is solid at room temperature. In some recipes, such as cookie press cookies and ice cream cones, it functions better than any other oil. Because it is high in saturated fats it should not be eaten in large quantities, but, according to Harvard authority Dr. Vigen K Babayan, "There's no danger unless you greatly overdo it. Not all saturated fats are alike, and not all are bad." He says that animal fats and coconut oil are quite different, with animal fats containing long-chains of fatty acids, and coconut oil containing shorter-chain fatty acids which do not deposit as easily in blood vessels.[2] There are even reports that medium chain triglycerides, such as those in coconut oil, may suppress the synthesis of fat by the body.[3]

SWEETENERS

The dessert recipes in this book are minimally sweetened. As we get used to eating little or no refined sugar, our tastes change and minimally sweetened foods seem like a great treat.

CONCENTRATED SWEETENERS, such as **BEET SUGAR, CANE SUGAR, MOLASSES, HONEY,** and **MAPLE SYRUP,** have the most effect on blood sugar metabolism and may need to be completely avoided by individuals with candidiasis. They are used in some of the recipes in this book however (although in smaller amounts than in most recipes) as a concession to special social situations, especially those involving children. For purposes of rotation, beet sugar is in the same family as quinoa and spinach, and cane sugar is in the grain family.

FRUIT SWEETENERS are used in the majority of the dessert recipes in this book. Frozen fruit juice concentrates may be thawed and used as the liquid in a recipe, adding sweetness and acidity to the leavening process at the same time. Fruit purees improve the texture of many baked products as well as binding the crumbly ones more firmly together. Date sugar is also a great fruit sweetener. It is simply dried ground dates and behaves more like beet and cane sugars in baking than fruit juices do.

SUGAR ALCOHOLS such as xylitol, sorbitol, and erythritol are natural sweetening agents which occur in small amounts in some fruits and vegetables. They do not cause tooth decay or wide fluctuations in blood sugar. They are highly purified. Most of them are not absorbed so can cause diarrhea if eaten in large amounts. Erythritol is an exception to this; it is absorbed rapidly in the small intestine so does not usually cause diarrhea. Xylitol is made from birch trees and should be rotated with filberts. Since the rest of these sweeteners can be derived from a number of sources it is difficult to know which food group they should be rotated with. Because they may not be absorbed and their sources might be unknown, it is probably best to use them infrequently.

STEVIA is a potently sweet herb that is very helpful in the diets of patients with severe candidiasis. It is derived from the plant *Stevia rebaudiana* which is in the composite (lettuce) family. It is available in several forms–as a brownish powder, a brownish liquid, and as a white powder. The white powder is used in this cookbook because it is the purest form of the sweetening agents found in the plant. Stevia has a slight licorice-like taste which is most noticeable in bland recipes and almost undetectable in recipes containing strongly flavored ingredients such as cranberries and carob.

FOS (fructooligosaccharides) is among the newest sweeteners. It is expensive but is an alternative to sugar that produces very normal appearing and tasting treats for special occasions like birthday parties. FOS has no aftertaste and tastes just like sugar except that it is less potently sweet. It is a long chain carbohydrate which is made from sugar, so if it is cooked too long, it breaks down into sugar again. FOS should be used with caution and only occasionally because it can worsen bacterial dysbiosis caused by unfriendly bacteria such as *Klebsiella*. Like the sugar alcohols, it is highly refined. It cannot be easily rotated because you will probably not be able to determine whether it was made from beet or cane sugar. Therefore, it is best used infrequently.

OTHER FOODS AND INGREDIENTS

The more different kinds of foods you eat on a rotation diet, the better off you will be, both nutritionally and also with your allergies. To expand your repertoire of fruits and vegetables, see the grocery shopping and "Vegetables" chapters of *Easy Cooking for Special Diets* as described on the last pages of this book.

Many ingredients not usually found in your kitchen may be used in cooking for an allergy rotation diet. Other less-common ingredients include:

UNBUFFERED VITAMIN C CRYSTALS have already been mentioned as a component in the leavening process. They are also useful for adding tartness to salads instead of using vinegar or lemon juice. Different brands of vitamin C differ in how tasty they are in salads. Be sure to purchase a brand of vitamin C crystals that is free of corn. Because hypoallergenic brands of vitamin C are usually extremely pure, most doctors allow their patients to have vitamin C on every day of a rotation diet.

AGAR is derived from seaweed, and can be used instead of gelatin for individuals allergic to beef or pork. It is available as a powder or as flakes. Generally speaking, it takes less of the powder than of the flakes to produce gelling.

GUAR GUM and **METHYLCELLULOSE** add fiber to foods. In yeast bread recipes which are made with low-gluten flours, the guar gum is essential to trap the gas made by the yeast so the bread will rise. Guar gum and methylcellulose may be added to ice cream recipes to promote a smooth texture. To purchase these thickeners, see "Sources of Special Foods," page 220.

Footnotes:

1. Crook, William G., M.D. *The Yeast Connection Cookbook,* Professional Books, Jackson, TN 38303, 1989, page 24.

2. Babayan, Vigen K., M.D. *The Denver Post.* "Food Pharmacy" column, March 28, 1990.

3. Kaunitz, Hans, M.D. "Medium Chain Triglycerides (MCT) In Aging and Arteriosclerosis," *Advances in Human Nutrition,* Volume 3, Chem-Orbital, Park Forest, IL 60466, 1986, pages 115-121.

Muffins, Crackers, Breakfast Foods, and Breads Made without Yeast

"What can we eat for breakfast?" "What can I take in my lunch?" These seem like difficult questions when wheat and yeast must be eliminated from your diet. The recipes in this chapter provide answers to those questions.

Baking for allergies is different from "regular" baking in several ways. Alternative flours do not have to be sifted before measuring them. However, it is important to stir them in case they have settled during storage. Simply stir the flour with a large spoon, lightly spoon it into the measuring cup, and level it off with a knife.

Speed and efficiency are also more important in allergy baking than in "regular" baking. Before you begin baking, preheat your oven. Prepare the baking pans ahead of time; oil and flour them with the same oil and flour used in the recipe. Be careful not to over-mix as you stir the liquid ingredients into the dry ingredients. Mix the dry ingredients together in a large bowl and the liquid ingredients together in another bowl or cup. Working quickly, stir the liquid ingredients into the dry ingredients until they are just mixed, put the batter into the pans, and pop them into the preheated oven.

To test quick breads and muffins for doneness, insert a toothpick into the center of the pan. If it comes out dry, it is time to remove the pan from the oven. Allow breads to cool completely before you slice them to eat or to put in the freezer.

By following these special instructions for allergy baking, you should be able to easily produce delicious baked goods that you or your family can eat without problems.

Barley Muffins

These go well with any meal of the day.

2 cups barley flour
¼ teaspoon salt (optional)
1 teaspoon baking soda
¼ teaspoon unbuffered vitamin C crystals
¼ cup oil
1¼ cups water

Mix the dry ingredients together in a large bowl. Mix together the water and oil, pour them into the dry ingredients, and stir until they are just mixed in. Put the batter into an oiled and floured muffin tin, filling the cups about ⅔ full. Bake at 400°F for 30 to 35 minutes, or until the muffins begin to brown. Makes about 12 muffins.

Apple and Spice Muffins

The chunks of apple are like little treasures in these sweet and spicy grain-free muffins.

1¾ cups quinoa flour
¼ cup tapioca flour
2 teaspoons baking soda
½ teaspoon unbuffered vitamin C crystals
2 teaspoons cinnamon
1½ cups peeled and chopped apples
1 cup unsweetened applesauce
¼ cup apple juice concentrate, thawed
¼ cup oil

Mix the dry ingredients together and stir the chopped apples into them. Mix together the applesauce, apple juice and oil, and add them to the dry ingredients, stirring until just mixed. Put the batter into an oiled and floured muffin tin, filling the muffin cups about ¾ full. Bake at 375°F for 20 to 25 minutes. Makes about 16 muffins.

Pear Muffins

This variation on "Apple and Spice Muffins" will add some variety to your diet.

Prepare "Apple and Spice Muffins" above, except omit the applesauce and apple juice concentrate, and instead use 1¼ cups pear juice. (If you purchase pears canned in pear juice, this can be the juice drained from the fruit used in this recipe.) Also, substitute 1½ cups fresh peeled and chopped or canned chopped pears for the chopped apples. If canned pears are used, fold them into the batter after it is mixed instead of mixing them with the dry ingredients.

Oat Muffins

These are a good change from oatmeal for breakfast on days when oats are on your rotation schedule.

2 cups oat flour
¼ teaspoon salt (optional)
1 teaspoon baking soda
¼ teaspoon unbuffered vitamin C crystals
¼ cup oil
1 cup water

Mix the dry ingredients together in a large bowl. Mix together the water and oil, pour them into the dry ingredients, and stir until they are just mixed in. Put the batter into an oiled and floured muffin tin, filling the cups about ⅔ full. Bake at 400°F for 30 to 35 minutes, or until the muffins begin to brown and pull away from the side of the pan. Makes about 10 muffins.

Pineapple Muffins

Delicately flavorful, these muffins are a hit with young and old alike, especially when you make them with milo flour.

2 cups milo flour OR 2 cups teff flour OR 2¼ cups spelt flour
1 teaspoon baking soda
¼ teaspoon unbuffered vitamin C crystals
½ cup pineapple canned in its own juice or fresh pineapple with juice to cover, pureed
½ cup pineapple juice concentrate, thawed
⅓ cup oil

Mix the flour, baking soda, and vitamin C crystals in a large bowl. Combine the pureed pineapple, pineapple juice concentrate, and oil and stir them into the dry ingredients until they are just mixed in. Put the batter into an oiled and floured muffin tin (or use paper muffin cup liners), filling the cups about ⅔ full. Bake at 400°F for 15 to 20 minutes, or until the muffins begin to brown. Makes about 12 muffins.

Banana Muffins

The natural sweetness of the chestnut flour and bananas combine to make this an exceptionally tasty grain-free treat. To obtain chestnut flour, see "Sources of Special Foods," page 218.

2¼ cups chestnut flour, sifted if lumpy
1 teaspoon baking soda
½ teaspoon unbuffered vitamin C crystals
¼ teaspoon ground cloves (optional)
1¾ cup pureed ripe bananas (You may substitute pureed peaches).
¼ cup oil

Mix together the chestnut flour, baking soda, vitamin C crystals, and cloves in a large bowl. Stir the bananas and oil together, add them to the flour mixture, and stir until they are just mixed in. Spoon the batter into oiled and floured muffin cups, filling them a little over ¾ full. Bake at 375°F for 18 to 20 minutes. Makes 12 to 13 muffins.

Millet Surprise Muffins

These muffins are fragile, but the jelly surprise inside them helps to hold them together. Use paper muffin cup liners for added stability..

1 cup millet flour
¾ cup tapioca flour
¾ teaspoon baking soda
⅛ teaspoon unbuffered vitamin C crystals
1 teaspoon cinnamon
¾ cup apple juice concentrate, thawed
⅓ cup oil
2 to 3 tablespoons unsweetened apple butter or all-fruit jelly or jam (optional)

Mix the flours, baking soda, vitamin C crystals, and cinnamon in a large bowl. Combine the juice and oil and stir them into the dry ingredients until just mixed in. Fill about 12 oiled and floured muffin cups ⅓ full with the batter, add ½ teaspoon jelly or jam to the center of each muffin cup, and then top the jelly or jam with additional batter to fill the cups about ⅔ full. Or, omit the jelly or jam and fill the muffin cups ⅔ full with the batter. Bake at 400°F for 15 to 20 minutes. Makes about 12 muffins.

Spelt Surprise Muffins

If apple butter or pear-apple spread is used rather than a grape-based jelly or jam, this recipe contains only three food families. These muffins are also excellent without the jelly surprise.

2½ cups spelt flour
1½ teaspoons baking soda
¼ teaspoon unbuffered vitamin C crystals
⅓ cup oil
1 cup apple juice concentrate, thawed
2 to 3 tablespoons unsweetened apple butter or all-fruit jelly or jam (optional)

Mix together the flour, baking soda, and vitamin C crystals in a large bowl. Mix the oil and apple juice concentrate and stir them into the dry ingredients until they are just mixed in. Fill each of 12 oiled and floured muffin cups about ⅓ full of the batter, add ½ teaspoon of jelly or jam to the center of each muffin cup, and top the jelly with additional batter to fill the muffin cups ⅔ full. Or, omit the jelly or jam and fill the muffin cups ⅔ full of batter. Bake at 350°F for 15 to 18 minutes. Makes 12 muffins.

Kamut Surprise Muffins

These are great with blueberries! See the "Blueberry Muffins" recipe on page 26.

2¼ cups kamut flour
1½ teaspoon baking soda
¼ teaspoon unbuffered vitamin C crystals
¼ cup oil
1¼ cups apple juice concentrate, thawed
2 to 3 tablespoons unsweetened apple butter or all-fruit jelly or jam (optional)

Mix together the flour, baking soda, and vitamin C crystals in a large bowl. Mix the oil and apple juice concentrate and stir them into the dry ingredients until they are just mixed in. Fill each of 10 to 11 oiled and floured muffin cups about ⅓ full of the batter, add ½ teaspoon of jelly or jam to the center of each muffin cup, and top the jelly with additional batter to fill the muffin cups ⅔ full. Or, omit the jelly or jam and fill the muffin cups ⅔ full of batter. Bake at 350°F for 25 to 30 minutes. Makes 10 to 11 muffins.

Rye Surprise Muffins

This recipe contains only two food families if the muffins are sweetened with grape juice rather than maple syrup, grapeseed oil is used, and all-grape jelly is used in the center of the muffins.

2 cups rye flour
¾ teaspoon baking soda
¼ teaspoon unbuffered vitamin C crystals if water and maple syrup are used;
    ⅛ teaspoon if grape juice is used
⅓ cup grapeseed or any other oil
1 cup unsweetened white grape juice OR ¼ cup maple syrup plus ¾ cup water
2 to 3 tablespoons unsweetened all-fruit jelly or jam (optional)

Mix the flour, baking soda, and vitamin C crystals in a large bowl. Mix the juice or maple syrup plus water with the oil, pour them into the dry ingredients, and stir until they are just mixed in. Fill 12 oiled and floured muffin cups ⅓ full of batter, add ½ teaspoon jelly or jam to the center of each muffin cup, and top the jelly or jam with additional batter to fill the cups about ⅔ full. Or, omit the jelly or jam and just fill each muffin cup ⅔ full of batter. Bake at 400°F for 18 to 20 minutes. Makes about 12 muffins.

Blueberry Muffins

These are as delicious as ever when made without wheat, milk, eggs, or sugar.

1 cup fresh blueberries or unsweetened frozen blueberries, not thawed
1 batch of one of the following recipes:
    Oat Muffins, page 22
    Barley Muffins, page 20
    Spelt Surprise Muffins, omitting the jelly or jam, page 24
    Kamut Surprise Muffins, omitting the jelly or jam, page 24
    Rye Surprise Muffins, omitting the jelly or jam, page 25
    Apple and Spice Muffins, omitting the chopped apple, page 21
    Stevia-Sweetened Spice Muffins, page 26 (below)

Mix the muffin batter as directed in the recipe. Quickly fold in the blueberries. Bake as directed in the recipe, or for 5 to 10 minutes longer if you are using frozen blueberries. Makes one or two more muffins than what the recipe would make without the blueberries.

Stevia-Sweetened Spice Muffins

Here are muffins for the person who must avoid fruit sweeteners as well as refined sugar. They are also grain-free and made with high-protein flours.

1¾ cups amaranth flour plus ½ cup arrowroot
    OR 1½ cups quinoa flour plus ½ cup tapioca flour
2 teaspoons baking soda
½ teaspoon unbuffered vitamin C crystals
2 teaspoons cinnamon (optional)
¼ teaspoon ground cloves (optional)
¼ teaspoon white stevia powder
1 cup water
¼ cup oil

Stir together the amaranth flour and arrowroot OR the quinoa flour and tapioca starch with the baking soda, vitamin C crystals, cinnamon, cloves, and stevia powder.

Combine the water and oil and stir them into the dry ingredients. (The dough will be stiffer than most muffin batter). Put the dough into an oiled and floured muffin tin and bake at 375°F for 20 to 25 minutes. Makes 10 to 12 muffins.

Quinoa Crackers

These make great snacks, as well as being a delicious addition to a simple soup or salad meal.

3 cups quinoa flour
1 cup tapioca flour
¼ cup sesame seeds
2 teaspoons baking soda
½ teaspoon unbuffered vitamin C crystals
1 teaspoon salt
1¼ cups water
½ cup oil

Mix together the quinoa flour, tapioca flour, sesame seeds, baking soda, vitamin C crystals, and salt in a large bowl. Combine the water and oil and stir them into the dry ingredients until the dough sticks together, adding a few more tablespoons of water if necessary. Divide the dough into thirds. Roll each third to about ⅛ inch thickness on an ungreased cookie sheet. Cut the dough into 2 inch squares and bake at 350°F for 15 to 25 minutes, or until the crackers are crisp and lightly browned. Makes about 9 dozen crackers.

"Graham" Crackers

A traditional favorite made grain-free.

Prepare "Quinoa Crackers," above, except omit the sesame seeds and salt, and substitute an equal amount of thawed apple juice concentrate for the water. Lightly oil the cookie sheets before rolling the dough out on them. Bake at 350°F for 10 to 15 minutes, watching the crackers carefully to prevent burning. Remove the crackers from the cookie sheet immediately, using a spatula to pry them off if necessary.

Zesty Rye Crackers

These tasty crackers are great for snacks!

4 cups rye flour
1 to 2 teaspoons onion powder (optional)
1½ teaspoons caraway seeds (optional)
2 teaspoons baking soda
½ teaspoon vitamin C crystals
1 teaspoon salt
1 cup water
½ cup oil

Combine the flour, onion powder, caraway seeds, baking soda, vitamin C crystals, and salt in a large bowl. Mix together the water and oil and pour them into the flour mixture. Stir until the dough sticks together, adding another few tablespoons of water if necessary to form a stiff but not crumbly dough. Divide the dough into thirds. Roll each third to about ⅛ inch thickness on an ungreased cookie sheet and cut the dough into 2 inch squares. Sprinkle the crackers with additional salt if desired. Bake at 375°F for 15 to 20 minutes, or until the crackers are crisp and lightly browned. Makes about 9 dozen crackers.

Oat Crackers

These delicious crackers remind me of Scottish shortbread.

4 cups quick oats, uncooked
½ teaspoon salt (optional)
⅓ cup oil
⅔ cup water

Combine the oats and salt. Add the oil and mix it into the dry ingredients thoroughly. Add the water and mix the dough with a spoon and your hands until the dough sticks together. Divide the dough in half and roll each half to about ⅛ inch thickness on an ungreased cookie sheet. Cut the dough into 1½ inch to 2 inch squares. Bake at 350°F for 20 to 25 minutes. Makes 4 to 5 dozen crackers.

Saltines

The delicious nutty flavor of spelt shines in these crackers.

2 cups spelt flour
½ teaspoon salt
½ teaspoon baking soda
¼ teaspoon unbuffered vitamin C crystals
¼ cup oil
½ cup water

Combine the flour, salt, baking soda, and vitamin C crystals. Add the oil and stir until it is thoroughly mixed in to form small crumbs. Add the water two tablespoons at a time, mixing well after each addition. Knead the dough on a lightly floured board for one to two minutes. Divide the dough in half and roll each half out on an oiled baking sheet with an oiled rolling pin to about a 10 inch by 14 inch rectangle. The dough should be very thin, about ⅟₁₆ to ⅛ inch thick. Cut the dough into 2 inch squares and prick each square three times with a fork. Sprinkle the tops of the crackers with additional salt if desired. Bake at 350ºF for 10 to 14 minutes, or until the crackers are golden brown and crisp. Makes 6 to 7 dozen crackers.

Honey "Graham" Crackers

These honey-sweetened crackers are just like the ones you remember from your childhood.

2½ cups spelt flour
½ teaspoon salt
¾ teaspoon baking soda
¼ teaspoon unbuffered vitamin C crystals
½ cup milk-free margarine (not low-fat) or goat butter at room temperature
⅜ cup (¼ cup plus 2 tablespoons) honey
⅛ cup (2 tablespoons) water

Combine the dry ingredients in a bowl. Cut in the margarine or butter with a pastry cutter until well blended. Mix the honey and water together thoroughly. Stir the honey and water into the flour mixture, using your hands to mix and knead it until it forms a soft dough. Divide the dough in half. Flour the dough and rolling pin and roll each half on a floured baking sheet to about ⅛ inch thickness. Cut into 1½ inch by 3 inch rectangles and prick them with a fork. Bake at 350°F for 8 to 11 minutes, or until they begin to brown. Remove them from the oven and re-cut them on the original cut lines if necessary. Cool on paper towels. Makes 3 to 4 dozen crackers.

Milo Crackers

The slightly coarse texture of milo flour adds to the appeal of these tasty crackers.

1¼ cups milo flour
¾ cup arrowroot
1 teaspoon baking soda
¼ teaspoon unbuffered vitamin C crystals
¼ to ½ teaspoon salt, to taste
¼ cup oil
½ cup water

Combine the milo flour, arrowroot, baking soda, vitamin C crystals, and salt in a large bowl. Mix together the oil and water and add them to the dry ingredients, mixing with your hands to form a stiff dough. Divide the dough in half and roll each part out onto an ungreased cookie sheet with an oiled rolling pin. Cut the dough into 1½ inch squares and bake at 350°F for 20 to 25 minutes. Makes about 4 dozen crackers.

Coconut Milk Wafers

These are a tasty treat with an incredible crunch.

1 cup tapioca or water chestnut flour
¼ teaspoon baking soda
⅛ teaspoon vitamin C crystals
Coconut milk - 7 to 8 tablespoons with tapioca flour
      or 12 to 13 tablespoons with water chestnut flour
Melted coconut oil, or any other kind of oil

Mix the tapioca or water chestnut flour, baking soda, and vitamin C crystals. Add the coconut milk one tablespoon at a time to make a very stiff dough. Drop teaspoonfuls of the dough onto an oiled cookie sheet and flatten them to ⅛ inch or less thickness with your hand. Bake at 350°F for 10 to 15 minutes, or until the edges begin to brown. Turn them over and bake 5 minutes more. Makes 2 to 3 dozen wafers.

Canola Seed Crackers

The canola seeds add interest and flavor to both the grain and non-grain versions of this recipe, but the crackers are also delicious without the seeds.

Amaranth:

> 3 cups amaranth flour
> 1 cup arrowroot
> ¼ cup canola seeds (optional)
> 2 teaspoons baking soda
> ½ teaspoon unbuffered vitamin C crystals
> 1 teaspoon salt
> ¾ cup water
> ½ cup canola or other oil

Barley:

> 4 cups barley flour
> ¼ cup canola seeds (optional)
> 2 teaspoons baking soda
> ½ teaspoon unbuffered vitamin C crystals
> 1 teaspoon salt
> ⅞ cup water (¾ cup plus 2 tablespoons)
> ½ cup canola or other oil

Choose one set of ingredients above. Combine the flour(s), optional canola seeds, baking soda, vitamin C crystals, and salt in a large bowl. Mix together the water and oil and pour them into the flour mixture. Stir until the dough sticks together, adding another few tablespoons of water if necessary to form a stiff but not crumbly dough. Divide the dough into thirds. Roll each third to about ⅛ inch thickness on an ungreased cookie sheet and cut the dough into 2 inch squares. Sprinkle the tops of the crackers lightly with additional salt if desired. Bake at 375°F for 15 to 20 minutes, or until the crackers are crisp and lightly browned. Makes about 9 dozen crackers.

Kamut Poppy Seed Crackers

These crackers are a crunchy golden delight.

2 cups kamut flour
2 tablespoons poppy seeds (optional)
¾ teaspoon baking soda
¼ teaspoon unbuffered vitamin C crystals
½ teaspoon salt
⅔ cup water
⅓ cup oil

Combine the flour, optional poppy seeds, baking soda, vitamin C crystals, and salt in a large bowl. Mix together the water and oil and pour them into the flour mixture. Stir until the dough sticks together, adding a few tablespoons of water if necessary to form a stiff but not crumbly dough. Divide the dough in half. Roll each part to about ⅛ inch thickness on an lightly oiled cookie sheet and cut the dough into 2 inch squares. Sprinkle the tops of the crackers lightly with additional salt if desired. Bake at 350°F for 13 to 17 minutes, or until the crackers are crisp and lightly browned. Makes about 4 dozen crackers.

Chestnut Wafers

With the natural sweetness of chestnut flour, these grain-free crackers can be eaten as a cookie.

2½ cups chestnut flour
1 cup arrowroot
½ teaspoon baking soda
¼ teaspoon unbuffered vitamin C crystals
¼ teaspoon salt
¾ cup water
¼ cup oil

Mix the chestnut flour, arrowroot, baking soda, vitamin C crystals, and salt in a large bowl. Stir together the water and oil and mix them into the dry ingredients, kneading with your hands if necessary. Divide the dough in half and roll each half out to between ⅛ and ¼ inch thickness on an oiled cookie sheet. Cut the dough into 1½ inch squares and bake at 375°F for 8 to 12 minutes. Makes about 4 dozen crackers.

Cassava Crackers

These crackers are crunchy and crumbly. Save the crumbs to use in place of croutons in salads or as breading for broiled fish. (See the "Crispy Broiled Fish" recipe on page 78). To obtain cassava meal by mail order, see "Sources of Special Foods," page 217.

2 cups cassava meal
½ teaspoon baking soda
¼ teaspoon unbuffered vitamin C crystals
¼ teaspoon salt
¾ cup water
¼ cup oil

Mix the cassava meal, baking soda, vitamin C crystals and salt together in a large bowl. Combine the water and oil and stir them into the dry ingredients. Roll and press the crumbly mixture firmly into a 12 by 15 inch pan. (The thickness of the dough layer will be between ⅛ and ¼ inch). Cut the dough into 1½ inch squares and bake at 375°F for 35 to 40 minutes. Makes about 3½ dozen crackers.

Rye Pancakes

Try these and the following pancake recipes with "Mock Maple Syrup," page 197.

2 cups rye flour
1 teaspoon baking soda
½ teaspoon unbuffered vitamin C crystals
3 tablespoons oil
2¼ cups water or unsweetened white grape juice

Mix together the flour, baking soda, and vitamin C crystals. Combine the oil and water or juice and stir them into the flour mixture with a wire whisk, adding a few tablespoons more water if necessary to make a thin batter. (This batter may thicken as it stands and require the addition of more water, 1 to 2 tablespoons at a time, after part of the pancakes have been cooked). Heat a lightly oiled griddle over medium heat or an electric griddle to 350°F. Pour about ⅛ cup batter for each pancake onto the griddle and cook them until they look dry around the edges on the top and are very brown on the bottom. Turn and cook the other side until brown. Makes about 2 to 2½ dozen 3-inch pancakes.

Barley Pancakes

These are so delicious that you will never miss the wheat, milk, and eggs.

2 cup barley flour
1 teaspoon baking soda
½ teaspoon unbuffered vitamin C crystals
½ teaspoon salt
1 tablespoon sugar (optional)
3 tablespoons oil
2½ to 3 cups water

Mix together the flour, baking soda, and vitamin C crystals. Combine the oil and 2½ cups of water and stir the liquids into the flour mixture with a wire whisk, adding a few tablespoons more water if necessary to make a thin batter. (This batter has a pronounced tendency to thicken as it stands and will require the addition of more water, 1 to 2 tablespoons at a time, after part of the pancakes have been cooked. You may have to use up to 3 cups of water (total amount) with additional tablespoons of water added several times as the pancakes are cooking). Heat a lightly oiled griddle over medium heat or an electric griddle to 350°F. Pour about ⅛ cup batter for each pancake onto the griddle and cook them until they look dry around the edges on the top and are light brown on the bottom. Turn and cook the other side until light brown. Makes about 2 to 2½ dozen 3-inch pancakes.

Spelt Pancakes

These pancakes rise like the lightest and fluffiest pancakes you have ever eaten.

2 cups spelt flour
1½ teaspoons baking soda
½ teaspoon unbuffered vitamin C crystals
½ teaspoon salt
2 cups water OR 1¾ cups water plus ¼ cup thawed apple juice concentrate
    OR 1 cup water plus 1 cup apple juice
3 tablespoons oil

Mix together the flour, baking soda, vitamin C crystals, and salt. Combine the oil with the water or water and juice and stir them into the flour mixture with a wire whisk, adding a few tablespoons more water if necessary to make a thin batter. (This batter may thicken as it stands and may require the addition of more water, 1 to 2 tablespoons at a time, after part of the pancakes have been cooked). Heat a lightly oiled griddle over medium heat or an electric griddle to 350°F. Pour about ⅛ cup batter for each pancake onto the griddle and cook them until they look dry around the edges on the top and are light brown on the bottom. Turn the pancakes and cook them until the other side is light brown. Makes about 2½ dozen 3 to 4-inch pancakes.

Kamut Pancakes

These pancakes are kamut at its best – light, fluffy, and delicious!

2½ cups kamut flour
1¼ teaspoons baking soda
½ teaspoon unbuffered vitamin C crystals
¼ teaspoon salt
2 cups water
¼ cup thawed apple juice concentrate
3 tablespoons oil

Mix together the flour, baking soda, vitamin C crystals, and salt. Combine the oil, water, and juice and stir them into the flour mixture with a wire whisk, adding a few tablespoons more water if necessary to make a thin batter. (This batter may thicken as it stands and may require the addition of more water, 1 to 2 tablespoons at a time, after part of the pancakes have been cooked). Heat a lightly oiled griddle over medium heat or an electric griddle to 350°F. Pour about ⅛ to ¼ cup of batter for each pancake onto the griddle and cook them until they look dry around the edges on the top and are light brown on the bottom. Turn the pancakes and cook them until the other side is light brown. Makes about 2 dozen 3 to 4-inch pancakes.

Quinoa Pancakes

These pancakes are a delight to those who must avoid all grains. Try them with "Strawberry Sauce" or "Pineapple Sauce," page 177.

1½ cups quinoa flour
½ cup tapioca flour
1 teaspoon baking soda
½ teaspoon unbuffered vitamin C crystals
1½ teaspoons cinnamon (optional)
3 tablespoons oil
2 cups water or apple juice

Mix together the flours, baking soda, vitamin C crystals, and cinnamon. Combine the oil with the water or juice and stir them into the flour mixture with a wire whisk to make a thin batter. Lightly oil a pancake griddle and heat it over medium heat or heat an electric griddle to 350°F. Pour ⅛ to ¼ cup of batter onto the griddle for each pancake. If the first batch of pancakes you cook is too thick, add an extra 2 to 4 tablespoons of water or juice to the batter until it is thin enough. Cook the pancakes until they are dry on the top and light brown on the bottom, then turn and cook them until the second side is light brown. Makes about 2 dozen 3-inch pancakes or 1½ dozen 4-inch pancakes.

Barley Waffles

Although these waffles are a little more time-consuming to prepare than other breakfast foods, they are a real treat for breakfast and at other times during the day.

2 cups barley flour
2 teaspoons baking soda
¾ teaspoon unbuffered vitamin C crystals
½ teaspoon salt
2 tablespoons oil
2½ cups water

Preheat a lightly oiled waffle iron to medium-high. While the iron is heating, combine the flour, baking soda, vitamin C crystals, and salt in a large bowl. Mix the oil and water, stir them into the dry ingredients, and allow the batter to stand for about 10 minutes while the iron is heating. Pour enough batter into the iron to almost reach the edges (about 1 cup for a large iron) and bake for 15 minutes. Do not try to open the iron until each waffle should be almost done. Makes 3 to 4 9-inch square waffles.

Quinoa Granola

This granola is good for snacks and to take on outings as well as for breakfast. For several granola varieties to use on other days of a rotation diet, see The Ultimate Food Allergy Cookbook and Survival Guide *as described on the last pages of this book.*

1½ cups quinoa flour
½ cup tapioca flour
1½ cups chopped nuts
½ cup sesame seeds
1½ teaspoons cinnamon
⅓ cup oil
¾ cup unsweetened applesauce
¼ cup apple juice concentrate, thawed
⅔ cup chopped dried pears, chopped dates, raisins, or other dried fruit

Combine the flours, nuts, seeds, and cinnamon in a large bowl. Mix the oil, apple-sauce, and juice and pour them into the dry ingredients. Stir until the dough sticks together, adding a little more apple juice concentrate or water if necessary. Spread the dough in a lightly oiled 11 by 15 inch pan. Bake at 300°F for 1 hour, or until light brown, breaking the dough into chunks and stirring it every 15 minutes. Cool the granola completely and stir in the dried fruit. Makes about 8 servings of cereal.

Applesauce Bread

2 cups quinoa flour
½ cup tapioca flour
2 teaspoons baking soda
½ teaspoon unbuffered vitamin C crystals
2 teaspoons cinnamon
¼ cup oil
1 cup unsweetened applesauce
¾ cup apple juice concentrate, thawed

Combine the flours, baking soda, vitamin C crystals, and cinnamon in a large bowl. Mix together the oil, applesauce, and juice, and stir them into the dry ingredients until they are just mixed in. Pour the batter into an oiled and floured 8 by 4 inch loaf pan and bake at 350°F for 45 to 55 minutes, or until the bread is brown and a toothpick inserted into the center of the loaf comes out dry. Cool the loaf in the pan for about 10 minutes, and then remove it from the pan to finish cooling. Makes one loaf.

Banana Bread

This sweet and moist bread can be made in either a grain or a non-grain version.

3 cups spelt flour OR 2 cups amaranth flour plus ½ cup arrowroot
2 teaspoons baking soda
½ teaspoon unbuffered vitamin C crystals
½ teaspoon ground cloves (optional)
½ cup chopped nuts (optional)
1¾ cups mashed ripe bananas
¼ cup oil

Stir together the flour(s), baking soda, vitamin C crystals, cloves, and nuts in a large bowl. Combine the mashed bananas and oil and stir them into the dry ingredients until they are completely mixed in, but be careful not to over-mix. (The batter will be stiff). Put the batter into an oiled and floured 9 by 5 inch loaf pan and bake at 350°F for 55 to 60 minutes, or until the bread is lightly browned and a toothpick inserted in the center comes out dry. Remove it from the oven and allow it to cool in the pan for 10 minutes. Remove it from the pan to cool completely. Makes one loaf.

No-Yeast Bread

These breads are a very versatile answer to the question of how to make a sandwich for lunch without yeast. This bread holds together best if you toast it well before you make a sandwich with it.

Amaranth:

> 3⅜ cups (3¼ cups plus 2 tablespoons) amaranth flour
> 1⅛ cups (1 cup plus 2 tablespoons) arrowroot
> 3 teaspoons baking soda
> ¾ teaspoon unbuffered vitamin C crystals
> 1½ teaspoons salt
> ⅜ cup (¼ cup plus 2 tablespoons) oil
> 1½ cups water

Quinoa:

> 2¼ cups quinoa flour
> ¾ cup tapioca flour
> 2 teaspoons baking soda
> ½ teaspoon unbuffered vitamin C crystals
> 1 teaspoon salt
> ¼ cup oil
> 1½ cups water

Spelt:

>   3½ cups spelt flour
>   2 teaspoons baking soda
>   ½ teaspoon unbuffered vitamin C crystals
>   1 teaspoon salt
>   ½ cup oil
>   1¼ cups water

Barley:

>   3 cups barley flour
>   1½ teaspoons baking soda
>   ½ teaspoon unbuffered vitamin C crystals
>   1 teaspoon salt
>   ⅜ cup (¼ cup plus 2 tablespoons) oil
>   2 cups water

Kamut:

>   3¼ cups kamut flour
>   1¾ teaspoons baking soda
>   ¾ teaspoon unbuffered vitamin C crystals
>   1 teaspoon salt
>   ⅓ cup oil
>   1¾ cups water

Rye:

>   3 cups rye flour
>   1½ teaspoons baking soda
>   ½ teaspoon unbuffered vitamin C crystals
>   1 teaspoon salt
>   ⅓ cup oil
>   1½ cups water

Choose one set of ingredients, above. Combine the flour(s), baking soda, vitamin C crystals, and salt in a large bowl. Stir together the oil and water and mix them into the dry ingredients until they are just mixed in. Put the batter into an oiled and floured 8 by

4 inch loaf pan. Bake at 350°F for 45 to 60 minutes for the kamut bread or for 35 to 45 minutes for the other kinds of bread, or until the bread is lightly browned and a toothpick inserted in the center of the loaf comes out dry. Gently remove the loaf from the pan immediately and cool it completely on a wire rack before slicing it to eat or to put in the freezer. Makes one loaf.

No-Yeast Sandwich Buns

These are great with burgers of any kind, fresh sliced vegetables, and the condiments of your choice made from the recipes in this book.

Prepare one batch of any variety of "No-Yeast Bread," above. Put the batter into oiled and floured glass custard cups, filling them ½ to ⅔ full. Bake at 350°F for 30 to 45 minutes, or until the buns are lightly browned and a toothpick inserted in the center of one bun comes out dry. Remove them from the cups immediately and allow them to cool completely. Carefully slice them in half horizontally with a serrated knife. Makes 7 to 11 buns.

Barley Sandwich Bread

If you want to pick your barley bread sandwich up rather than possibly eating it with a knife and fork, try this recipe. The addition of guar gum to this bread makes it less fragile than barley "No-Yeast Bread."

3 cups barley flour, divided
2 teaspoons guar gum
1 teaspoon salt
2 cups water
⅜ cup (¼ cup plus 2 tablespoons) oil
1½ teaspoons baking soda
½ teaspoon unbuffered vitamin C crystals

Combine 2½ cups of the flour, the guar gum, and the salt in an electric mixer bowl. Add the water and oil and beat the dough for 3 minutes on medium speed. Combine the remaining ½ cup flour with the baking soda and vitamin C crystals, quickly stir them into the dough mixture in the bowl, and beat it on medium speed for 30 seconds. Put the dough into an oiled and floured 8 by 4 inch loaf pan and bake at 350°F for 55 to 65 minutes, or until a toothpick inserted in the center of the loaf comes out dry. Remove from the pan immediately. Makes 1 loaf.

Spelt Sandwich Bread

Beating the batter for this bread develops the gluten in the spelt flour and gives the bread a firmer texture than spelt "No-Yeast Bread."

3½ cups spelt flour, divided
1 teaspoon salt
1¼ cups water
½ cup oil
2 teaspoons baking soda
½ teaspoon unbuffered vitamin C crystals

Combine 3 cups of the flour and the salt in an electric mixer bowl. Add the water and beat on medium speed for 3 minutes or until the dough becomes cohesive and climbs up the beaters. Beat in the oil. Mix together the remaining ½ cup flour, baking soda, and vitamin C crystals and stir or, if necessary, briefly knead them into the dough. Then beat the dough on medium speed for 30 seconds. Put the dough into an oiled and floured 8 by 4 inch loaf pan. Bake at 350°F for 50 to 60 minutes, or until it is brown. Remove it from the pan immediately. Makes one loaf.

Oat Biscuits

These are wonderful fresh out of the oven or served with stew or soup.

2 cups oat flour
1 teaspoon baking soda
¼ teaspoon unbuffered vitamin C crystals
½ teaspoon salt
¼ cup oil
½ cup water

Stir together the flour, baking soda, vitamin C crystals, and salt. Blend in the oil with a pastry cutter until the mixture is crumbly. Stir in the water and pat the dough to about ½ inch thickness on an oat-floured board. Cut the dough in circles with a biscuit cutter or drinking glass and put them on an ungreased baking sheet. Bake at 400°F for 20 to 25 minutes. Makes 10 to 12 biscuits.

Barley Biscuits

The flavor of these barley biscuits is especially delicious when they are hot.

2 cups barley flour
1 teaspoon baking soda
¼ teaspoon unbuffered vitamin C crystals
½ teaspoon salt
⅜ cup (¼ cup plus 2 tablespoons) oil
½ cup water

Stir together the flour, baking soda, vitamin C crystals, and salt. Blend in the oil with a pastry cutter until the mixture is crumbly. Stir in the water and pat the dough to about ½ inch thickness on a barley-floured board. Cut the dough in circles with a biscuit cutter or drinking glass and put them on an ungreased baking sheet. Bake at 400°F for 20 to 25 minutes. Makes 10 to 12 biscuits.

Kamut Drop Biscuits

These biscuits are quick and easy to make.

2⅔ cups kamut flour
1½ teaspoons baking soda
¼ teaspoon unbuffered vitamin C crystals
½ teaspoon salt
¼ cup oil
¾ cup water

Stir together the flour, baking soda, vitamin C crystals, and salt. Combine the oil and water in a separate cup. Stir the liquid ingredients into the dry ingredients until just mixed. Drop the dough by heaping tablespoons on a lightly greased baking sheet. Bake at 350°F for 20 to 30 minutes. Makes about 12 biscuits.

Spelt Biscuits

These biscuits will split into layers that just invite a little all-fruit jam or jelly.

2 cups spelt flour
1 teaspoon baking soda
¼ teaspoon unbuffered vitamin C crystals
½ teaspoon salt
¼ cup oil
½ cup water

Stir together the flour, baking soda, vitamin C crystals, and salt. Blend in the oil with a pastry cutter until the mixture is crumbly. Stir in the water. Knead the dough about 25 times on a spelt-floured board; then pat or roll it to ⅜ inch thickness. Cut the dough in circles with a biscuit cutter or drinking glass and put them on an ungreased baking sheet. Bake at 400°F for 20 to 25 minutes. Makes about 10 2-inch biscuits.

Spelt Biscuit Sandwich Buns

These sandwich buns will stand up to almost anything without falling apart.

Prepare "Spelt Biscuit" dough, above, knead it, and roll it out to ½ inch thickness. Cut it into 3 to 4 inch circles using a large coffee mug. Bake as directed above. Makes 4 to 5 buns.

Teething Biscuits

It is never too early to start rotating the foods of children born into a family with allergic tendencies. These teething biscuits are tough and great for gumming, but watch your children at all times when they are eating these just in case they manage to gum off a piece that they could choke on.

Quinoa:

> 1 cup quinoa flour
> ½ cup tapioca flour
> 3 tablespoons oil
> ½ cup apple juice concentrate, thawed

Amaranth:

> 1 cup amaranth flour
> ½ cup arrowroot
> 3 tablespoons oil
> ⅜ cup pineapple juice concentrate, thawed

Rye:

> 1½ cups rye flour
> 3 tablespoons oil
> ¼ cup plus 3 tablespoons grape juice concentrate, thawed

Combine the flour(s) in a bowl. Mix the oil and juice together and stir them into the flour. Knead the dough to absorb all the flour and form a very hard dough. Roll the dough out to ⅜ inch thickness on a floured board and cut it into 1 by 3 inch bars with a knife. Transfer the bars to a lightly oiled baking sheet. Bake at 300°F for 35 to 40 minutes, or until they begin to brown. Turn off the oven and leave them in for 1 more hour. Makes about 1½ dozen teething biscuits.

Yeast-Leavened Bread, Rolls, and Treats

Yeast bread has been called "the staff of life." This chapter provides recipes for people who tolerate yeast-containing foods (at least occasionally in rotation) but cannot eat the wheat breads and baked goods found at their grocery store.

One of the most exciting developments in cooking since the first edition of *Allergy Cooking with Ease* was written was the advent of bread machines. Now making wheat-free yeast bread can be as easy as measuring out ingredients and pushing a few buttons. Most bread machines can make very good spelt bread and satisfactory kamut bread. To make breads with other, lower gluten flours, one needs to use a bread machine on which you can control the length of the last rising cycle. You can even make non-yeast breads and cakes with most machines. For more about bread machine baking, see *Easy Breadmaking for Special Diets* which is discussed on the last pages of this book.

It is not difficult to make yeast bread by hand, and while it requires intermittent attention over a few hours, the actual amount of time you spend working on it is not that great. Success in making yeast bread depends on two factors: taking good care of the yeast so it will produce gas, and trapping the gas in the dough so the dough will rise properly.

The most important factor in taking good care of the yeast is temperature, both of the liquid used to dissolve the yeast and of the place the dough is set to rise. A yeast thermometer is a very useful tool for determining the temperature of both the liquid and the rising place.

For quick-rise yeast (which is used in the recipes in this book) the temperature of the dissolving liquid should be between 115°F and 120°F. The yeast dissolves best if you sprinkle it over the whole surface of the liquid rather than adding it in one lump. The temperature of the other ingredients is also important. If you have refrigerated other ingredients used in the recipe, such as oil or flour, allow them to warm up to room temperature before you use them.

You should allow the dough to rise in a warm (85°F to 90°F) place. The inside of your oven is an ideal place because it is draft-free and can be kept warm regardless of the room temperature. In a gas oven, the pilot light keeps the inside of the oven at just the right temperature for yeast bread dough to rise. You can use an electric oven for a rising place by heating it to 350°F for five minutes as you start making the bread, then turning it off and leaving the door open for long enough to allow it to cool to about 90°F, and then closing the door.

Another factor in taking good care of yeast is the provision of some food, usually some type of sugar, to support its metabolism. All of the yeast bread recipes in this book contain either some type of fruit sweetener, honey, maple syrup, or sugar. The recipes containing fruit sweeteners tend to be a little heavier than those using the more refined sugars. "Spelt Yeast Bread" is an exception to this, being very light in spite of using apple juice to feed the yeast.

Although fruit sweeteners provide food for yeast, they also add acid to the yeast's environment. If they are used in small amounts, this is usually not a problem. However, when you try to make yeast dough very sweet using fruit sweeteners, the larger amount of fruit sweetener can contribute enough acid to inhibit the growth of the yeast causing long rising times. With some types of dough, you can just wait longer for your dough to rise. If this is not the case, try using SAF Gold™ yeast, a strain of yeast specially bred to be resistant to acid and high concentrations of sweeteners. (See "Sources" page 220).

Along with keeping the yeast happy, you have to trap the gas it makes in order to get yeast bread dough to rise properly. Wheat and spelt flour are naturally high in gluten, a protein found in grains. When you beat or knead wheat or spelt dough, the gluten molecules join together to make long strands of gluten which trap the gas that the yeast produces. Kamut and rye flours contain less gluten than wheat and spelt but still have enough to allow the bread to rise. Adequate beating and/or kneading is vital to developing the gluten in breads made with these flours so that they will rise properly.

Other flours, such as barley, oat, and quinoa, do not contain enough gluten to trap the gas from the yeast on their own. However you can add guar gum to the dough to trap the gas, although the bread will not be as light as wheat or spelt bread. Do not allow guar-gum-containing dough to rise to more than double its original volume during the final rising period, or it may collapse during baking. To purchase guar gum, see "Sources of Special Foods," page 220.

Yeast bread is tested for doneness after baking by different criteria than baking-soda-raised breads. When a loaf of yeast bread is done it will be nicely browned and will have pulled away from the sides of the pan slightly. Remove the bread from the pan immediately after removing it from the oven. If you tap the loaf on the bottom and it sounds hollow, this also indicates that it is done.

Finally, making yeast bread is good for the soul of the cook as well as the bodies of the eaters. It is therapeutic and satisfying to make, and your house will smell wonderful as it bakes. Go for it! You can do it!

Spelt Yeast Bread

This bread is so light that you will not believe that it is made with an alternative flour. Most of the spelt recipes in this book are made with whole spelt flour. For white (sifted) spelt bread recipes, see Easy Breadmaking for Special Diets *as described on the last pages of this book.*

2½ cups water plus ½ cup thawed apple juice concentrate, warmed to 115°F
    OR 1 cup water plus 2 cups apple juice, warmed to 115°F
2 packages quick-rise yeast
2 teaspoons salt
¼ cup oil
8 to 9 cups spelt flour, divided

Combine the water, juice, and yeast in a large electric mixer bowl and let the mixture stand for about 10 minutes or until it is foamy. Add 4½ cups of the spelt flour and beat on medium speed for 5 to 8 minutes. During this time the gluten in the dough will develop into long strands and the dough should become cohesive and begin to climb up the beaters. Beat in the oil and salt. Stir in another 1 to 2 cups of spelt flour. Put the dough on a floured board and knead it for 10 minutes, kneading in enough of the remaining flour to make a firm and elastic dough. Put the dough into an oiled bowl and turn it once so that the top of the ball is also oiled. Cover it with a towel and let it rise in a warm (85°F to 90°F) place until it has doubled in volume, about 45 minutes to 1 hour. Punch down the dough and shape it into two or three loaves. Put each loaf into an oiled 9 by 5 inch loaf pan if you made two loaves or an oiled 8 by 4 inch loaf pan if you made three loaves. (See note on preparing the pans below). Let the loaves rise until they have doubled again, about 45 minutes. Bake at 375°F for 40 to 45 minutes. Immediately run a knife around the edges of the loaves and remove them from the pans. Cool them on a wire rack. Makes 2 or 3 loaves.

Note on preparing the pans: This bread is sometimes difficult to remove from the pan after baking, especially if it has been baked for the full baking time. If you prefer your bread quite brown, you may want to line the pans with parchment or waxed paper after oiling them and also oil the paper.

Spelt Sandwich or Dinner Buns

These buns are as light and tasty as the best from any bakery.

Prepare "Spelt Yeast Bread" dough, above. After the first rising period, divide the dough into 20 to 24 balls for sandwich buns or into about 30 balls for dinner buns. Place them on oiled baking sheets and let them rise until doubled in volume, about 20 minutes. Bake at 375°F for 20 to 30 minutes, or until they are nicely browned. Immediately remove them from the baking sheets with a metal spatula. Makes 20 to 24 sandwich buns or about 30 dinner buns.

Oat Yeast Bread

This bread has a homey and hearty flavor.

1½ cups warm (115°F) water
½ cup date sugar
1 package quick-rise yeast
2¾ cups oat flour
2¼ teaspoons guar gum
½ teaspoon salt
3 tablespoons oil
Oatmeal

Mix together the warm water, date sugar, and yeast, and let the mixture stand for about 10 minutes or until it is foamy. Stir together the dry ingredients in a large electric mixer bowl. Add the yeast mixture and oil and beat the dough for three minutes at medium speed. Scrape the dough from the beaters and the sides of the bowl into the bottom of the bowl. Oil the top of the dough and the sides of the bowl, and cover the bowl with a towel. Put the bowl in a warm (85°F to 90°F) place and let the dough rise for 1 to 1½ hours. Beat the dough again for three minutes at medium speed. Oil an 8 by 4 inch loaf pan and coat the inside of it with oatmeal. Put the dough in the pan and allow it to rise in a warm place for about 20 minutes, or until it barely doubles. Preheat the oven to 350°F. Bake the loaf for about 75 minutes, loosely covering it with foil after the first 15 minutes to prevent excessive browning. Makes one loaf.

Quinoa Yeast Bread

Spicy and flavorful, this is great bread for those who can tolerate yeast occasionally but cannot have grains.

    1 cup water
    ½ cup apple juice concentrate, thawed
    l package quick-rise yeast
    2 cups quinoa flour
    2¼ teaspoons guar gum
    1 teaspoon cinnamon (optional)
    ¼ teaspoon salt
    3 tablespoons oil
    Sesame seeds

Heat the water and apple juice concentrate to about 115°F. Stir in the yeast and let the mixture stand for about 10 minutes or until it is foamy. Stir together the dry ingredients in a large electric mixer bowl. Add the yeast mixture and oil and beat the dough for three minutes at medium speed. Scrape the dough from the beaters and the sides of the bowl into the bottom of the bowl. Oil the top of the dough and the sides of the bowl, and cover the bowl with a towel. Put the bowl in a warm (85°F to 90°F) place and let the dough rise for 1 to 1½ hours. Beat the dough again for three minutes at medium speed. Oil an 8 by 4 inch loaf pan and coat the inside of it with sesame seeds. Put the dough in the pan and allow it to rise in a warm place for about 20 minutes, or until it barely doubles. Preheat the oven to 375°F. Bake the loaf for about 65 minutes, loosely covering it with foil after the first 15 minutes to prevent excessive browning. Makes one loaf.

Raisin Bread

This traditional favorite is excellent grain-free when made with quinoa. For raisin bread made with white spelt flour, see Easy Breadmaking for Special Diets *(page 234).*

Prepare "Quinoa Yeast Bread," above. After the second beating, stir ½ cup raisins into the dough. Put the dough into the pan, allow it to rise the final time, and bake it as directed above. Makes one loaf.

Rye Yeast Bread

This sturdy bread is excellent for sandwiches of all kinds. Since it is made with all whole-grain rye, expect it to be dense. However, its flavor is great!

⅓ cup water
1 cup white grape juice
1 package quick-rise yeast
1 teaspoon salt
3 tablespoons oil
1 tablespoon caraway seed (optional)
4 to 4½ cups rye flour

Warm the water and grape juice to about 115°F and stir in the yeast. Let the mixture stand for about 10 minutes or until it is foamy. Stir in the salt, oil, caraway seed, and 2 cups of the flour, and beat it with a spoon or mixer until it is smooth. Add enough of the rest of the flour to make a soft dough. Knead the dough on a floured board for 10 minutes. Place the dough in an oiled bowl, turn it over so the top of the ball is also oiled, and cover it with a towel. Let it rise in a warm (85°F to 90°F) place for about 45 minutes, or until it is doubled in volume. Shape the dough into a loaf, place it in an oiled 8 by 4 inch loaf pan, and let it rise in a warm place again for about 30 minutes, or until it doubles in volume. Bake at 425°F for 10 minutes, then lower the oven temperature to 350°F for an additional 35 to 45 minutes of baking. Remove it from the oven when the loaf is brown and has pulled away from the sides of the pan slightly. Makes one loaf.

Rye Sandwich Buns

These are excellent with hamburgers and many other types of sandwiches

Prepare "Rye Yeast Bread" dough, above. After the first rising period, divide the dough into nine pieces. Shape the pieces into flattened balls and place them on an oiled baking sheet. Allow them to rise in a warm place for about 30 minutes, or until they have doubled in volume. Bake at 375°F for 20 to 25 minutes, or until they are lightly browned. Slice them in half horizontally with a serrated knife. You can freeze any that will not be used soon. Makes 9 buns.

Quick Barley Yeast Bread

Because this bread does well with a single rising period, it can be made more quickly than most of the other yeast breads.

2⅝ cups (2½ cups plus 2 tablespoons) warm (115°F) water plus 3 tablespoons sugar
    OR 2½ cups warm (115°F) water plus 3 tablespoons honey OR 2¼ cups water
    plus ⅜ cup orange or pineapple juice concentrate warmed to 115°F
1½ packages quick-rise yeast
¼ cup oil
1½ teaspoons salt
3¼ teaspoons guar gum
6 cups barley flour

Mix the water with the sugar, honey, or fruit juice concentrate in a large electric mixer bowl. Stir in the yeast and allow the mixture to stand for about 10 minutes or until it is foamy. Add the oil and salt to the yeast mixture. Stir the guar gum into half of the flour and add this flour mixture to the liquid ingredients in the mixer bowl. Beat at medium speed for three minutes. Mix in the rest of the flour with the mixer and your hands and knead the dough on a floured board for 5 to 10 minutes. Shape the dough into a loaf and press it into an oiled 8 by 4 inch or 9 by 5 inch loaf pan. Place the loaf in a warm (85°F to 90°F) place and allow it to rise for 20 to 30 minutes, or until the dough is just to the top of the pan. Bake at 375°F for 65 to 85 minutes, or until it is golden brown. Makes one loaf.

Barley Sandwich Buns

While these buns are not exactly light, they are still excellent with hamburgers of all kinds.

Prepare "Barley Yeast Bread" dough, above. After kneading, divide the dough into twelve pieces. Shape the pieces into flattened balls and put them on an oiled baking sheet. Let them rise in a warm (85°F to 90°F) place until barely double in volume, about 20 minutes. Bake them at 375°F for 45 to 50 minutes, or until they are lightly browned. Makes 12 buns.

Kamut Yeast Bread

Kamut bread is quick to make because it needs only one rising time right in the baking pan.

2½ cups water plus ½ cup thawed apple juice concentrate, warmed to 115°F
    OR 1 cup water plus 2 cups apple juice, warmed to 115°F
2 packages quick-rise yeast
2 teaspoons salt
¼ cup oil
6 to 6½ cups kamut flour, divided

Combine the water, juice, and yeast in a large electric mixer bowl and let the mixture stand for about 10 minutes or until it is foamy. Add 4 cups of the flour and beat on medium speed for 4 minutes. Beat in the oil and salt. Stir in another 1 to 1½ cups of flour. Put the dough on a floured board and knead it for 10 minutes, kneading in enough of the remaining flour to make a firm and elastic dough. Shape the dough into two loaves. Put each loaf into an oiled 8 by 4 inch loaf pan. Let the loaves rise until they reach the top of the pans, about 20 to 30 minutes. Bake at 375°F for 40 to 45 minutes. Remove the loaves from the pans immediately. Cool on a wire rack. Makes 2 loaves.

Kamut Sandwich or Dinner Buns

These are great with burgers of any kind. Try some of the recipes in this book such as "Heart Healthy Burgers" or "Lentil Burgers" on pages 83 and 84.

Prepare "Kamut Yeast Bread" dough, above. Put the dough into an oiled bowl and turn it once so that the top of the ball is also oiled. Cover it with a towel and let it rise in a warm (85°F to 90°F) place until it has doubled in volume, about 30 minutes to l hour. Punch down the dough and divide it into 16 to 18 pieces for sandwich buns or 20 to 24 pieces for dinner rolls. Shape each piece into a ball, put the balls on an oiled cookie sheet, and allow them to rise again for about 20 to 30 minutes. Bake at 375°F for 20 to 30 minutes. Makes 16 to 18 sandwich buns or 20 to 24 dinner rolls.

Pita (Pocket) Bread

These are great for pocket sandwiches, or cut them in half and use them for pocket tacos.

⅓ batch "Spelt Yeast Bread" dough, page 48
Oil
Spelt flour

Make the dough for "Spelt Yeast Bread" as directed in the recipe and let it rise in a warm (85°F to 90°F) place for 30 to 60 minutes. Punch down the dough and knead it for 3 to 5 minutes on a very lightly oiled board. Using a very lightly oiled rolling pin, roll the dough out to about ¼ inch thickness. Fold the dough in half and roll it out to ¼ inch thickness again. Repeat this process 15 to 20 times. Cut the dough into eight pieces and roll each piece into a 6 to 7 inch circle, flouring both sides of each piece well while you are rolling it and when it is finished. Place the circles on floured baking sheets. Bake in a pre-heated 475°F oven for 5 to 8 minutes, or until they begin to brown. Immediately remove them from the baking sheet and wrap them with a damp dishcloth to keep them soft. Cool them completely before removing them from the dishcloth. To serve, cut them in half with a saw-toothed bread knife, also using the knife to open any places where the top and bottom did not separate. Makes 8 pitas.

Pretzels

These make delicious and nutritious snacks.

⅓ batch "Spelt Yeast Bread" dough, page 48
Salt, coarse if possible

Prepare the "Spelt Yeast Bread" dough and allow it to rise the first time as directed in the recipe. Punch down and knead the dough a few times. Divide it into 24 pieces and roll each piece into a 12 to 15 inch long rope. Place the ropes on oiled baking sheets and shape them into pretzel (open knot) shapes. Sprinkle them with salt and allow them to rise for about 20 minutes. Bake at 350°F for 20 to 25 minutes, or until they are lightly browned. Remove them from the baking sheet immediately with a metal spatula and cool them on a wire rack. Makes 24 3-inch pretzels.

English Muffins

These are delicious split, toasted, and spread with a little all-fruit jam.

1 cup warm (115°F) water
1 tablespoon apple juice concentrate, thawed
1 package quick-rise yeast
2½ to 2¾ cups spelt flour, divided
¼ cup oil
½ teaspoon salt

Combine the water, juice, and yeast in a large electric mixer bowl and let it stand for about 10 minutes or until it is foamy. Mix in 1½ cups of the flour and beat on medium speed for 3 to 5 minutes, or until the gluten is developed and the dough climbs up the beaters. Beat in the oil and salt. Knead in enough of the remaining flour to make a soft dough. Roll the dough out to about ⅜ inch thickness on a thoroughly floured board. Thoroughly flour the top of the dough before and after rolling it. Cut it into 3 inch rounds using a large round biscuit cutter, mug or wide-mouthed glass. Sprinkle flour on a baking sheet. Transfer the rounds to the baking sheet and allow them to rise in a warm (85°F to 90°F) place for about 45 minutes, or until they double in volume. Heat an ungreased griddle or skillet over medium heat or an electric griddle or skillet to 375°F. Carefully transfer the rounds to the griddle and bake them for 6 to 7 minutes on each side, or until each side is brown. Cool them on a wire rack. To split them, make a shallow cut with a knife all around the center of the outside edge of each muffin, then gently pull the top and bottom of the muffins apart. The muffins split more easily when cool. Makes about 16 muffins.

Spelt Waffles

These waffles are light, fluffy, and delicious served with fruit.

1 package active dry or quick-rise yeast
¼ cup apple juice concentrate, warmed to 115°F
2¼ cups water, warmed to 115°F
1 teaspoon salt
¼ cup oil
3¼ cups spelt flour

Dissolve the yeast in the water and apple juice and allow it to stand for 10 minutes, or until foamy. Add the rest of the ingredients and beat with a wire whisk until smooth. Let the batter rise in a warm (85°F) place for 1½ hours, stirring it down one or two times. Stir it down again and refrigerate it for 4 hours to overnight. Bake in an oiled waffle iron heated to "medium" for 6 to 8 minutes, or until the waffles begin to brown. Makes four 9 inch square waffles.

Kamut Waffles

The batter for these waffles (and the spelt waffles, above) can be made the evening before you want to have them for breakfast.

     1 package active dry or quick-rise yeast
     ¼ cup apple or pineapple juice concentrate, warmed to 115°F
     2¼ cups water, warmed to 115°F
     1 teaspoon salt
     ¼ cup oil
     2¼ cups kamut flour
     ½ cup arrowroot

Dissolve the yeast in the water and juice and allow it to stand for 10 minutes, or until foamy. Add the rest of the ingredients and beat with a wire whisk until smooth. Let the batter rise in a warm (85°F) place for 1½ hours, stirring it down one or two times. Stir it down again and refrigerate it for 4 hours to overnight. Bake in an oiled waffle iron heated to "medium" for 10 minutes, or until the waffles begin to brown. Makes three 9 inch square waffles.

Cinnamon Swirl Bread

This is a great breakfast bread especially when toasted.

1 batch "Rye Yeast Bread" dough OR ⅓ batch "Spelt Yeast Bread" dough, page 48,
   OR ½ batch "Kamut Yeast Bread" dough, page 53
2 tablespoons honey, Grape Sweet™ or Fruit Sweet™ OR ¼ cup apple juice
   concentrate OR 2 to 4 tablespoons sugar
2 teaspoons cinnamon
2 teaspoons oil (only if sugar is used for the sweetener)
½ cup raisins (optional)

Make the bread dough as directed in the recipe and let it rise once. While it is rising, if you are using apple juice concentrate for the sweetener, boil it down to 2 tablespoons in volume and let it cool. When the dough is doubled, punch it down and roll it into an 18 by 8 inch rectangle. If you are using sugar for the sweetener, brush the rectangle with the oil. Spread the rectangle with the sweetener, cinnamon, and raisins. Roll it up tightly, starting with the short edge, and pinch the final edge onto the outside of the roll. Place the roll into an oiled 8 by 4 inch loaf pan with the seam side down. Allow it to rise again and bake it as directed in the bread recipe. Makes one loaf.

Spelt Sweet Roll Dough

You can use this dough to make several yeast bread treats – cinnamon rolls (page 62), doughnuts (page 60), or "Tea Ring" (page 59). If you use sugar or honey as the sweetener, the dough will be lighter than if you use apple juice.

½ cup apple juice concentrate plus ⅝ cup water warmed to 115°F OR 1 cup warm
   (115°F) water plus ⅓ cup sugar OR ¾ cup warm (115°F) water plus ⅓ cup honey
1 package quick-rise yeast
3 tablespoons oil
½ teaspoon cinnamon (optional)
¼ teaspoon salt
3 to 3½ cups spelt flour, divided

In a large electric mixer bowl, stir the yeast into the warm water and sweetener. Let the mixture stand for 10 minutes or until it is foamy. Add the oil, cinnamon, salt, and 2¼ cups of the spelt flour. Beat the dough on medium speed for 4 to 6 minutes, or until it becomes cohesive and climbs up the beaters. Knead in enough of the rest of the flour to make a firm and elastic dough. Then knead it for another 10 minutes. Let the dough rise in a warm (85°F to 90°F) place for about 45 minutes to 1 hour, or until it has doubled in volume. Shape and bake it as directed in the individual recipe. The number of rolls, doughnuts, etc. this recipe makes is given in the recipes that follow.

Kamut Sweet Roll Dough

This golden dough is lightly sweetened and tastes great in all kinds of treats such as "Tea Ring," page 59, or "Cinnamon Rolls," page 62.

    1 cup water, warmed to 115°F
    ¼ cup honey
    1 package quick-rise yeast
    3 tablespoons oil
    ¼ teaspoon salt
    3 to 3½ cups kamut flour, divided

In a large electric mixer bowl, stir the yeast into the warm water and honey. Let the mixture stand for 10 minutes or until it is foamy. Add the oil, salt, and 2¼ cups of the flour and beat the dough on medium speed for 4 to 6 minutes. Knead in enough of the rest of the flour to make a firm and elastic dough. Then knead it for another 10 minutes. Let the dough rise in a warm (85°F to 90°F) place for about 45 minutes to 1 hour, or until it has doubled in volume. Shape and bake it as directed in the individual recipe. The number of rolls, etc. this recipe makes is given in the recipes that follow.

Tea Ring

Serve this for an old fashioned tea party or as a not-too-sweet but elegant dessert.

1 batch or "Rye Yeast Bread" dough (page 51) OR ¼ batch "Spelt Yeast Bread"
    dough (page 48) OR 1 batch "Spelt Sweet Roll Dough" made using apple juice
    (page 57) OR ⅔ batch "Spelt Sweet Roll Dough" made using sugar or honey
    (page 57) OR 1 batch of "Kamut Sweet Roll Dough" (page 58)
⅓ cup all-fruit (unsweetened) blueberry preserves, or other all-fruit preserves
⅓ cup chopped nuts
1½ teaspoons cinnamon

Prepare the dough as directed in the individual recipe and allow it to rise the first time. Punch it down and knead it a few times, then roll it into a 12 by 12 inch square. Spread all but a 1 inch margin on one edge of the square with the preserves; sprinkle the preserves with the nuts and cinnamon. Roll the square up, beginning with the edge opposite the edge with no toppings. Pinch the edge without toppings to the outside of the roll. Place the roll, seam side down, on a oiled baking sheet. Using a sharp knife, make eleven cuts at one-inch intervals that extend ¾ of the way through the roll from one side. Form the roll into a circle, using the uncut side as the center of the ring. Turn the slices down on their sides all facing the same way. Allow the ring to rise about 30 minutes to one hour, or until it is doubled in volume. Bake at 350°F for 20 to 30 minutes, or until it is lightly browned. Remove it from the baking sheet to a serving dish immediately. Makes one tea ring.

No-fry Doughnuts

These are a delightful dessert for "kids" of all ages and are easier to make than you would expect.

Quinoa-Cinnamon:

> ½ cup apple juice concentrate, thawed
> ½ cup water
> 1 package quick-rise yeast
> 2½ cups quinoa flour
> 1¾ teaspoons guar gum
> 1 teaspoon cinnamon
> ⅛ teaspoon salt (optional)
> 3 tablespoons oil
> Additional oil
> Optional coating: ¼ cup sugar plus 1 teaspoon cinnamon

Rye:

> 1 cup water plus ⅓ cup maple syrup OR 2 ⅔ cups white grape juice boiled down
>   to 1⅓ cups
> 1 package quick-rise yeast
> 3¼ to 3¾ cups rye flour
> ¼ tsp salt (optional)
> 3 tablespoons oil
> Additional oil
> Optional coating: ¼ cup maple sugar

Spelt:

> 1 batch of "Spelt Sweet Roll Dough," page 57
> Additional oil
> Optional coating: ⅓ cup sugar plus 1½ teaspoons cinnamon (Only about ⅔ of this
>   mixture will be needed if the dough is sweetened with apple juice).

Carob:

    ⅔ cups apple juice concentrate, thawed
    ⅔ cup water
    1 package quick rise yeast
    3 cups rye flour
    ⅓ cup carob powder
    ¼ teaspoon salt (optional)
    3 tablespoons oil
    Additional oil
    Optional coating: ½ cup carob powder or ¼ cup sugar

If you are making spelt doughnuts, prepare the "Spelt Sweet Roll Dough" as directed in the recipe, allow it to rise the first time, punch it down, and begin following the directions in this recipe in the next paragraph. If you are making another type of doughnuts, choose one set of ingredients above. Heat the juice or syrup and water to 115°F. Stir in the yeast and let the mixture stand about 10 minutes, or until it is foamy. Stir the dry ingredients and 3 tablespoons oil into the yeast mixture in a large mixer bowl. (For the rye doughnuts, start with 3¼ cups flour, and add more if needed to make a soft dough). For the quinoa dough, beat the dough for 3 minutes at medium speed. The rye dough and carob doughs may be kneaded by hand for a few minutes instead if they are too stiff for your mixer. Scrape the dough from the beaters and sides of the bowl. Oil the top of the dough and the sides of the bowl and cover the bowl with a towel. Put the dough in a warm (85°F to 90°F) place and let it rise for 45 minutes to 1 hour, or until it has doubled in volume. Beat the quinoa dough for 3 more minutes on medium speed; punch the rye and carob doughs down.

Roll out the dough to about ½ inch thickness on a floured board and cut it with a floured doughnut cutter. Transfer the doughnuts to an oiled cookie sheet with a spatula. Brush the tops of them with oil. Let them rise again until they have doubled in volume, about 20 to 30 minutes. Bake at 400°F for 10 to 15 minutes, or until they are golden brown. Immediately brush them with oil and sprinkle them with or shake them in a bag with the coating, if desired. Makes about 11 to 12 quinoa, carob, or apple-juice-sweetened spelt doughnuts, 12 to 13 rye doughnuts, or 15 to 16 spelt doughnuts if the dough is made with sugar or honey.

Cinnamon Rolls

These rolls are a great treat any time of the day – for breakfast, for an after school snack, or for dessert. To make cinnamon rolls with additional alternative flours, see Easy Breadmaking for Special Diets *as described on the last pages of this book.*

1 batch "Rye Yeast Bread" dough (page 51) OR ⅓ batch "Spelt Yeast Bread" dough
    (page 48) OR 1 batch "Spelt Sweet Roll Dough" made with apple juice (page 57)
    OR ⅔ batch "Spelt Sweet Roll Dough" made with sugar or honey (page 57)
    OR 1 batch of "Kamut Sweet Roll Dough" (page 58)
2 tablespoons Fruit Sweet™, Grape Sweet™, honey or sugar OR ¼ cup apple juice
    concentrate boiled down to 2 tablespoons volume
1 tablespoon oil (only if sugar is used above)
1½ teaspoons cinnamon
⅓ cup raisins (optional)

Prepare the dough and allow it to rise the first time as directed in the individual recipe. Punch it down and roll it out on an oiled board with an oiled rolling pin into a 12 by 12 inch square. Spread the square with oil only if sugar is used for the sweetener. Spread it with the sweetener and sprinkle it with the cinnamon and raisins. Roll the square up starting from one side. Cut the roll into 9 slices and place them cut side down into an oiled 8 or 9 inch square baking pan. Allow the rolls to rise in a warm (85°F to 90°F) place for about 20 to 30 minutes, or until they double in volume and fill the pan. Bake at 375°F for 20 to 30 minutes, or until they are lightly browned. Makes 9 cinnamon rolls. If you wish to use a whole batch of "Spelt Sweet Roll Dough" made with sugar or honey in this recipe, roll the dough out to a 12 by 18 inch rectangle, spread it with 1½ times the given amounts of toppings, roll it up starting on the long side, cut the roll into 12 slices, and bake in a 13 by 9 inch pan to make 12 rolls.

Main Dishes

Main dishes do not pose the same degree of difficulty for the person with food allergies that breads and breakfast foods do. There are many recipes in ordinary cookbooks for broiling, roasting, or baking plain fish, meat, or poultry, or see *Easy Cooking for Special Diets* as described on the last pages of this book. However, if you want to make a casserole or one-dish meal, it is more difficult to find a suitable recipe. This chapter provides such recipes, as well as recipes for those who cannot use ordinary meats, wheat pasta, and other common main dish ingredients. It contains vegetarian recipes and recipes using goat, rabbit, duck, fish, buffalo, and wild game. To get buffalo and wild game by mail order, see "Sources of Special Foods," page 216.

Wild game sometimes has a gamey taste or is tough. To reduce the gamey taste, rub or sprinkle the frozen meat liberally with salt before placing it in the refrigerator to thaw. A crock pot is ideal for cooking game because the long, slow cooking tenderizes the meat.

Stuffed Zucchini

This is a tasty way to use the larger zucchinis from summer gardens.

4 large (about 10 inch long) zucchini squash
1 cup cracker crumbs from cracker recipes in this book
8 ounces goat cheese, shredded
¼ teaspoon salt
⅛ to ¼ teaspoon pepper (optional)
3 teaspoons oil

Wash the zucchinis, cut off the stems, and cut them in half lengthwise. Scoop out the seeded part of the pulp and chop about half of it to make 1½ cups chopped pulp. Mix this with the cracker crumbs, cheese, salt, and pepper. Oil one 9 by 13 inch and one 9 by 9 inch baking pan with the oil. Put the zucchini halves in the pans cut side up and fill them with the pulp mixture. Bake them uncovered at 350°F for 45 minutes, or until the zucchini is tender. This dish may be made ahead and refrigerated and then baked about 1 hour at 350°F. Makes 6 to 8 servings.

Stuffed Acorn Squash

This is a delicious one-dish meal using winter squash.

3 medium acorn squash, about 4½ to 5 pounds total weight
3 medium apples, about 1 pound total weight,
      OR 1½ cups fresh or canned pineapple
¼ cup raisins (optional)
2 cups crumbled goat's or sheep's milk feta cheese, about 12 ounces drained weight
½ teaspoon cinnamon (optional)
1 tablespoon oil

Cut the squash in half lengthwise and remove the seeds. Place them cut side down in an oiled baking dish and bake them at 350°F for 30 minutes. Peel, core, and finely chop the apples, or chop the pineapple into small pieces. Mix the raisins, cheese, cinnamon, and oil with the fruit. Turn the squash cut side up and heap the fruit and cheese mixture into the centers of the squash halves. Bake them for an additional 30 to 45 minutes, or until the squash is tender. Makes six servings.

Note on feta cheese: Feta cheese is produced from milk by a rapid process involving rennet and salt rather than fermentation. Therefore, some doctors allow it on a low-yeast diet. As with any food, what determines if you can eat it is your individual tolerance for it.

No Meat or Tomato Chili

The paprika and vitamin C crystals add the color and tang of tomatoes to this vegetarian chili.

½ cup cold water or bean liquid
1 teaspoon tapioca starch or arrowroot
$\frac{1}{16}$ to ¼ teaspoon chili powder, or to taste
1 teaspoon paprika (optional - for color)
⅛ teaspoon salt, or to taste (optional)
1½ to 2 cups cooked pinto or kidney beans
½ to ⅝ teaspoon tart-tasting unbuffered vitamin C crystals

Combine the water or bean liquid and tapioca starch or arrowroot in a saucepan. Add the chili powder, paprika, and salt and bring the mixture to a boil, stirring it often. Add the beans, crushing a few of them against the side of the pan, and simmer the chili for a few minutes. Stir in the vitamin C crystals. Serve the chili alone or over cooked rice, quinoa, or baked potatoes. Makes one to two servings.

Two-Food-Family Vegetarian Chili

The textured vegetable protein in this recipe, which is derived from soy beans, seems to be meat but is not.

¾ cup textured vegetable protein (optional)
¾ cup boiling water (needed only if you are using the textured vegetable protein)
5 cups cooked kidney or other type of beans, drained
3 cups tomato sauce or fresh peeled and chopped or pureed tomatoes
½ cup water
½ teaspoon salt
⅛ to ¼ cup canned diced green chiles OR ¼ to 1 teaspoon chili powder, to taste

Combine the textured vegetable protein and boiling water in a large saucepan and allow to stand for 5 to 10 minutes, or until the water is all absorbed. Add the beans, tomato sauce or tomatoes, water, salt, and chiles or chili powder and bring the chili to a boil. Reduce the heat and simmer it for 15 to 30 minutes. Makes 4 to 6 servings.

Italian Rice Meal-in-a-Bowl

This makes a easy and satisfying hot lunch.

1 cup peeled and pureed fresh tomatoes OR 1 8-ounces can tomato sauce
1 cup water
½ teaspoon salt
¾ cups uncooked brown rice
1 cup shredded goat cheese, divided
½ cup sliced pitted black olives

Combine the tomatoes or tomato sauce, water, and rice in a large saucepan and bring them to a boil. Reduce the heat and simmer them, covered, for 40 minutes. Remove the pan from the heat, fluff the rice with a fork, and fold in the olives and ¾ cup of the cheese. Let the rice stand in the pan for a few minutes. Sprinkle it with the remaining cheese before serving it. Makes 4 servings.

Quinoa Stuffed Peppers

Because quinoa contains high-quality protein, this is a very satisfying vegetarian dish.

1½ cups quinoa
3 cups water
1 pound frozen chopped spinach
2 tablespoons oil
2 teaspoons salt
¾ teaspoon pepper
3 tablespoon chopped fresh or 3 teaspoons dry sweet basil
2 tablespoons paprika (optional - for color)
6 green bell peppers, seeded
Additional oil

Wash the quinoa thoroughly by putting it in a strainer and rinsing it under running water until the water is no longer foamy. Combine it with 3 cups of water in a saucepan. Bring it to a boil, reduce the heat, and simmer it for 15 to 20 minutes. Cook the spinach in the 2 tablespoons of oil, adding no water, for 5 to 10 minutes, or until it is barely tender. Mix the quinoa and spinach with the seasonings and stuff the mixture into the peppers. To cook the peppers in the traditional Italian way, put a little oil into a heavy frying pan, lay the peppers in the pan on their sides, cover the pan, and fry the peppers slowly, turning them to brown all sides, for 30 to 45 minutes. Or, if you would rather bake the peppers, parboil them for 5 minutes before stuffing them, stuff them, and bake them in an oiled casserole dish at 350ºF for 45 minutes. Makes 4 to 6 servings.

Turkey Pot Pie

Turn that leftover turkey into meals in your freezer using this recipe.

1 batch of any kind of pie crust, page 179
2 cups cooked, cubed turkey (or chicken)
2 cups cooked, cubed vegetables, such as potatoes, carrots, celery, green beans,
    peas, or a combination of vegetables
1¼ to 1½ cups turkey gravy, white sauce, or clear sauce, below

Make one of the following binders for the pie filling:

TURKEY GRAVY: Add 3 tablespoons rye, spelt, kamut, or barley flour to about 3 to 4 tablespoons of turkey drippings and cook the mixture over medium heat, stirring it, for a few minutes. Gradually add 1 cup water while stirring the mixture, and cook it for a few minutes more, or until it is thick and smooth. Season it to taste with salt if desired.

GRAIN-FREE TURKEY GRAVY: Combine ¼ cup cold water with 2 tablespoons arrowroot in a jar and shake it until the lumps are gone. Stir this into 1 cup of chicken or turkey broth or pan juices. Cook the mixture over medium heat, stirring, until it comes to a boil and thickens.

WHITE SAUCE: Combine 1¼ cups cold water and 4 tablespoons spelt, rye, or barley flour in a jar and shake it until the lumps are gone. Cook the mixture over medium heat, stirring, until it becomes thick and bubbly. Simmer it for a few minutes more and season it to taste with salt if desired.

CLEAR SAUCE: Combine 1½ cups cold water and 2 tablespoons arrowroot or tapioca starch in a saucepan. Cook the mixture over medium heat, stirring it often, until it boils and thickens. Season it to taste with salt if desired.

Make the pie crust as directed in the recipe. If you are using a rye or spelt crust, roll out half of it on a floured pastry cloth and put it into a pie dish. For any other kind of crust, press half of it into a pie dish. Combine the turkey, vegetables, and gravy or sauce and put them into the bottom crust of the pie. Roll out the top crust of a spelt or rye pie and put it over the filling; crimp the edges together and prick the top of the crust. If you are using any other kind of crust, sprinkle crumbs of the crust evenly over the pie filling. Bake at 350°F for 45 minutes or until the crust begins to brown. This pie can be frozen before baking and baked without thawing at 350°F for about one hour. Serves 4 to 6.

Biscuit Topping for Casseroles

Use these toppings for the buffalo, duck, or bean casseroles on the following pages or for a casserole filling of your own creation.

Barley:

   ⅞ cup barley flour (¾ cup plus 2 tablespoons)
   ¾ teaspoon baking soda
   ¼ teaspoon unbuffered vitamin C crystals
   ¼ teaspoon salt
   ⅜ cup water (¼ cup plus 2 tablespoons)
   2 tablespoons oil

Amaranth:

   ¾ cup amaranth flour
   ¼ cup arrowroot
   ¾ teaspoon baking soda
   ¼ teaspoon unbuffered vitamin C crystals
   ¼ teaspoon salt
   ⅜ cup water (¼ cup plus 2 tablespoons)
   2 tablespoons oil

Quinoa:

   ⅝ cup quinoa flour (½ cup plus 2 tablespoons)
   2 tablespoons tapioca flour
   ¾ teaspoon baking soda
   ¼ teaspoon unbuffered vitamin C crystals
   ¼ teaspoon salt
   ⅜ cup water (¼ cup plus 2 tablespoons)
   2 tablespoons oil

Rye:

  ¾ cup rye flour
  ¾ teaspoon baking soda
  ¼ teaspoon unbuffered vitamin C crystals
  ¼ teaspoon salt
  ⅜ cup water (¼ cup plus 2 tablespoons)
  2 tablespoons oil

Spelt:

  ⅞ cup spelt flour (¾ cup plus 2 tablespoons)
  ¾ teaspoon baking soda
  ¼ teaspoon unbuffered vitamin C crystals
  ¼ teaspoon salt
  ⅜ cup water (¼ cup plus 2 tablespoons)
  2 tablespoons oil

Kamut:

  ¾ cup kamut flour
  ¾ teaspoon baking soda
  ¼ teaspoon unbuffered vitamin C crystals
  ¼ teaspoon salt
  ⅜ cup water (¼ cup plus 2 tablespoons)
  2 tablespoons oil

Choose one set of ingredients, above. Combine the flour(s), baking soda, vitamin C crystals, and salt in a bowl. Mix together the water and oil and stir them into the flour mixture until just mixed. Spread the batter over the casserole filling of your choice and bake it at 350°F for 35 to 45 minutes, or until the topping browns. Makes enough topping for a casserole serving 4 to 6 people.

Bean-n-Biscuit

In this vegetarian casserole, the protein in the beans and the protein in the grain combine to give you a complete protein.

¼ small onion, chopped (optional)
1 tablespoon oil (optional – only needed if you are using the onion)
1½ cups water OR 1½ cups tomato sauce
      OR 1 pound Italian plum tomatoes plus 1 cup water
2 tablespoons arrowroot or tapioca starch
1 10-ounces package frozen green lima beans (about 1 ½ cups beans)
1½ cups cooked kidney beans, drained
1½ cups cooked white beans, such as canellini or navy beans, drained
½ teaspoon salt, or to taste (optional)
¼ teaspoon pepper (optional)
⅛ teaspoon chili powder, or to taste (optional)
1 batch of "Biscuit Topping for Casseroles," page 68

If you are using the onion, sauté it in the oil until it begins to brown. If you are using the fresh tomatoes, remove the stem ends from them and cut them into eighths. Combine the water or tomato sauce with the arrowroot or tapioca flour in a saucepan. Cook them over medium heat, stirring often, until the mixture thickens and boils. Stir in the beans, tomatoes (if you are using them), onion, and seasonings. Return the mixture to a boil and pour it into a 3-quart casserole dish. Top it with the biscuit topping of your choice, and bake it at 350ºF for 35 to 45 minutes, or until the topping browns. Makes 4 to 6 servings.

Macaroni and Cheese

Children love this traditional favorite. To keep the pasta firm, it is best to make it right before serving time with most types of pasta, but you can make it ahead of time and freeze it if you use spelt pasta.

10 to 12 ounces uncooked pasta, any type and shape
1 batch of either "Cheese Sauce I" OR "Cheese Sauce II," on the next page

Prepare the cheese sauce while bringing the water to a boil for the pasta. When the cheese sauce is almost finished, cook the pasta according to the directions for cooking pasta on page 85 and the cooking time for the type of pasta you are using given on the package or on page 88 or 89 if you made your own pasta. Do not overcook the pasta or it will get mushy standing in the cheese sauce. When the pasta is cooked, drain it, combine it with the hot cheese sauce, and serve it immediately. Makes 4 servings.

CHEESE SAUCE I:

5 ounces goat's or sheep's milk feta cheese, crumbled (about 1 cup crumbled cheese)
¾ cup water
4½ teaspoons arrowroot or tapioca flour

Blend all of the ingredients in a blender until they are smooth. Pour the mixture into a saucepan and heat it over medium heat until it thickens slightly and barely boils. Use it with pasta for "Macaroni and Cheese" or as a sauce for vegetables.

CHEESE SAUCE II:

3 tablespoons arrowroot OR 2 tablespoons rye or barley flour plus 2 tablespoons oil
¼ teaspoon salt
Dash of pepper (optional)
2 cups goat milk
8 to 10 ounces goat jack or cheddar cheese, shredded

To thicken the sauce with the arrowroot, combine the arrowroot, seasonings, and milk in a saucepan. Cook the mixture over medium heat, stirring it occasionally, until it thickens and just begins to boil.

To thicken the sauce with the rye or barley flour, combine the flour, oil, and seasonings in a saucepan. Cook the mixture over medium heat, stirring constantly, until it begins to bubble. Add the milk very gradually while stirring it and cook it until it thickens and just begins to boil.

After the sauce has thickened, remove the pan from the burner and add the cheese. Stir it until the cheese has melted, and then combine it with cooked pasta for "Macaroni and Cheese" or serve it with cooked vegetables.

Buff-n-Biscuit

Meat, vegetables, and bread – this casserole has everything you could want for a meal in one dish.

5 to 6 stalks celery (about ½ pound)
½ medium onion (optional)
2 teaspoons oil
1 pound ground buffalo
¾ to 1 teaspoon salt, or to taste (optional)
¼ teaspoon pepper (optional)
2 teaspoon paprika (optional - for color)
1¼ cups water, divided
2 tablespoons arrowroot or tapioca starch
1 batch of "Biscuit Topping for Casseroles," page 68

Slice the celery into ¼ inch slices and chop the onion. Sauté them in a skillet with the oil until they begin to brown. Remove them to a 3-quart casserole dish. Put the buffalo in the remaining oil in the skillet and cook it, stirring it occasionally, until it is well browned. Drain the fat from the pan, and add the salt, pepper, paprika, and 1 cup of the water. Simmer the mixture for 30 minutes, adding more water while it is cooking, if necessary, to bring it back to its original level. Combine the arrowroot or tapioca starch with the remaining ¼ cup cold water and add the mixture to the pan. Return the meat mixture to a boil and simmer it until it thickens. Put the meat into the casserole dish with the celery and onion and stir them together. Top them with the biscuit topping of your choice, and bake at 350°F for 35 to 45 minutes, or until the topping browns. Makes 4 to 6 servings.

Duck-n-Biscuit

Here is a great way to use up that leftover duck or other poultry.

¾ pound cooked duck, skinned and cut into ¾ inch cubes (about 2½ cups cubes)
¾ pound butternut squash, pared, seeded, and cut into ¾ to 1 inch cubes
     (about 3 cups cubes)
½ pound small zucchini, sliced into ½ inch slices (about 3 cups slices)

½ to ¾ teaspoon salt, or to taste
¼ teaspoon pepper (optional)
1½ cups water
2 tablespoons arrowroot or tapioca flour
1 batch of "Biscuit Topping for Casseroles," page 68

Combine the water and arrowroot or tapioca flour in a saucepan. Cook it over medium heat until it thickens and boils. Stir in the duck, vegetables, and seasonings, return it to a simmer, and heat it through for a few minutes. Pour the mixture into a 3-quart casserole dish, top it with the biscuit topping of your choice, and bake it at 350°F for 35 to 45 minutes, or until the topping browns. Makes 4 to 6 servings.

Pasties

This is a great meal to have in the freezer for the days when you're too busy to cook.

⅓ batch "Spelt Yeast Bread" dough, page 48, OR 1 batch "Rye Yeast Bread" dough,
    page 51, OR ½ batch "Kamut Yeast Bread" dough, page 53
1 tablespoon spelt, kamut, or rye flour (the same type as used in the dough)
2 teaspoons oil
½ cup water
⅛ teaspoon salt
2 cups chopped leftover meat or cooked ground meat of any kind
    (10 to 12 ounces weight of ground meat before cooking)
2 cups cooked vegetables, any kind or combination

Prepare the yeast bread dough and allow it to rise the first time. Combine the flour and oil in a saucepan and heat the mixture over medium heat until it begins to bubble. Then cook it for 1 to 2 minutes, stirring it constantly. Add the water and salt and cook it until it boils and thickens. Stir in the meat and vegetables. Divide the dough into twelve pieces. Roll each piece out into a 6-inch circle on a lightly floured board. Put one-twelfth of the meat and vegetable filling on each circle. Fold the circles in half over the filling, press the edges together, and prick the tops of the pasties with a fork. Put them on two oiled baking sheets. Let them rise for about 15 minutes. Bake them at 375°F for 15 to 20 minutes, or until they are lightly browned. Makes 12 pasties.

Game Stroganoff

This is an elegant way to prepare game meat.

1 to 1½ pounds elk, antelope, venison, buffalo, or other game steak, cut into
    thin strips about 2 inches long
¾ pound mushrooms, sliced (optional)
1 small onion, minced (optional)
3 tablespoons oil
1½ cups water
1 to 1½ teaspoons salt, or to taste
2 tablespoons arrowroot
¾ cup wine or additional water
4 cups cooked noodles

Sauté the vegetables in the oil until they are tender and remove them from the pan.
Brown the meat in the oil remaining in the pan. Add the 1½ cups water and the salt and
simmer the meat, covered, for 45 minutes. Add the vegetables, return the mixture to a
boil, and simmer it for a few minutes. Combine the arrowroot with the wine or additional water and stir them into the meat and vegetable mixture. Simmer the mixture
until it thickens. Serve it over hot cooked noodles. Makes 4 servings.

Crock Pot Game Roast

*The long, slow cooking of the crock pot gives this roast a delicious flavor while
tenderizing it.*

1 2- to 3-pound antelope, elk, venison, buffalo, or other game roast
½ to ¾ teaspoon salt
3½ cups water, or enough to barely cover the roast

The day before cooking this dish, rub the frozen roast with the salt and allow it to
thaw overnight in the refrigerator. In the morning, place the roast in a 3-quart crock pot
and add enough water to barely cover the roast. Cook it on low for 8 to 10 hours. Serves
4 to 6.

Game Roast Dinner

If you start this in the crock pot in the morning, you will have a delicious complete dinner ready for you at the end of the day.

1 2- to 3-pound antelope, elk, venison, buffalo, or other game roast
½ to ¾ teaspoon salt
2 to 3 pounds sweet potatoes, or a combination of sweet potatoes, carrots, and/or parsnips
6½ cups water, or enough to barely cover the roast and vegetables

The day before cooking this dish, rub the frozen roast with the salt and allow it to thaw overnight in the refrigerator. In the morning, place the vegetables in a 3-quart crock pot, put the roast on top of them, and add enough water to barely cover the roast. Cook it on low for 8 to 10 hours. Remove the roast and vegetables from the liquid in the crock pot and place them on a serving dish. Serves 4 to 6.

Game Chili

The game meat is so well disguised in this recipe that even a fussy eater will like it.

1½ pounds ground antelope, elk, venison, buffalo, or other game meat
1 tablespoon oil (optional)
3 cups tomato sauce or pureed fresh tomatoes
½ to ¾ teaspoon chili powder, or to taste
¼ teaspoon salt
½ cup water
5 cups kidney or other cooked beans, drained

In a large saucepan, brown the meat in the oil or without the oil. Pour off as much of the fat as possible. Add the rest of the ingredients, adding more water if you prefer a juicier chili. Simmer the chili for 30 minutes. Makes 4 to 6 servings.

Game Stew

To decrease the number of food families in this recipe to three, omit the bay leaf and black pepper and either use three seeded and chopped green peppers instead of the carrots and celery or omit the potatoes.

2 to 3 pounds of elk, antelope, venison, buffalo, or other game round steak, cut
    into cubes
5 carrots (about 1 pound), peeled and cut into 1 inch pieces
5 stalks of celery, cut into 1 inch pieces
2 to 3 potatoes, peeled and cut into 1 inch cubes (optional)
½ cup tapioca
1 bay leaf (optional)
2 teaspoons salt, divided
¼ teaspoon pepper (optional)
3 cups water

The day before you plan to serve this stew, rub the frozen meat with 1 teaspoon of the salt and allow it to thaw overnight in the refrigerator. In the morning, cut the meat into cubes, trimming off all of the fat, and combine it with the vegetables, tapioca, bay leaf, remaining 1 teaspoon salt, pepper, and water in a 3-quart crock pot. Stir the mixture well to evenly distribute the tapioca and cook it on low for 8 to 10 hours or on high for 6 hours. Any leftover stew freezes well. Makes 8 servings.

Zucchini Stew

Zucchini does not seem mushy when it is frozen in this stew, so this is a perfect dish to make in the summer when zucchini is abundant and freeze to eat in the winter. It can be made with any game meat or even beef if you tolerate it.

1 to 1¼ pounds ground antelope, elk, venison, buffalo, or other game meat
2 tablespoons finely chopped onion, or to taste (optional)
1 tablespoon oil
1¼ pounds Italian plum tomatoes, stemmed and cut into quarters
    OR 1 1-pound can peeled tomatoes
6 tablespoons tomato paste (optional) OR 1 8-ounce can tomato sauce
    (optional - omit the water, below, if the sauce is used)

1 teaspoon salt
¼ teaspoon pepper (optional)
¼ to ½ cup water
2 to 2½ pounds zucchini, sliced about ⅜ inch thick

In a large saucepan, brown the meat and onion in the oil. Drain off all of the fat. Add the tomatoes, tomato paste or sauce, salt, pepper, and ¼ cup of water (omit it if tomato sauce was used) and simmer the stew for about 15 minutes. Add the zucchini and simmer it for about an additional 15 minutes, or until the zucchini is just tender. (For very large zucchini, the simmering time will be longer.) Add the additional ¼ cup water if the stew begins to dry out during cooking. Makes 4 to 6 servings.

Golden Game Stew

The sweetness of the vegetables used in this stew is a perfect complement to the game meat.

1½ pounds antelope, elk, venison, buffalo, or other game round steak
1½ pounds (about 2 to 3 large) sweet potatoes, peeled and cut into 1inch cubes (about 4 cups cubes)
1½ pounds carrots, cut into ¾ to 1 inch slices (optional)
½ cup tapioca
2 teaspoons salt, divided
¼ teaspoon pepper (optional)
2 whole cloves (optional)
1 bay leaf (optional)
1 cup water
1½ pounds butternut squash, pared, seeded, and cut into 1 inch cubes (optional) (about 4 cups cubes)

The day before you plan to serve this stew, rub the frozen meat with 1 teaspoon of the salt and allow it to thaw in the refrigerator overnight. Cut it into 1 inch cubes and combine it with the sweet potatoes, tapioca, remaining 1 teaspoon salt, pepper, clove, bay leaf, and water in a 3-quart crock pot. Cook the stew on high for 6 hours or on low for 8 to 10 hours. If you are using the squash, add it 2 hours before the end of the cooking time. Leftovers from this recipe freeze well. Makes 6 to 8 servings.

Crispy Broiled Fish

This is a grain-free change from plain broiled fish. To obtain cassava meal by mail order, see "Sources of Special Foods," page 217.

1 pound cod, halibut, haddock, turbot, or other fish fillets or steaks
Oil
Salt
1 to 2 tablespoons cassava meal or crumbs from cassava crackers

Brush oil on both sides of the fish and sprinkle it lightly with salt. Pat the cassava meal or cracker crumbs onto both sides of the fish. Broil it at 450°F for 10 minutes per inch of thickness of the fish, turning the fish over halfway through the broiling time. Makes 2 servings.

Salmon Loaf or Patties

When made as patties, this recipe is delicious served on any type of sandwich buns with "Pine Nut Dressing" and fresh vegetables.

1 15-ounce can salmon
½ cup finely crushed cracker crumbs, made from "Quinoa Crackers," page 27,
    "Saltines," page 29, "Canola Seed Crackers," page 31, Kamut Poppy Seed
    Crackers," page 32, or any other crackers you can eat
Oil

Drain the salmon, reserving the liquid. Remove the skin from the meat, if desired. Knead together the fish and the cracker crumbs, adding a little of the reserved fish liquid if necessary to help the mixture stick together. Press it into an oiled 7 by 7 inch glass baking dish. Bake it uncovered at 350°F for 25 to 30 minutes, or until it begins to brown on top. Or, form the mixture into four patties and fry them on both sides in a little oil. (These patties are fragile). Makes 4 servings.

Roast Duck with Cherry Sauce

This makes an elegant but easy dinner for guests.

1 duck, weighing about 5 pounds
Salt
1 16-ounce can tart cherries, packed in water
1 cup apple juice concentrate
4 teaspoons arrowroot or tapioca flour

Clean the duck and cut off the excess skin and fat. Rub the inside of the cavity with salt. Place it on a rack in an uncovered roasting pan and bake at 325°F for 3 to 3½ hours, or until brown. At least ½ hour before the end of the roasting time or up to two days ahead, drain the cherries, reserving the liquid. Combine ½ cup of the cherry liquid with the apple juice concentrate and arrowroot or tapioca flour in a saucepan. Cook this mixture over medium heat until it thickens and begins to boil. Stir in the cherries and return it to a boil. Serve the sauce warm over or along side of the duck. The cherry sauce is best made 1 to 2 days ahead so the sweetness of the apple juice can permeate the cherries, and then reheated right before serving time. Makes 2 to 4 servings.

Crispy Oven-Fried Chicken

Chicken does not have to be laden with wheat, eggs, and fat to be delicious, as this recipe demonstrates.

1 chicken, weighing about 3 to 4 pounds
½ cup rye, barley, rice, spelt, kamut, or oat flour, or cassava meal
¼ teaspoon salt
⅛ teaspoon pepper (optional)
3 tablespoons oil (optional)

Wash and clean the chicken and cut it into serving size pieces. Combine the flour or meal, salt, and pepper in a bag. If you are using the oil, put it in a shallow bowl, dip each piece of chicken in it, turning it to coat all of the sides, and allow the excess oil to drip off. Put each chicken piece into the bag and shake it to coat it with flour or meal. Place the chicken pieces in a baking dish and bake them, uncovered, at 350°F for 1½ to 2 hours, or until nicely browned. Makes 4 servings.

Italian-Style Baked Rabbit

This is an old family recipe when made with the wine, but is also delicious made with water or juice.

1 rabbit, weighing about 2 to 2½ pounds
1 clove garlic (optional)
¼ to ½ teaspoon salt, or to taste
⅛ teaspoon pepper (optional)
2 teaspoons dry sweet basil, or 1 tablespoon finely chopped fresh sweet basil
¾ cup white wine, white grape juice, apple juice, or water

Cut the rabbit into serving size pieces and place them in a 13 by 9 inch baking dish. Cut the garlic into quarters and put the pieces of garlic between the pieces of rabbit in the dish. Pour the wine, juice, or water over the rabbit. Sprinkle it with the salt, pepper, and sweet basil. Cover it with foil or a glass baking dish lid and bake it at 350°F for 1 hour. Uncover it and bake it 30 minutes to 1 hour longer, or until it is brown and the liquid has evaporated. Serves 4 to 6.

Tender Goat Chops or Steak

Broiled goat can be tough if thoroughly cooked to the well-done stage. Long cooking with water makes it tender.

1 to 1½ pounds goat chops, round steak, shoulder steak, or other cut of meat
Salt
Pepper (optional)
Water

Place the chops or steak in a glass baking dish that has a lid and add water to a depth of about ¾ of the thickness of the meat. Sprinkle the meat with salt and pepper. Cover the dish with its lid and bake it at 350°F for 2 hours, uncovering it the last half hour to allow most of the water to evaporate if necessary. Makes 4 servings.

Goat Ribs

These ribs are delicious either barbecue-style or plain for those who cannot eat tomatoes.

Rib (center) section of a small goat (about 3½ pounds)
About 6 to 8 cups water
Salt
2 cups catsup (optional) - about 2 batches of "Easy Catsup," page 198, or
    1 batch of "Fresh Tomato Catsup," page 198

Flatten out the center section of a small goat, breaking a few ribs if necessary to flatten it. Place it in a large roaster and add water to ½ to ¾ the depth of the meat. Salt the meat. Cover it and bake it at 350°F for 1½ hours. Uncover it and bake it 1 hour longer, or until the top of the meat has browned nicely. For plain ribs, serve it at this point. For barbecue-style ribs, pour off as much of the liquid as possible from the roaster. Pour the catsup over the meat and bake it, uncovered, for another ½ to 1 hour, basting it often. Makes 6 servings.

Braised Goat

This is a traditional Italian way to prepare young goat for Easter.

1 quarter of a young goat (about 4 pounds)
Oil
Salt
Pepper (optional)
Rosemary (optional)

Rub the goat with oil. Sprinkle all sides of the meat generously with the salt, pepper, and rosemary. Place it on a rack in a roasting pan and bake it, uncovered, at 400°F for 30 to 45 minutes, or until it begins to brown. Add 1 inch of boiling water to the bottom of the roaster, cover it, and bake it at 350°F for an additional 2 hours. Makes 6 to 8 servings.

Sloppy Goat Sandwiches

This is a delicious way to use leftover "Braised Goat" on the previous page.

6 ounces small pieces or scraps of cooked goat meat
½ cup catsup, either "Easy Catsup," page 198, or "Fresh Tomato Catsup," page 198
Bread or sandwich buns (see the preceding two chapters for recipes)

Mix the meat and catsup in a saucepan and heat them over medium heat until the mixture begins to boil. Reduce the heat and simmer for a few minutes to heat the meat through thoroughly. Serve it on bread or sandwich buns. Makes 2 servings.

Buffalo Loaf

The fresh vegetables added to this meatloaf give it such an excellent flavor that it doesn't really need the optional catsup.

1 pound ground buffalo
¼ small onion, finely chopped (optional)
½ small green pepper, finely chopped (about ⅓ cup chopped)
1 cup grated carrots
¼ cup arrowroot or tapioca flour
¾ teaspoon salt, or to taste (optional)
¼ teaspoon pepper (optional)
¼ teaspoon dry mustard (optional)
½ cup water, divided
¼ cup catsup, (optional – "Easy Catsup," page 198, or "Fresh Tomato Catsup," page 198)

Mix together the buffalo, vegetables, arrowroot or tapioca flour, seasonings, and ¼ cup of the water, and shape the mixture into a loaf. Place it into a 2- to 3-quart covered casserole dish with the remaining ¼ cup water. Cover the casserole dish with its lid and bake the meatloaf at 350°F for 45 minutes. Then uncover it and bake it for another 30 minutes. Top it with the catsup during the last 15 minutes of baking, if desired. Makes 6 servings.

Braised Buffalo Burgers

This recipe is for those who like their burgers well-done but find thoroughly broiled buffalo tough.

1 pound ground buffalo
½ teaspoon salt, or to taste (optional)
⅛ to ¼ teaspoon pepper (optional)
2 tablespoons tapioca starch or arrowroot
2 tablespoons water

Mix all the ingredients together thoroughly. Shape the mixture into four patties. Place the patties in a covered casserole and add water to a depth of ¼ to ½ inch. Cover the casserole with its lid and bake the burgers at 350°F for 30 minutes. Uncover them and bake them an additional 15 minutes. Turn the burgers over and bake them for another 15 minutes, or until the second side is browned on the top. Makes 4 servings.

Heart Healthy Burgers

Combining turkey and/or buffalo with grain and vegetables in these burgers gives them a great taste, makes them lower in fat, and adds fiber and vitamins to the meat.

8 ounces of ground turkey PLUS 4 ounces of ground buffalo
    OR 12 ounces of ground turkey, buffalo, or other meat of your choice
½ cup cooked rice or other cooked grain or grain alternative of any kind
½ cup cooked vegetables, any kind or combination (peas, carrots, beans, or a
    combination of these vegetables are good)
½ teaspoon salt (optional)
¼ teaspoon pepper

Put the cooked vegetables and grain in a food processor or blender and puree, or puree them with a hand blender. To do this with a hand blender, puree the vegetables first. Then add the grain and blend the mixture some more. It does not have to be perfectly liquefied; a few chunks remaining in the burgers are nice. Combine the puree with the meats and seasonings. Form the mixture into 5 patties. Place the patties on a broiler pan and broil at 500°F about 3 to 4 inches from the heat. Broil the burgers for 8 minutes, then turn them and broil the other side for 8 minutes. Cut one of the burgers to make sure the inside is no longer pink before serving. Serve the burgers on split buns with the toppings of your choice. Makes 5 servings. If you are not feeding five people, these burgers freeze well, either before or after cooking.

Lentil Burgers

These vegetarian hamburgers are excellent with any type of bread or sandwich buns and fresh vegetables or homemade condiments (pages 198 to 200).

    1 pound dry lentils
    Water
    2 tablespoons chopped onion (optional)
    2 teaspoon salt, or to taste (optional)
    ¼ teaspoon pepper (optional)
    ½ cup tapioca flour, arrowroot, or water chestnut flour
    Oil

Wash the lentils and soak them overnight in about 2 quarts of water. In the morning, drain and rinse them 2 to 3 times, and drain them again. Add the onion, if you are using it, and enough water to the lentils to barely cover them (about 4 cups water), and bring them to a boil. Reduce the heat, and simmer them, covered, for 1½ to 2½ hours, or until they are tender and the water is almost completely absorbed. Mash them with a potato masher, mashing in the starch, salt, and pepper. Return the mixture to the heat and cook it over low heat, stirring it often, for about 30 minutes, or until it is very thick and the whiteness of the starch has disappeared. (The mixture may be refrigerated at this point, if you wish). Form the mixture into patties and fry them in a small amount of oil on both sides. These patties freeze well and may be reheated. Makes 8 to 10 patties.

Pasta and Ethnic Dishes

When I was diagnosed as being allergic to all of the major ingredients in most Italian dishes, my husband's comment was that my "Italian license" was going to be revoked. But being allergic to wheat (or even all grains), milk, eggs, tomatoes, and beef does not mean that one can no longer enjoy Italian or other ethnic foods. Commercially made pasta is available for people with food allergies (See "Sources of Special Foods," pages 218 to 219), and this chapter also provides recipes for making pasta.

You can make pasta sauces with ingredients other than tomatoes. (See the recipes in this chapter for "Pesto" and "Garlic, Pepper, and Oil Sauce"). You can use meat other than beef or pork in sauce recipes or omit meat altogether. You can use goat or sheep cheese, if you tolerate it, or simply omit the cheese. Don't give up your Italian license! It is worth a little extra effort to make and enjoy these foods.

TO COOK PASTA

For each pound of pasta to be cooked, bring at least 4 quarts of water to a rolling boil. Add 1 to 2 teaspoons of salt to make the water boil even faster. Add the pasta, stir it to keep it from sticking together, and rapidly return it to a boil. Begin timing the cooking of the pasta when the water returns to a boil. Reduce the heat enough to keep it from boiling over and boil it until the pasta is *al dente,* or offers some resistance "to the tooth." In *The Romagnoli's Table,* Margaret and G. Franco Romagnoli describe *al dente* as being "bitable but not raw, can be felt under the teeth but is neither crunchy not rubbery; it means that each piece of pasta retains its individuality and texture, yet is just tender enough to please." The only foolproof way to determine when pasta is *al dente* is to remove a piece of it from the boiling water and bite it. The length of time it will take to cook the pasta varies with the type and size of the pasta and if it is home-made or dried. It ranges from 2 to 4 minutes for some homemade pastas to 12 minutes for some commercial pastas. Approximate cooking times are given in the following recipes. Begin testing the pasta a few minutes before the time should be up until you become familiar with each type of pasta. When the pasta is *al dente,* pour it and the water through a large colander set in the sink. Then immediately pour the pasta into a bowl containing a generous amount of sauce or oil and toss it to coat the pasta thoroughly. You do not have to let it stand in the colander long enough to be drained until it is dry; a little water left on it keeps the strands from sticking together. Serve it immediately with oil, salt (optional), and pepper (optional) or with the sauce of your choice.

Pasta for Rolling By Hand

It is not difficult to roll and cut pasta by hand, or you can roll and cut the spelt or rye pasta dough with a crank-type pasta machine.

Spelt:
    4 cups spelt flour
    1¼ cups water

Rye:

    4 cups rye flour
    ½ teaspoon salt (optional)
    1 cup water

Kamut:

    4 cups kamut flour
    ½ teaspoon salt (optional)
    1½ cups water

Quinoa:

    2 cups quinoa flour
    2 cups tapioca flour
    ½ teaspoon salt (optional)
    1 cup plus 2 tablespoons water

Amaranth:

    3 cups amaranth flour
    ½ cup arrowroot
    ¾ cup water

Barley:

    4 cups barley flour
    1½ cups water

Chestnut:

    4½ cups chestnut flour
    ¾ cup water

Measure the flour(s) onto a large board or into a large bowl. Make a crater in the center of the flour and gently pour the water into it. Begin stirring the water and flour together in the center of the crater with a fork. If you are using a board rather than a bowl, shore up the walls of the crater with your other hand as you stir. When the dough in the center of the crater becomes very thick, set aside the fork and mix the dough with your hand until all, or almost all, of the flour is mixed in. The dough will be very stiff. Knead the dough on a lightly floured board for 10 minutes. Then lightly oil the board and the ball of dough. Place the dough on the board, cover it with an inverted bowl, and let it rest for at least 30 minutes.

Roll the dough out as thinly as possible with a rolling pin on a floured board, or, for the more fragile types of dough, on a floured pastry cloth. For lasagne, layer the pasta in the pan with the other ingredients. For manicotti, cut the dough into squares with a sharp knife. For noodles, flour the dough well and either fold the dough (for less breakable types like rye and spelt), roll it up like a jelly roll, or for most fragile types of dough, like chestnut, leave it flat. Cut the dough into noodles of the desired width.

If you have a crank-type pasta machine, after the dough has rested, the rye or spelt dough may be rolled to about ¼ inch thickness and then cut into 4 to 6 pieces for rolling through the machine. Flour each piece well and roll it through the rollers several times, starting with the widest spacing and working down to the desired thickness of the dough. Use the sheets of dough for lasagne or manicotti at this point, or flour them well and roll them through the cutters for noodles.

Spread the noodles on a lightly floured cloth, separating the strands, and allow them to dry, or cook them immediately. (See "To Cook Pasta," page 85). The amaranth pasta is not suitable for cutting into noodles and boiling (it turns to mush in any type of sauce), but only for use in lasagne or manicotti. The cooking time for pasta is affected by many factors including the thickness of the noodles, the altitude, etc. Pasta should be tested for being *al dente* as described on page 85, but approximate cooking times are:

Spelt – 10 to 13 minutes
Rye – 6½ to 8 minutes
Kamut – 3 to 5 minutes
Barley – 2 to 3 minutes
Quinoa – 3½ to 4 minutes
Chestnut – 2½ to 3 minutes.

Pasta Made with an Extrusion Machine

If you enjoy pasta often or wish to make a variety of shapes, an extrusion machine is a good investment.

Spelt:

> 4 cups plus 1 to 2 tablespoons spelt flour
> 200 milliliters water

Rye:

> 3½ cups rye flour
> 185 milliliters water

Kamut:
> 4 cups kamut flour
> 225 milliliters water

Barley:

> 4 cups plus 1 to 2 tablespoons barley flour
> 250 milliliters water

Quinoa:

> 3½ cups quinoa flour
> 212 milliliters water

Stir the flour, gently spoon it into the measuring cup, level it off with a knife, and put it in the mixing chamber of the machine. Carefully measure the water. (Most measuring cups have milliliter markings, which give a more precise measurement, as well as cup markings.) Turn on the machine and add the water to the flour as directed in the machine's instructions. After a few minutes of mixing, take a few crumbs of the dough between your thumb and index finger and pinch them together. (This is called the "pinch test"). They should stick together, but the dough should be dry rather than sticky. If the dough is sticky, add 1 tablespoon of flour to the machine, allow it to mix a few more minutes, and do the pinch test again. If it is still sticky, continue to add flour 1 tablespoon at a time, mixing and doing a pinch test after each addition, until the proper consistency is reached. If the crumbs of dough do not stick together when the pinch test is performed, add 1 teaspoon of water to the machine, allow it to mix for a few minutes, and do another pinch test. If it is still too dry, add water 1 teaspoon at a time, mixing and performing a pinch test between each addition, until the proper consistency is reached. Make a note of the final amount of water and flour you used for future reference.

Allow the pasta to extrude according to the machine's instructions. Lay the strands of pasta on a lightly floured cloth to dry, separating the strands as you lay them down, or cook them immediately. For macaroni, extrude pasta with a hole in the middle of it, let the strands dry for a few hours, cut them into the desired lengths, and allow them to finish drying or cook them immediately. The cooking time is affected by many factors, including the size and shape of the pasta. Cook the pasta according to the directions given in "To Cook Pasta" on page 85, testing it often to avoid overcooking it. Note the cooking times for each type and shape of pasta for future reference. The approximate cooking times given below are for spaghetti:

Spelt – 12 to 14 minutes
Rye – 6½ to 8 minutes
Kamut – 4 to 6 minutes
Barley – 2½ to 3 minutes
Quinoa – 3 to 3½ minutes.

Pesto

The protein supplied by the nuts makes pasta served with this tomato-free sauce a very satisfying main dish.

3½ cups parsley, spinach, or sweet basil leaves, washed, stemmed, and dried
    (about ¼ pound as purchased)
1 to 2 cloves of garlic (optional)
½ cup pine nuts
½ cup olive or other oil
¼ to ½ teaspoon salt, or to taste
⅛ teaspoon pepper (optional)

Chop the garlic in a food processor or blender using a pulsing action. Add the parsley, spinach, or sweet basil and pulse to chop the leaves as finely as possible. Add the nuts and process continually until they are ground. Add the oil gradually while processing. Add the seasonings and process until they are blended in. Serve the sauce over warm cooked pasta. This sauce is very rich, so a little goes a long way. Makes about 1 cup of sauce.

Garlic, Pepper, and Oil Sauce

This is a very simple yet flavorful way to serve pasta without using tomatoes.

5 tablespoons oil, preferably olive oil
1 to 2 cloves of garlic, peeled (optional)
3 tablespoons finely chopped Italian (flat-leaf) parsley (if necessary, substitute
    2 tablespoons dry parsley)
1 teaspoon pepper, or to taste
⅛ teaspoon salt (optional)
1 pound pasta

Sauté the garlic in the olive oil until it is lightly browned, then remove and discard the garlic. Cook and drain the pasta. (See "To Cook Pasta" on page 85). Pour the warm olive oil over the pasta, sprinkle it with the parsley, pepper, and salt, and toss it thoroughly to mix all the ingredients. Makes 4 to 6 servings.

Easy Vegetarian Spaghetti Sauce

If you can eat canned tomato products but wish to avoid meat, this is the sauce for you.

2 tablespoons olive or other oil
1 clove of garlic, peeled and cut into quarters (optional)
1 18-ounce can tomato paste
1 28-ounce can tomato puree
2 cups water
1 tablespoon fresh chopped or l teaspoon dry oregano
1 teaspoon fresh chopped or ½ teaspoon dry sweet basil
1 teaspoon salt (optional)
⅛ teaspoon pepper (optional)

Sauté the garlic in the olive oil in a large kettle until it begins to brown. Then remove and discard the garlic. Add the tomato paste and cook it slowly, stirring it frequently, for about 10 minutes, or until it begins to darken slightly. Add the tomato puree, water, and seasonings and simmer the sauce for about 2 hours, stirring it frequently. Freeze any leftover sauce in meal-size portions. Makes 6 to 7 cups of sauce.

Fresh Tomato Sauce

If you can eat tomatoes but cannot tolerate canned tomato products, this multi-purpose recipe is the one to use.

4 pounds ripe Italian plum tomatoes
4 tablespoons olive or other oil
1 clove of garlic, minced (optional)
⅛ teaspoon pepper OR about ½ inch of a dried red chili pepper pod, seeded
    and crumbled (optional)
½ to 1 teaspoon salt, or to taste
1 tablespoon chopped fresh or 1 teaspoon dry sweet basil, or to taste (optional)

Scald the tomatoes in boiling water for 2 minutes, then slip the skins off. Puree them in a food processor or blender. Sauté the garlic in the olive oil in a large sauce pot. When the garlic is brown, remove and discard it. Add the pureed tomatoes and seasonings and partially cover the pan with its lid. Simmer the sauce, stirring it frequently, for 45 minutes to 1 hour or until it is very thick. If you wish to serve meatballs with this sauce, make and brown them as directed in "Easy Spaghetti Sauce With Meatballs," below, and add them to a double batch of this sauce for its simmering time. To use this sauce on pizza, omit the pepper and 1 tablespoon fresh or 1 teaspoon dry sweet basil and instead add 1 tablespoon chopped fresh or 1 teaspoon dry oregano, 1 teaspoon chopped fresh or ½ teaspoon dry thyme, and 1 teaspoon chopped fresh or ½ teaspoon dry sweet basil. A single batch of this recipe makes about 2½ cups of sauce.

Easy Spaghetti Sauce with Meatballs

The meatballs for this sauce are delicious when made with alternative meats.

2 pounds lean ground beef, pork, buffalo, turkey, or game meat
1 tablespoon chopped fresh or 1 teaspoon dry parsley (optional)
1½ teaspoons salt, divided
½ teaspoon pepper, divided (optional)
2 tablespoons olive or other oil
1 clove of garlic, peeled (optional)
1 28-ounce can tomato puree
1 12-ounce can tomato paste
1 cup water
1 teaspoon chopped fresh or ¼ teaspoon dry oregano (optional)
1 teaspoon chopped fresh or ¼ teaspoon dry sweet basil (optional)

Mix together the meat, ½ teaspoon salt, ¼ teaspoon pepper, and the parsley and press them firmly into about 10 meatballs. Put the oil, meatballs, and garlic in a large kettle, and cook the meatballs slowly, uncovered, turning them to brown all the sides. Remove the clove of garlic and drain off all of the fat. Add the tomato puree, tomato paste, water, 1 teaspoon salt, ¼ teaspoon pepper, oregano, and sweet basil and simmer the sauce, stirring it frequently, for 1½ to 2 hours. Remove the meatballs after the first hour of simmering to keep them from falling apart. Any sauce and meatballs that you do not use immediately freeze very well. Makes about 5 cups sauce and 10 meatballs.

Easy Meat Sauce for Lasagne

Use this sauce for lasagne or if you prefer ground meat in your spaghetti sauce.

1½ pounds lean ground beef, pork, buffalo, turkey, or game meat
1 12-ounce can tomato paste
1 16-ounce can tomato puree
3 cups water
1 teaspoon salt (optional)
⅛ teaspoon pepper (optional)

Brown the meat in a large sauce pot. Drain off the fat. Add the tomato paste, tomato puree, water, and seasonings and simmer the sauce, stirring it frequently, for 1½ to 2 hours. If you wish to, you can allow the sauce to settle after cooking and skim off 1 cup of relatively meat-free sauce from the top of the pan to serve on the side with the lasagne. Makes 8 to 9 cups of sauce, or enough for one batch of lasagne made with the recipe in this book.

Easy Pizza Sauce

If can tolerate canned tomatoes and want your pizza in a jiffy, use this sauce.

1 6-ounce can tomato paste
1 8-ounce can tomato sauce
½ cup water
2 tablespoons olive or other oil (optional)
1 tablespoon chopped fresh or 1 teaspoon dry oregano
1 teaspoon chopped fresh or ½ teaspoon dry thyme
1 teaspoon chopped fresh or ½ teaspoon dry sweet basil

Combine all of the ingredients in a saucepan and simmer them for 45 minutes, stirring frequently. Makes enough sauce for 2 pizzas.

Manicotti

This delicious meat-free dish is nice to prepare ahead and freeze.

2 cups of "Easy Vegetarian Spaghetti Sauce," page 91, or "Fresh Tomato Sauce,"
    page 91
1 pound goat or sheep feta cheese or goat or cow ricotta, drained
¼ cup sheep or cow Romano cheese (optional)
¼ teaspoon salt (optional - with cow ricotta only)
⅛ teaspoon pepper (optional)
2 teaspoons chopped fresh or dry parsley (optional)
1 batch of "Pasta for Rolling By Hand," page 86

Using a potato masher, mash together the cheese(s), salt, pepper, and parsley.
Prepare the pasta, roll it out into thin sheets as directed in the pasta recipe, and cut it
into 4 to 5 inch squares. Place 2 to 3 tablespoons of the cheese filling on each square
and roll them up diagonally. Put about ½ cup of the sauce in the bottom of a 9 by 12
inch baking dish. Lay the manicotti in the dish with the seam side of the pasta down.
Put another ½ cup of the sauce on top of the manicotti. Bake them, covered, at 350°F
for 30 minutes. Serve the manicotti with the remaining sauce on the side. Any leftover
pasta dough may be cut into noodles and dried for future use. Makes 4 to 6 servings.

Polenta

*This northern Italian dish is traditionally made with cornmeal flour (not grits),
but may also be made with cassava meal. The flavor comes from the sauce.*

2 cups cornmeal flour OR 1⅓ cups cassava meal (See "Sources of Special Foods,"
    page 218, for a mail order source for cassava meal).
4 cups water
1 to 1½ teaspoons salt, or to taste
Any tomato-based pasta sauce, pages 91 to 93, OR "Pesto," page 90
Grated goat cheese of crumbled goat or sheep feta cheese (optional)

Combine the cornmeal flour or cassava meal with 2 cups of cold water. Bring the rest of the water and the salt to a boil in a large sauce pot. Add the wet meal a little at a time, stirring constantly. Return the mixture to a boil and cook it over very low heat for 1 hour for the cornmeal flour or for 30 minutes for the cassava meal, stirring it frequently. It will become very stiff. Spread it on a platter and top it with the sauce and optional cheese, serving more sauce and cheese on the side. Any leftovers that do not have sauce on them may be packed into an oiled loaf pan, refrigerated overnight, sliced into ½ inch thick slices, and pan fried in a small amount of oil for breakfast. Makes 4 servings.

Lasagne

This dish may be prepared a day ahead to serve to a large crowd of guests for a dinner party.

1 batch of "Pasta for Rolling By Hand," page 86
1½ pounds goat ricotta cheese OR sheep or goat feta cheese
½ teaspoon salt (optional - omit with feta cheese)
¼ teaspoon pepper (optional)
1 tablespoon finely chopped fresh or dried parsley
1½ pounds goat jack cheese (optional)
1 tablespoon oil
1 batch "Easy Meat Sauce for Lasagne," page 93, OR 1½ batches of "Fresh Tomato
    Sauce," page 91, OR ½ batch of "Easy Vegetarian Spaghetti Sauce," page 91

Prepare the pasta as directed in the recipe. While the dough is resting, mash together the ricotta or feta cheese, salt, pepper, and parsley with a potato masher. Thinly slice the jack cheese if you are using it. Use the oil to grease the sides and bottom of a 9 by 13 inch baking dish. Divide the pasta dough into three pieces. Roll one piece out to the size of the pan on a floured pastry cloth, invert the cloth into the pan, and peel the cloth off of the pasta. (If you are using spelt or rye pasta you can just pick it up to put it in the pan). Cover the pasta with about ¾ cup of tomato sauce without meat or 1½ to 2 cups of sauce with meat. Top this with half of the ricotta or feta mixture and half of the sliced jack cheese. Roll out another piece of pasta and add it to the pan and repeat the layers of sauce and cheese. Roll out the final piece of pasta and add it to the pan. Top it with about 1 cup of sauce. Cover the pan with foil and bake it at 350°F for 1 hour, or until it is bubbly and hot all the way through. If you make the lasagne ahead and refrigerate it, increase the baking time to 1½ hours. Cut any leftovers into meal-size portions and freeze them. Makes 8 to 10 servings.

Pizza

This is very satisfying to both body and soul even if it is made without the meat and cheese.

Pizza toppings:

½ batch of "Easy Pizza Sauce," page 93, OR ½ batch of "Fresh Tomato Sauce," page 91, made with the spices listed for pizza

1 to 1½ cups grated goat jack cheese, about 4 to 6 ounces (optional)

¼ to ½ pound ground meat of any kind, cooked, crumbled, and drained of fat (optional)

½ to 1 cup total amount of assorted vegetable toppings, such as sliced black olives, chopped green peppers, etc.

Pizza dough – choose one of the following:

Yeast dough:

    ⅓ batch of "Spelt Yeast Bread," page 48

    1 batch of "Rye Yeast Bread," page 51

    ½ batch of "Barley Yeast Bread," page 53

    ½ batch of "Kamut Yeast Bread," page 52

Non-yeast pizza dough (choose one of the ingredient lists below):

Spelt:

    3½ cups spelt flour

    2 teaspoons baking soda

    ½ teaspoon unbuffered vitamin C crystals

    ½ teaspoon salt

    ½ cup oil

    1¼ cups water

Rye:

   3 cups rye flour
   1½ teaspoons baking soda
   ½ teaspoon unbuffered vitamin C crystals
   ½ teaspoon salt
   ⅜ cup oil
   1¼ cups water

Kamut:

   3 cups kamut flour
   1½ teaspoons baking soda
   ½ teaspoon unbuffered vitamin C crystals
   ½ teaspoon salt
   ⅓ cup oil
   1⅔ cups water

Barley:

   2½ cups barley flour
   ½ cup arrowroot
   1½ teaspoons baking soda
   ½ teaspoon unbuffered vitamin C crystals
   ½ teaspoon salt
   ⅜ cup oil
   1¼ cups water

Amaranth:

   3 cups amaranth flour
   1½ cups arrowroot
   2¼ teaspoons baking soda
   ¾ teaspoon unbuffered vitamin C crystals
   ¾ teaspoon salt
   ½ cup oil
   1½ cups water

Quinoa:

  3 cups quinoa flour
  1½ cups tapioca flour
  2¼ teaspoons baking soda
  ¾ teaspoon unbuffered vitamin C crystals
  ¾ teaspoon salt
  ½ cup oil
  1½ cups water

Chestnut:

  2½ cups chestnut flour
  1½ cups arrowroot
  1 teaspoon baking soda
  ½ teaspoon unbuffered vitamin C crystals
  ½ teaspoon salt
  ⅜ cup oil
  1¼ cups water

If you are making your pizza with yeast dough, prepare the dough as directed in the bread recipe and set it in a warm place to rise the first time. Prepare the tomato sauce as directed in the sauce recipe, grate the cheese if you are using it, cook and drain the meat if you are using it, and chop the vegetables. If you are using a non-yeast pizza dough, begin making it at this point, after all of the toppings are ready. Combine the flour(s), baking soda, vitamin C crystals, and salt in a large bowl. Combine the water and oil and stir them into the flour mixture until just mixed. Pat the dough into an oiled and floured 12 inch pizza pan with a floured hand. If you are using a yeast dough, stretch it out into a very lightly oiled 12 inch pizza pan. Top the dough with the sauce, cheese, meat and vegetables. Bake at 400°F for 25 to 30 minutes, or until the edge of the pizza is brown. Makes one 12 inch pizza.

Pesto Pizza

This is just as delicious as the usual type of pizza and it gives people who are sensitive to tomatoes pizza they can eat.

1 recipe of any pizza dough on pages 96 to 98
¾ cup pesto made with sweet basil, page 90
1 to 1½ cups shredded goat jack cheese, about 4 to 6 ounces (optional)
½ cup sliced black olives (optional)

Prepare the pizza dough and pat or stretch it into a prepared pan as directed in the previous recipe. Spread the pesto on the dough, sprinkle it with the cheese, and top it with the olives. Bake at 400°F for 25 to 30 minutes, or until the edge of the pizza begins to brown. Makes one 12 inch pizza.

Pasta e Fagioli

This traditional Italian soup is quite easy to make.

1 to 2 large stalks of celery (use 2 if you are omitting the onion and garlic)
2 slices nitrate-free bacon or salt pork (optional)
1 small onion (optional)
1 clove of garlic (optional)
3 tablespoons olive or other oil
3 to 4 Italian plum tomatoes, peeled and coarsely chopped (about 4 to 6 ounces)
6 cups hot water
1½ teaspoons salt
⅛ teaspoon pepper (optional)
2 cups cooked cannelini beans or other white beans, drained
2 cups small pasta or spaghetti broken into 1 to 2 inch pieces

Place the celery, pork, onion, and garlic on a chopping board and chop them together until they are almost the consistency of a paste. Sauté this mixture in the oil in a large sauce pot until it begins to brown. Add the tomatoes and cook them for a few minutes. Add the water, salt, and beans, and boil the soup for 5 minutes. Add the pasta and boil the soup for an additional 2 to 12 minutes, or until the pasta is *al dente*. (The cooking time depends on what type of pasta is used. See "To Cook Pasta" on page 85). Serve the soup immediately since most alternative pastas become mushy upon standing in liquid. Makes 4 to 6 servings, or about 8 cups of soup.

Tortillas

These are not just for Mexican food. Eat them with breakfast or dinner, or make a sandwich using them in place of the bread for lunch. For more Mexican main dish recipes to make with tortillas, see Easy Breadmaking for Special Diets *as described on the last pages of this book.*

Garbanzo:

> 2 cups garbanzo flour
> ½ teaspoon salt
> ½ cup water

Quinoa:

> 2 cups quinoa flour
> ½ teaspoon salt
> ¾ cup water

Amaranth:

> 2¼ cups amaranth flour
> ½ teaspoon salt
> ¾ cup water

Rye:

> 2 cups rye flour
> ½ teaspoon salt
> ¾ cup water

Spelt:

> 2 cups spelt flour
> ½ teaspoon salt
> ½ cup plus 2 tablespoons water

Kamut:

> 2 cups spelt flour
> ½ teaspoon salt
> ¼ cup oil
> ¾ cup water

Stir together the flour and salt. For the kamut tortillas, cut the oil into the flour and salt with a pastry cutter until thoroughly blended. For all of the types of tortillas, add the water to the flour mixture and stir and knead to form a stiff dough. Divide the dough into portions – 4 for large (8 to 9 inch) tortillas or 6 for small (6 to 7 inch) tortillas. Flour each portion well and roll it out to about ⅛ inch thickness on a well floured board, turning the dough over and flouring it on both sides while rolling it.

For soft tortillas, such as for the "Enchilada Casserole," page 103, heat a heavy frying pan over medium heat. One at a time, put each tortilla into the pan and cook it for about 3 minutes on the first side or until it begins to brown in spots on the underside. Turn it with a spatula and cook it for about 3 minutes on the second side also. Cool on a dishtowel or a wire rack.

For crisp tortillas, such as for "Tostadas," page 104, heat about ½ inch of oil in a frying pan until a small piece of dough sizzles when put into the oil. One at a time, put each tortilla into the oil and cook it until the edges turn brown. Carefully turn it with a large slotted spatula and cook it until the second side browns. Drain and cool the crisp tortillas on paper towels or dishtowels to absorb the oil. Makes 4 large or 6 small tortillas.

Easy Refried Beans

If these beans are fried with soy oil and served on top of "Garbanzo Tortillas" on the previous page, you have a one-food-family meal.

1 pound Anasazi or pink, red, or speckled beans
Water
½ to 2 teaspoons salt, or to taste
3 tablespoons oil

Wash the beans and cover them with 3 to 4 times their volume of cold water. Soak them overnight OR bring them to a boil, boil them for 2 minutes, turn off the heat, and let them stand for 1 hour. Drain the water and rinse them two or three times until the rinse water is clear. (This removes some of the hard-to-digest carbohydrates). Cover them with water, bring them to a boil, and then cook them over medium heat until they are very soft, about 2 to 2½ hours for anasazi beans. (The cooking time may vary for other types of beans). Drain almost all of the water, add salt to taste, and mash the beans with a potato masher. Put the oil in a large frying pan, add the beans, and cook them until they are dry, turning them with a spatula as they are cooking. This recipe makes about 4 cups of refried beans.

Mexican Sauce

This spicy sauce may be made with canned tomato puree or with fresh tomatoes.

4½ pounds Italian plum tomatoes OR 1 28-ounce can tomato puree
¼ onion, finely chopped (optional)
1 tablespoon oil (needed only if you are using the onion)
½ clove garlic, finely chopped (optional)
⅛ teaspoon ground cumin
¼ teaspoon oregano
2 teaspoons chili powder, or more to taste
1 teaspoon salt (optional)

If you are using the fresh tomatoes, quarter them, remove the seeds, and puree them in a blender or food processor. If you are using the onion, sauté it in the oil until it is soft. Combine the fresh or canned tomato puree, onion, garlic, cumin, oregano, chili powder, and salt in a saucepan and cook the sauce over medium heat, stirring it about every 10 minutes, until it is thickened. For the fresh tomatoes, cook the sauce uncovered for about 1 hour. For the canned tomato puree, cook it covered for 30 to 40 minutes. This recipe makes about 3 cups of sauce.

Avocado Sauce

Use this sauce with "Enchilada Casserole," page 103, "Tostadas," page 104, or as a dip for fresh vegetables.

1 large (about ½ pound in weight) ripe avocado
⅛ teaspoon tart-tasting unbuffered vitamin C crystals
1 tablespoon finely chopped onion (optional)
¼ teaspoon salt (optional)
⅛ teaspoon pepper (optional)

Thoroughly mash the avocado with the vitamin C crystals, onion, salt, and pepper. Makes about ⅔ cup of sauce.

Enchilada Casserole

This vegetarian casserole is great for a make-ahead meal.

1 batch of soft "Tortillas," page 100, or commercial spelt tortillas*
3 cups "Easy Refried Beans," page 102, OR 1½ 16-ounce cans of vegetarian
    refried beans
1 batch of "Mexican Sauce," page 102
1 cup shredded goat jack cheese (optional)
Sliced avocado or "Avocado Sauce," page 103 (optional)
Sliced black olives (optional)

Make four soft tortillas about the same size as an 8 or 9 inch round baking dish as directed in the tortilla recipe. Put one of the tortillas in the baking dish, spread it with 1 cup of the beans, and top the beans with ⅓ cup of the "Mexican Sauce" and ¼ cup of the cheese. Repeat the layers two more times. Top the casserole with the last tortilla, ⅓ cup sauce, and ¼ cup cheese. Bake it at 350°F for 30 minutes, or until it is bubbly. Cut the casserole into wedges and serve it with more "Mexican Sauce," avocado slices or "Avocado Sauce," and sliced olives, if desired. Makes 6 servings.

*Note: If you tolerate spelt, some health food stores carry commercially made whole spelt or white spelt tortillas. If your store does not have them, ask them to order the from Rudi's Organic Bakery. See "Sources," page 220, for ordering information.

Tostadas

These make a delicious and nutritious vegetarian lunch. If they are made with garbanzo tortillas and bean sprouts, you can keep the number of food families used down to one plus the number of toppings used.

6 large crisp tortillas, fried as in the recipe on page 100
1 batch of "Easy Refried Beans," page 102, OR 2 16-ounce cans of vegetarian
    refried beans, warmed
3 to 5 cups of bean sprouts or shredded lettuce
Shredded goat jack cheese (optional)
Sliced black olives (optional)
Chopped tomatoes (optional)
Sliced avocado or "Avocado Sauce," page 103 (optional)
"Mexican Sauce," page 102 (optional)

While the tortillas are still warm from being fried as in the "Tortilla" recipe, spread them with the warmed beans and top them with the desired toppings listed above. This recipe makes 6 tostadas.

Asian Game or Chicken

This is a healthy way to prepare game meat or chicken.

1 to 1½ pounds antelope, elk, buffalo, or venison steak OR 2 whole boned
    and skinned chicken breasts
2 tablespoons oil
2½ to 3 cups water, divided
1 cup celery, sliced diagonally
1 5-ounce can sliced water chestnuts, drained
1 green pepper, seeded and cut into ½ inch pieces
¾ teaspoon salt, or to taste
¼ teaspoon pepper, or to taste
¼ cup arrowroot, tapioca flour, or water chestnut starch
½ cup bean sprouts (optional)
½ pound fresh mushrooms plus 1 tablespoon oil OR one 4-ounce can sliced
    mushrooms, drained (optional)
3 to 4 cups cooked rice, quinoa, or noodles, or puffed amaranth cereal

Cut the meat into thin strips about 1½ to 2 inches long. Brown them in the 2
tablespoons oil in a frying pan. Add 2 cups of the water and the celery, water chestnuts,
green pepper, salt, and pepper, and simmer the mixture for 30 minutes. While it is
simmering, if you plan to use the fresh mushrooms, sauté them in the 1 tablespoon oil
in another pan. At the end of the simmering time, add the bean sprouts and mushrooms to the large pan (if you are using them). Mix the starch and ½ cup cold water
and add them to the pan. Return the mixture to a boil and simmer it until it is thick,
adding an additional ½ cup hot water if it is too thick. Serve it over cooked rice, quinoa,
or noodles or on puffed amaranth cereal. Makes 4 to 6 servings.

Vegetables, Side Dishes, and Soups

Vegetables, side dishes, and soups round out any meal. Some of them can be a meal all by themselves. Most commonly on an allergy diet, vegetables are eaten either plain or with a little oil and salt, so this chapter does not include a lot of vegetable recipes. For a complete discussion on how to prepare both common and less-usual vegetables, refer to the vegetable chapter in *Easy Cooking for Special Diets* as described at the end of this book. For recipes made with even more exotic vegetables, see *The Ultimate Food Allergy Cookbook and Survival Guide,* also described at the end of this book.

Harvard Beets

This recipe eliminates the sugar, vinegar, and cornstarch found in most Harvard beets.

½ cup apple juice concentrate, thawed, OR ½ cup water plus ¼ teaspoon stevia
   working solution, page 207
2 teaspoons arrowroot or tapioca flour
¼ teaspoon salt (optional)
2 whole cloves
¾ teaspoon tart-tasting unbuffered vitamin C crystals
2 cups sliced cooked beets

Combine the juice or water and stevia with the starch, salt, and cloves in a saucepan. Bring the mixture to a boil and simmer it until it is thick and clear. Stir in the vitamin C crystals and beets, return the mixture to a boil, and then reduce the heat and simmer it until the beets are heated through. Makes 2 to 4 servings.

Dried Beans

Cooked dried beans have many uses and freeze well, so do not hesitate to cook a large batch.

Wash the beans to remove any sand or dirt, and pick out and discard any bad-looking beans. Soak them in about 3 times their volume of water overnight. In the morning, rinse the beans 2 to 3 times with fresh water to remove some of the hard-to-digest substances that may cause intestinal gas. Cover them with about twice their volume of water and bring them to a boil. Reduce the heat and simmer them until they are tender to soft. (From the standpoint of digestibility, it is better to cook beans to the point of softness rather than just cook them until they are tender). The cooking time varies with the hardness of the water, type and age of the beans, altitude, etc., but some general guidelines are:

Anasazi beans – 2 to 2½ hours
Black beans – 2 to 3 hours
Garbanzo beans – 2 to 3 hours
Kidney beans – 2½ to 3 hours
Lentils – 1 to 2 hours
Lima beans – 1 to 1½ hours
Navy beans – 3 to 3½ hours
Pinto beans – 2 hours
Small white beans – 2 to 3 hours
Split peas – 1½ to 2½ hours

Salt the beans after cooking them; they will not soften properly if salted before cooking. When trying to determine how many dried beans you need to cook for a recipe, a rule of thumb is that 1 cup of dried beans will yield 2 to 2½ cups of cooked beans.

Vegetables with Cheese Sauce

When served with bread or crackers, this dish is satisfying enough to make a meal.

1 pound broccoli, cauliflower, spinach, or the vegetable of your choice, fresh
    or frozen
1 recipe of either "Cheese Sauce I" or "Cheese Sauce II," page 71

If you are using frozen vegetables, cook them according to the package directions. If you are using fresh broccoli or cauliflower, steam or boil it for 10 to 15 minutes. (The cooking time depends on many factors, including the size of the pieces). If you are using fresh spinach, put it in a pan with the water that clings to the leaves after washing it and cook it, stirring it often, for 3 to 10 minutes. Prepare the cheese sauce as directed in the recipe. Pour the cheese sauce over the vegetables and serve. Makes 4 to 6 servings.

Sugar- and Tomato-Free Baked Beans

From the flavor of these beans, one would never guess that they contain no sugar, tomatoes, or meat. They are easy to make in a crock pot.

2 pounds small white or small navy beans
Water
6 cups white grape, apple, or pineapple juice OR 6 cups water plus ⅛ teaspoon
    white stevia powder
1 tablespoon salt
½ teaspoon pepper
3 tablespoons finely chopped onion, or 2 teaspoons dried onion flakes (optional)
2 tablespoons finely chopped fresh sweet basil OR 1 tablespoon dried sweet basil
1 tablespoon paprika

Sort over and wash the beans. Soak them in 2 to 3 times their volume of water overnight. In the morning, drain them and rinse them 2 to 3 times with fresh water. Then simmer them in about 2 times their volume of fresh water for ½ to 1 hour, or until they begin to soften. Drain them and place them in a roaster with the juice or water and stevia and the seasonings. Bake them at 250°F for about 8 hours, stirring them often and adding more water as needed.

To cook the beans in a crock pot, after they have soaked and been rinsed, place them in a 3-quart crock pot with the juice or water. Cook them on high for 6 to 7 hours or on low for 8 to 10 hours, or until they are tender. Stir them every few hours, and while stirring them, smash a few beans against the side of the pot to thicken the sauce. After they are cooked, stir in the stevia, salt, and other seasonings. (Do not salt the beans before cooking or they will not soften properly). Makes 12 to 14 servings. This recipe may be halved, but may take less time to cook. Any leftover beans freeze well.

Quinoa Poultry Stuffing or Side Dish

This grain-free poultry stuffing is also excellent served as a side dish with meat, poultry, or fish and vegetables. Be sure to wash the soap-like coating off of the quinoa before using it.

2 cups sliced celery
¼ small onion, chopped (optional)
4 tablespoons oil
1 cup quinoa, thoroughly washed
2 cups water
½ to 1 teaspoon salt, or to taste
¼ teaspoon pepper
3 tablespoons finely chopped fresh parsley OR 1 tablespoon dried parsley
1 tablespoon finely chopped fresh sweet basil OR 1 teaspoon dried sweet basil
1 teaspoon finely chopped fresh rosemary OR ¼ teaspoon ground dried rosemary
    (optional)

Using a saucepan, sauté the celery and onion in the oil until they just begin to brown. Add the quinoa and water, bring the mixture to a boil, and simmer it for 15 to 20 minutes, or until the quinoa is translucent. Stir in the seasonings thoroughly and allow the quinoa to stand for a few minutes so that the flavors can blend. Serve it as a side dish or stuff it into a large chicken and then roast the chicken. If you use this stuffing for a turkey, double the recipe for a 12-pound turkey or triple it for a 24-pound turkey. Makes 4 to 6 servings.

Two-Food-Family Lentil Soup

The lentils in this easy and delicious vegetarian soup are one of the most easily tolerated legumes.

1 pound lentils
Water
3 to 5 carrots, peeled and sliced
3 stalks of celery, sliced
2 teaspoons salt
¼ teaspoon pepper (optional – omit it for only two food families)

Sort over and wash the lentils. In a 3-quart crock pot, soak them overnight in about three times their volume of water. Drain and rinse them two or three times in the morning. Add 5 cups of water and the carrots, celery, salt, and pepper to the drained lentils in the crock pot. Cook the soup on high for about 6 hours or on low for 8 to 10 hours. Add more boiling water before serving if you like your soup thinner. Makes about 2½ quarts of soup, or 5 to 8 servings. If you want to make a larger batch to freeze, use a 5-quart crock pot, double the amounts of all of the ingredients, and cook the soup on high for 8 to 10 hours. A double batch makes about 5 quarts of soup, or 10 to 16 servings.

Split Pea Soup

For the non-allergic members of your household, you can add a little warmed cubed ham to their serving bowls before ladling in this soup.

1 pound split peas
Water
2 to 3 carrots, peeled and sliced
2 to 3 stalks of celery, sliced
2 teaspoons salt
¼ teaspoon pepper (optional)
1 bay leaf (optional)

Sort over and wash the peas. In a 3-quart crock pot, soak them overnight in about three times their volume of water. Drain and rinse them two or three times in the morning. To the drained peas, add 5 cups of water and the carrots, celery, salt, pepper, and bay leaf. Cook the soup on high for about 6 hours or on low for 8 to 10 hours. Add more boiling water before serving it if you like your soup thinner. Makes about 2½ quarts of soup, or 5 to 8 servings. If you want to make a larger batch to freeze, use a 5-quart crock pot, double the amounts of all of the ingredients, and cook the soup on high for 8 to 10 hours. A double batch makes about 5 quarts of soup, or 10 to 16 servings.

Two-Food-Family Black Bean Soup

This is a very spicy soup. If you do not like spicy food, omit the black or red pepper or decrease the amount you use.

1 pound of black beans
Water
1 large or two small green peppers, seeded and cut into ½ inch square pieces
1 small onion, diced (optional – Omit it if you want to use only two food families).
1 tablespoon oil (Use soy if you want only two food families).
1¼ to 1½ pounds tomatoes OR 1 15-ounce can tomato sauce
2 teaspoons salt
¼ to ½ teaspoon black pepper OR ½ to 1 dry chili pepper, seeded and crumbled
    (Use the chili pepper if you want to use only two food families).

Sort through and wash the beans. Soak them overnight in about three times their volume of water. In the morning, rinse and drain them two or three times. Sauté the green pepper and onion in the oil until they are soft and slightly browned. If you are using the fresh tomatoes, peel and chop them to make about 2 cups of chopped tomatoes. Combine the drained beans, green pepper, onion, tomatoes or tomato sauce, seasonings and 2 to 3 cups of water in a saucepan, cover it, and heat it to boiling. Reduce the heat and simmer the soup for 2 to 3 hours, or until the beans are tender. Stir it occasionally while it is cooking, adding more water if necessary. Makes about 2½ quarts of soup, or about 8 servings.

"Cream" of Vegetable Soup

This recipe is a good way to use the excess zucchini from summer gardens as well as any leftover vegetables you may have on hand.

3 pounds zucchini
5 large carrots (about 1¼ pounds)
4 large stalks of celery
¼ onion, chopped (optional)
Water or broth (4 to 5 cups)
2 teaspoons salt, or to taste (only if you use water)
⅛ to ¼ teaspoon pepper (optional)
1 cup cooked vegetables, any kind (optional)

Peel the zucchini and carrots. Cut the zucchini, two of the carrots, and two of the stalks of celery into chunks. Combine the chunks of vegetables, enough water or broth to barely cover them (about 4 cups), salt (if you are using the water), and pepper in a large saucepan, bring them to a boil, reduce the heat, and simmer them for about 30 minutes, or until the vegetables are soft. While they are simmering, dice the remaining 3 carrots and 2 stalks of celery and simmer them until they are just tender in a little more water in a separate pan. When the chunks of vegetables are very soft, puree them and their cooking liquid in small batches in a food processor or blender. Return the puree to the pan and add the diced carrots and celery and optional cooked vegetables. If the soup is too thick, you may also add some of the cooking water from the diced carrots and celery. Reheat the soup to boiling and serve it. Makes 6 servings.

Duck Soup

Here is a poultry soup for people who are allergic to chicken. You can make it from the leftovers from a roasted duck.

Bones, meat scraps, and skin from a roasted duck which weighed about
    5 pounds before roasting
3 quarts (12 cups) water
2 stalks of celery with leaves, cut into chunks
1 carrot, cut into chunks
½ small onion, sliced (optional)
2 tablespoons chopped fresh parsley OR 1 tablespoon dried parsley
2 teaspoons salt, or to taste
3 peppercorns OR ¼ teaspoon pepper (optional)
1½ to 2 cups chopped cooked duck
1½ cups sliced celery (about 3 stalks)
2 cups peeled and sliced carrots (about 3 to 4 carrots)
One or more of the following extra ingredients (optional):
    2 potatoes, peeled and diced
    1 cup peas
    1 cup shredded cabbage

Combine the bones, meat scraps and skin from the duck with the water, celery and carrot chunks, onion, parsley, salt, and pepper in a large kettle. Bring the soup to a boil and skim the foam from the top of it. Reduce the heat and simmer the soup for about 2 hours. Strain the broth. If you wish to remove all of the fat from it, refrigerate it overnight and skim off the fat in the morning. Add the chopped duck, sliced celery, sliced carrots, and optional potatoes to the broth and bring it to a boil. Reduce the heat and simmer it until the vegetables are barely tender. Add the optional peas or cabbage if you wish to use them and simmer the soup until they are tender. Makes 6 servings.

Two-Food-Family Chicken Soup

This is old fashioned chicken soup just like Mom used to make. It can be easily limited to two food families if the optional ingredients are omitted.

1 3½ to 4 pound chicken, cleaned
3 quarts of water
1 to 1½ pounds carrots, peeled and sliced
3 stalks of celery, sliced
½ medium-sized onion, chopped (optional)
4 teaspoons salt
¼ teaspoon pepper (optional)
2 to 3 cups total of the following extra ingredients (optional):
    Cooked pasta
    Cooked rice
    Cooked barley
    Cooked peas
    Cooked beans

Put the chicken and water into a large kettle, bring them to a boil, and simmer them for about ½ hour. Skim off the foam from the top of the soup a few times while it is simmering. Add the carrots, celery, onion, salt, and pepper, return the soup to a boil, and simmer it for about another 2 hours. Refrigerate the soup overnight or until it is cool enough to handle. Skim off the fat and remove the chicken bones and skin from the meat, returning the meat to the pot. Add the optional extra cooked ingredients and reheat the soup. If not all family members can eat the optional ingredients, warm them separately and add them to the individual serving bowls as the soup is served. If you are using alternative pasta other than spelt pasta, do not allow it to stand in the soup too long before serving time or it will become mushy. Any leftover soup without pasta freezes well. Makes 8 servings.

Salads and Dressings

If you have to avoid lettuce and vinegar, making salads can pose a problem. But you can make salads with other leafy vegetables besides lettuce, such as cabbage and spinach, or with shredded vegetables, such as jicama, carrots, or zucchini. You can also make fruit salads, meat salads, or fish salads. Some individuals who are allergic to lettuce may even tolerate other members of the composite family to which lettuce belongs. For example, after over ten years of avoidance, I still reacted to lettuce but could eat Belgian endive occasionally with no problems.

Many people who cannot have yeast-containing foods such as vinegar substitute citrus fruit juices for vinegar in salads. If you are also allergic to citrus, you don't have to give up eating tasty salads. There is another substitute for vinegar in salads besides citrus fruit juices, corn-free unbuffered vitamin C crystals. Different brands differ in how they taste. Experiment with whatever brands you can find in your area, or order by mail. (See "Sources of Special Foods," page 220). Because of its purity, most doctors allow their patients to have vitamin C on every day of the rotation cycle.

Fruity Salad Dressing

This is the dressing to use when you want something slightly sweet.

½ cup oil
¼ cup apple, orange, or pineapple juice concentrate, thawed
1 tablespoon tart-tasting unbuffered vitamin C crystals
¼ teaspoon salt (optional)
Dash of pepper (optional)

Combine all of the ingredients in a glass jar and shake until the salt and vitamin C are dissolved. Serve this dressing over salad greens, sliced fruit, or avocado halves. Makes about ¾ cup of dressing.

Italian Dressing

This classic dressing is delicious on almost any kind of vegetable. Try it on shredded zucchini.

¾ cup oil
1½ teaspoons finely chopped fresh oregano OR ½ teaspoon dried oregano
   (optional)
¼ teaspoon finely chopped fresh thyme OR ⅛ teaspoon dried thyme (optional)
1 clove of garlic, crushed (optional)
1 teaspoon salt
2 teaspoons tart-tasting unbuffered vitamin C crystals
1½ teaspoons water

Combine the oil, spices, and crushed garlic in a glass jar and refrigerate them at least overnight. Remove and discard the garlic. Mix the salt and vitamin C crystals with the water until they dissolve and add them to the oil just before serving time. Shake the jar well before pouring the dressing on the salad. Makes about ¾ cup of dressing.

Avocado-Canola Seed Dressing

This rich dressing may be served with salad greens, sliced cucumbers (See the "Cucumber-Avocado Salad" recipe on page 120) or as a dip for fresh vegetables.

1 large ripe avocado
Water (about ⅓ cup)
1 teaspoon tart-tasting unbuffered vitamin C crystals, or to taste
⅛ teaspoon salt, or to taste (optional)
Dash of pepper, or to taste (optional)
1 tablespoon canola seeds (optional)

Peel the avocado and mash the pulp in a glass measuring cup. There should be about ⅔ cup of mashed avocado. Add water to the 1 cup mark. Transfer the avocado and water to a blender or food processor. Add the vitamin C crystals, salt, and pepper and puree the mixture until it is smooth. Stir in the canola seeds and serve the dressing immediately. Makes about 1 cup of dressing.

Pine Nut Dressing

This dressing may be used instead of mayonnaise. If you make it without the stevia, it is an excellent dip for artichokes.

½ cup pine nuts
¼ cup water
¼ cup oil
1 teaspoon tart-tasting unbuffered vitamin C crystals
$\frac{1}{16}$ teaspoon or a dash of salt
Dash of pepper (optional)
¼ teaspoon stevia working solution, page 207 (optional – Use it only if you want
   a sweet dressing).

Grind the nuts to a fine powder in a blender or food processor. Add the water and blend the mixture until it is smooth. Add the oil in the slowest stream possible while the blender or processor is running. Add the seasonings and blend briefly. If this dressing loses its tartness after being refrigerated for a while, mix ½ to 1 teaspoon vitamin C crystals with ½ to 1 teaspoon of water and stir it into the dressing. Makes about ¾ cup of dressing.

Waldorf Salad

This classic recipe is excellent when made with "Pine Nut Dressing," above. Stevia-sweetened dressing is especially good with this salad.

2 cups diced apple (about 2 small or 1½ large apples)
¾ cup diced celery (2 to 3 stalks)
¼ cup pine nuts or chopped larger nuts
¼ cup raisins (optional)
½ cup "Pine Nut Dressing," above

Combine the apple, celery, nuts, and raisins in a bowl. Stir in the dressing. Makes 2 to 4 servings.

Coleslaw

This old favorite is nutritious and satisfying when made with "Pine Nut Dressing,"
page 117.

> 1 pound cabbage, finely shredded (This is about 4 cups shredded cabbage,
>   or ½ of a large head).
> 1 medium-sized carrot, grated (optional)
> ½ cup "Pine Nut Dressing," page 117
> ⅛ to ¼ teaspoon tart-tasting unbuffered Vitamin C crystals, or to taste (optional)

Combine the cabbage and carrot in a large bowl. If more tartness is desired in the
dressing, thoroughly mix the vitamin C crystals into it in a separate bowl. Toss the
vegetables with the dressing and serve the salad. Makes 2 to 4 servings.

Cucumber Salad

This is an "old country" Italian salad when you make with the tomatoes. The juice
in the bottom of your bowl is delicious sopped up with bread, as my grandfather did.

> 2 medium-sized cucumbers, peeled and sliced
> 1 large ripe avocado, cut into cubes, OR 2 regular tomatoes, sliced, with the slices
>   quartered, OR 4 to 6 Italian plum tomatoes, sliced
> ¼ to ½ teaspoon tart-tasting unbuffered vitamin C crystals
> ⅛ teaspoon pepper
> ¹⁄₁₆ to ⅛ teaspoon salt (optional)
> ½ teaspoon water
> 2 tablespoons oil

Combine the cucumbers with the avocado or tomatoes in a large bowl. In a small
bowl or a glass jar, mix the vitamin C crystals, pepper, and salt with the water until the
vitamin C and salt are dissolved. Stir or shake the oil into the solution thoroughly. Pour
the dressing over the vegetables and toss the salad. Makes 2 to 4 servings.

Beet Salad

This is a delicious way to serve leftover beets.

¾ teaspoon tart-tasting unbuffered vitamin C crystals
⅛ teaspoon pepper
1/16 to ⅛ teaspoon salt (optional)
½ teaspoon water
2 tablespoons oil
3 to 4 cups cooked, sliced beets

In a small bowl or a glass jar, mix the vitamin C crystals, pepper, and salt with the water until the vitamin C and salt are dissolved. Stir or shake the oil into the solution thoroughly. Pour the dressing over the beets and toss. Makes 2 to 4 servings.

One-Food-Family Crunch Salad

If you make this salad with the nuts, it is satisfying enough to be a light meal.

¼ to ⅜ teaspoon tart-tasting unbuffered vitamin C crystals
Dash of salt (optional)
Dash of pepper (optional – Omit it for one food family).
½ teaspoon water
1 tablespoon canola or other oil (Use canola oil for one food family).
2 cups shredded cabbage
1 tablespoon canola seeds
¼ cup pine nuts or other nuts (optional – Omit them for one food family).

Mix the vitamin C crystals, salt, and pepper with the water in a small bowl or glass jar until the vitamin C crystals and salt are dissolved. Add the oil and mix or shake it until it is thoroughly combined. Pour the dressing over the cabbage and toss the salad. Stir in the canola seeds and nuts. Serves one as a main dish or two as a side dish.

Cucumber-Avocado Salad

This is a delicious way to use "Avocado-Canola Seed Dressing."

1 recipe of "Avocado-Canola Seed Dressing," page 116
2 large or 3 small (about 1½ pounds total weight) cucumbers

Peel and slice the cucumbers. Toss them with the dressing and serve. Makes 2 to 4 servings.

Carrot and Olive Salad

This tasty salad uses only two food families.

1½ cups grated carrots (about 2 small or 1½ medium sized carrots)
½ cup sliced black olives
2 tablespoons olive oil
2 tablespoons juice from the olives

Combine the carrots and olives in a bowl. Stir together the olive oil and olive juice in another bowl, pour them over the vegetables, and toss the salad. Makes 2 to 4 servings.

Garbanzo Bean Salad

Here is a simple and tasty way to use leftover cooked garbanzo beans.

¼ teaspoon tart-tasting unbuffered vitamin C crystals
Dash of pepper
Dash of salt
½ teaspoon water
1 tablespoon oil
1½ cups cooked garbanzo beans, drained

In a small bowl or a glass jar, mix the vitamin C crystals, pepper, and salt with the water until the vitamin C and salt are dissolved. Stir or shake the oil into the solution thoroughly. Pour the dressing over the beans and toss. Makes 1 to 2 servings.

Spinach Salad

This salad contains everything you could want for a light meal – vegetables in the spinach and beets, some starch in the crackers, and protein in the feta cheese, garbanzo beans, or sunflower seeds.

⅛ to ¼ teaspoon tart-tasting unbuffered vitamin C crystals
Dash of salt (optional)
Dash of pepper (optional)
½ teaspoon water
1 tablespoon oil
4 cups spinach leaves, washed, dried, and torn into bite-sized pieces
¼ cup crumbled crackers made from the recipes in this book
¼ cup crumbled goat or sheep feta cheese (about 1½ ounces drained weight)
　　OR ¼ cup cooked garbanzo beans, drained
1 cup diced or sliced cooked beets (optional)
¼ cup sunflower seeds (optional)

Combine the vitamin C crystals, salt, and pepper with the water in a small bowl or glass jar. Add the oil and mix or shake it until it is thoroughly combined. Pour the dressing over the spinach and toss. Stir in the rest of the ingredients. Serves one as a main dish or two as a side dish.

Belgian Endive Salad

Belgian endive is not as bitter as some types of endive. With the addition of cheese or nuts and crumbled crackers, this salad is satisfying enough to be a light meal all by itself.

⅜ teaspoon tart-tasting unbuffered vitamin C crystals
Dash of salt (optional)
Dash of pepper (optional)
½ teaspoon water
2 tablespoons oil
6 to 8 ounces Belgian endive, cut into bite-size pieces (about 2½ cups pieces)
⅓ cup crumbled "Quinoa Crackers," page 27, "Canola Seed Crackers," page 31,
    "Cassava Crackers," page 33, or other crackers
½ cup grated goat jack cheese OR ¼ cup sunflower seeds or chopped nuts

Combine the vitamin C crystals, salt, and pepper with the water in a small bowl or glass jar. Add the oil and mix or shake it until it is thoroughly combined. Pour the dressing over the endive and toss. Stir in the crackers and cheese or nuts. Serves one as a main dish or two as a side dish.

Christmas Salad

This salad is as delightful to look at as it is to eat. It makes any meal special even when it is not Christmas.

2 pounds jicama
Red dressing:
    ¼ cup fresh or frozen unsweetened raspberries
    ⅓ cup oil
    ¼ to ½ teaspoon tart-tasting unbuffered vitamin C crystals (Use the smaller
        amount if the raspberries are tart).
    ⅓ cup water OR apple or pineapple juice concentrate, thawed (Use the fruit
        juice if the raspberries are tart).
    Dash of salt (optional)

Green dressing:
    ½ cup diced green pepper
    ⅓ cup oil
    ¾ teaspoon tart-tasting unbuffered vitamin C crystals
    ¼ cup water
    Dash of salt (optional)
    Dash of pepper (optional)

Peel the jicama and shred it with a grater or a food processor. Make each dressing separately by the following method: Puree the raspberries or green pepper with the oil in a blender or food processor until there are no longer any visible chunks. Add the vitamin C crystals, water or juice, and seasoning(s) and blend again briefly. Divide the shredded jicama between 8 serving plates. Drizzle each plate with a little of both dressings – one dressing on each half of the plate, one in the center and the other around the edge, or whatever pattern you choose. Makes 8 servings.

Avocado and Almond Salad

This salad is slightly sweet and very satisfying.

1½ teaspoons tart-tasting unbuffered vitamin C crystals, or to taste
⅛ teaspoon salt (optional)
Dash of pepper (optional)
2 tablespoons apple, orange, or pineapple juice concentrate, thawed
4 tablespoons oil
8 cups spinach or other salad greens, washed, dried, and torn into bite-size pieces
¼ cup sliced almonds
1 large ripe avocado, peeled and cut into cubes

Mix the vitamin C crystals, salt, and pepper with the juice in a small bowl or glass jar until the vitamin C crystals and salt are dissolved. Add the oil and mix or shake it until it is thoroughly combined. Place the salad greens, almonds, and avocado cubes in a large bowl. Pour the dressing over them and toss the salad. Makes 4 servings.

Pita or Tortilla Salad

This vegetarian salad or sandwich is packed with nutrition.

2 cups coarsely chopped spinach, lightly packed into the measuring cup
1 medium-sized cucumber, peeled and cut into ½ inch cubes (about 1½ cups cubes)
1 large carrot, grated (about 1 cup grated)
1 large ripe avocado, cut into ½ inch cubes
1 cup goat jack cheese, cubed (about 4 ounces) OR ⅔ cup crumbled goat or sheep
     feta cheese (about 3 ounces) (optional)
¼ cup sunflower seeds OR ½ cup coarsely chopped almonds or other nuts
     (optional)
1½ teaspoons tart-tasting unbuffered vitamin C crystals
Dash of salt (optional)
Dash of pepper (optional)
2 teaspoons water
2 tablespoons oil
4 to 6 pitas, page 54, OR 4 large or 6 small tortillas, page 100 (optional)

Combine the spinach, cucumber, carrot, avocado cubes, cheese, and seeds or nuts in a large bowl. In a separate small bowl or glass jar, mix the vitamin C crystals, salt, and pepper with the water. Add the oil and mix or shake it until it is thoroughly combined. Pour the dressing over the vegetable mixture and toss it until all the ingredients are coated with the dressing. Serve the salad as is, stuff it into halved pita breads, or serve it on top of tortillas. Makes 4 to 6 servings.

Rabbit, Chicken, or Turkey Salad

Serve this salad alone, over salad greens, or in a sandwich made with tortillas, bread, or buns.

2 cups cubed cooked rabbit, page 80, chicken, or turkey
½ cup diced celery
⅓ cup "Pine Nut Dressing," page 117
⅛ to ¼ teaspoon salt, or to taste (optional)
Dash of pepper (optional)

Combine the rabbit or poultry and celery in a bowl. Stir the seasonings into the dressing and mix it into the meat thoroughly. Makes 2 to 4 servings.

Three Bean Salad

This is an incredibly easy salad to make from leftover cooked dried beans. Or, if you can tolerate canned beans, the salt-free ones often do not contain sugar or additives and make the preparation of this salad even easier.

1¼ cups cut green beans, cooked, drained, and chilled
1¼ cups cooked kidney beans, drained and chilled
1¼ cups cooked garbanzo beans, drained and chilled
2 tablespoons finely chopped onion (optional)
½ cup finely chopped green pepper (optional)
2 tablespoons apple juice concentrate, thawed, OR 2 tablespoons water
       plus ¼ teaspoon stevia working solution, page 207
¼ teaspoon salt
⅛ to ¼ teaspoon pepper (optional)
2 teaspoons tart-tasting unbuffered vitamin C crystals, or more to taste as tolerated
       (See the comment on bowel tolerance in this recipe).
¼ cup oil

Combine the beans, onion, and green pepper in a large bowl. In a separate small bowl, stir together the juice or water plus stevia, salt, and pepper until the stevia and salt are dissolved. Stir in the vitamin C crystals last. (They will not dissolve completely). Pour this mixture and the oil over the beans, toss them thoroughly, and serve the salad immediately. This salad loses its tartness rapidly if made very far ahead of serving time. To restore its tang, you may mix an additional ½ teaspoon vitamin C with 2 teaspoons of water and thoroughly stir it into the salad. However, some individuals do not have bowel tolerance for this great of an amount of vitamin C taken at one time, or even the amount originally in the recipe if a large serving is eaten. Makes 4 to 6 servings.

Pasta Salad

This is great as a side dish or as a summertime lunch or dinner. It is also a good way to use up leftover vegetables or pasta.

2 to 3 ounces dry pasta OR 1 to 1½ cups cooked pasta (If you are using spaghetti, break or cut it into 1 to 2 inch pieces).

2 tablespoons oil

1¼ cups assorted cooked dried beans, thawed frozen vegetables or lightly cooked fresh vegetables, cut into small pieces (such as carrots, peas, green beans, broccoli, etc.)

¾ to 1 teaspoon tart-tasting unbuffered vitamin C crystals, to taste or as tolerated (See the comment on bowel tolerance in this recipe).

⅛ teaspoon salt (optional)

⅛ teaspoon pepper (optional)

2 teaspoon water

Cook and drain the pasta. (See "To Cook Pasta" on page 85). Immediately toss it with the oil. Refrigerate the cooked pasta and vegetables until they are thoroughly chilled. Add the vegetables to the pasta and mix them gently. Combine the vitamin C crystals, salt, and pepper with the water in a small bowl or glass jar. Pour this mixture over the pasta and vegetables and toss the salad thoroughly. Serve it immediately, as this salad tends to lose its tartness upon standing. If it loses its tang, you may mix ½ teaspoon vitamin C crystals with 2 teaspoons water and thoroughly stir it into the salad. However, some individuals do not have bowel tolerance for this great of an amount of vitamin C taken at one time. Makes 2 to 3 servings.

Cookies

Nutritious fruit-sweetened cookies are a mother's best friend. They round out a brown-bagged lunch, are a good between-meal snack that will not ruin you child's appetite for the next meal and, best of all, your child will enjoy them. Cookies are easy to make, easy to store, and come in serving-size portions. They can make a restricted allergy diet seem more tolerable. They are truly a treat for kids of all ages.

This chapter contains many fruit-sweetened cookie recipes. It also contains some recipes minimally sweetened with refined sugar as a concession to the problem of "what the other kids are eating." If your children do not have yeast problems, it may not be practical to restrict them completely in regard to sugar. If you do, they may swap their sandwich for another child's Oreos™. If this becomes an issue (and your child can occasionally have some sugar) it can be addressed with cookies that are very much like Oreos™. (See the recipe on page 148). Once children have had a homemade cookie that looks like an Oreo™, they become much more agreeable about staying on their diets.

If you must avoid fruit sweeteners as well as sugar, you will enjoy the stevia-sweetened versions of several cookie recipes in this chapter ("Quinoa Brownies," "Carrot Cookies," "Quinoa Carob Chip Cookies," "Sugar Cookies," and "Carob Wafers"). For tips on measuring small amounts of stevia powder, see page 211. With the use of stevia, being on a strict low yeast diet does not mean that you cannot enjoy cookies.

Since the first printing of the original edition of *Allergy Cooking with Ease*, a new option in sweeteners has become available, fructooligosaccharides, or FOS. FOS is a supplement which promotes the growth of friendly intestinal bacteria such as *Lactobacillus* and *Bifidobacterium*. It does not support the growth of *Candida,* and thus is promoted for individuals with yeast problems. However, it can support the growth of some unfriendly intestinal bacteria such as *Klebsiella*, so it should not be used by people with bacterial dysbiosis caused by these bacteria. Unless you have had stool tests for these bacteria, you may not know if you have them. Therefore, FOS is best used as an occasional treat. Even in "normal" people, the consumption of large amounts of FOS can cause diarrhea. If you wish to use FOS occasionally in cookies, see the recipes in this chapter for "Blonde Brownies," and "FOS Sugar Cookies" on pages 129 and 141. More FOS-containing dessert and cookie recipes are found in *The Ultimate Food Allergy Cookbook and Survival Guide* as described on the last pages of this book.

Quinoa Brownies

These brownies are delicious and nutritious when made with apple juice, or if you must avoid fruit sweeteners, you can enjoy them made with stevia.

1 cup quinoa flour
¼ cup tapioca flour
⅓ cup carob powder, sifted to remove any lumps
1 teaspoon baking soda
¼ teaspoon unbuffered vitamin C crystals
¼ cup oil
¾ cup apple juice concentrate, thawed, OR ¾ cup water plus
    ⅛ teaspoon white stevia powder
¼ cup chopped nuts (optional)

In a large mixing bowl combine the quinoa flour, tapioca flour, carob powder, baking soda, vitamin C crystals, stevia (if you are using it rather than the apple juice), and optional nuts. Mix the oil with the water or apple juice and stir them into the dry ingredients until they are just mixed. Put the batter into an oiled and floured 9 by 5 inch pan and bake it at 350°F for 18 to 20 minutes. Cut it into squares. Makes 10 brownies.

Rye Brownies

Nobody but you will ever know these brownies are sweetened with grape juice - the carob hides the color.

2½ cups rye flour
⅜ cup (¼ cup plus 2 tablespoons) carob powder, sifted to remove any lumps
1½ teaspoons baking soda
1 cup grape juice concentrate, thawed
½ cup oil
¾ cup chopped nuts (optional)

Stir together the flour, carob powder, and baking soda in a large bowl. Mix the juice and oil together and stir them into the dry ingredients until they are just mixed in. Spread the batter in an oiled and floured 13 by 9 inch pan. Bake at 350°F for 18 to 20 minutes. (Do not over-bake these brownies – they should still be moist inside). Cool and frost them, if desired, with "Very Carob Frosting" or "Party Carob Frosting," page 166. Cut them into 1¾ inch squares. Makes about 3 dozen brownies.

Blonde Brownies

These are sweetened with FOS and are great as an occasional treat.

1½ cups rye flour
¼ cup uncooked rye flakes or cream of rye cereal
1 cup FOS*
¼ teaspoon baking soda
⅛ teaspoon unbuffered vitamin C crystals
⅛ teaspoon salt
½ cup water
3 tablespoons oil
1 teaspoon corn-free natural vanilla flavoring

Combine the flour, rye flakes, FOS, baking soda, vitamin C crystals, and salt in a large bowl. Mix together the water, oil, and vanilla and stir them into the dry ingredients until they are just mixed in. Spread the dough in a oiled and floured 8 inch square pan. Bake at 350°F for 30 to 35 minutes. Immediately cut into 2 inch squares. Cool the cookies before you remove them from the pan. Makes 16 cookies. If you wish to make a smaller batch, cut the amounts of all of the ingredients in half and bake in a 8 by 4 inch loaf pan to make 8 cookies.

*See the cautionary information about FOS in the introduction to this chapter on page 127.

Pineapple-Coconut Cookies

These fruit-sweetened cookies are a tropical delight.

1 cup unsweetened canned pineapple with its juice or fresh pineapple with
      juice to cover
¾ cup pineapple juice, concentrate, thawed
½ cup oil
2 cups rye flour
½ teaspoon baking soda
1 cup shredded unsweetened coconut

Puree the pineapple with its juice in a blender or food processor. Add the pineapple juice concentrate and oil and blend again briefly. In a mixing bowl, combine the flour, baking soda, and coconut. Stir the pineapple mixture into the dry ingredients until they are just mixed. Drop heaping teaspoonfuls of the dough onto an oiled cookie sheet. Bake at 350°F for 15 to 20 minutes, or until the cookies begin to brown. Makes about 3½ dozen cookies.

Oatmeal Raisin Cookies

These taste just like Mom used to make but contain no sugar. They are also an excellent source of fiber.

2 cups white raisins
2 cups white grape juice
½ cup oil
2 cups oat flour
2 cups oatmeal
1 teaspoon baking soda
1½ teaspoons cinnamon
1 cup brown raisins
½ cup chopped nuts (optional)

Soak the white raisins in the grape juice overnight, then puree them together in a blender or food processor. Add the oil and blend again briefly. Combine the oat flour, oatmeal, baking soda, cinnamon, brown raisins, and nuts in a mixing bowl. Stir in the raisin puree until it is just mixed into the flour mixture. Drop the batter by heaping teaspoonfuls onto an ungreased baking sheet and bake at 375ºF for 15 to 18 minutes, or until the cookies are lightly browned. Makes about 6 dozen cookies.

Carrot Cookies

These cookies are packed with nutrition and can be sweetened with either fruit juice or stevia. If you are just getting used to stevia, use the smaller amount.

3 cups quinoa or spelt flour
1 cup tapioca flour or arrowroot
1½ teaspoons baking soda
⅜ teaspoon unbuffered vitamin C crystals if you are using the apple juice OR
    ½ teaspoon unbuffered vitamin C crystals if you are using the stevia and water
1½ teaspoons cinnamon
2¼ cups grated carrots
1 cup raisins or chopped dates (optional)
1⅜ cups (1¼ cups plus 2 tablespoons) apple juice concentrate, thawed
    OR ¾ to 1 teaspoon white stevia powder plus 1⅜ cups (1¼ cups plus 2
    tablespoons) water
½ cup oil

Mix together the flours, baking soda, vitamin C crystals, cinnamon, and stevia, if you are using it, in a large bowl. Stir in the carrots and raisins or dates. Combine the juice or water and oil and stir them into the flour mixture until they are just mixed in. Drop the batter by heaping teaspoonfuls onto an ungreased cookie sheet and bake at 350ºF for 12 to 15 minutes. The stevia-sweetened cookies will not brown very much, but will feel dry when they are touched. Makes 4 to 5 dozen cookies.

Millet or Teff Apple Cookies

These fruit-sweetened cookies are fragile but delicious, especially when made with the carob chips.

2 cups millet or teff flour
½ teaspoon baking soda
½ cup unsweetened applesauce
¾ cup apple juice concentrate, thawed
½ cup oil
¾ cup chopped nuts OR milk-free unsweetened carob chips (optional)

Combine the flour and baking soda in a large bowl. Mix together the applesauce, juice, and oil in a small bowl, and then stir them into the flour until they are just mixed in. Quickly fold in the nuts or carob chips. Drop the batter by heaping teaspoonfuls onto an ungreased baking sheet. Bake at 350°F for 15 to 20 minutes, or until the cookies begin to brown. Makes about 3½ dozen 1½ inch cookies.

Quinoa Carob Chip Cookies

The high-protein quinoa flour makes these cookies very satisfying. If you make them with the stevia they are also excellent for low yeast diets.

3 cups quinoa flour
1 cup tapioca flour
1½ teaspoons baking soda
⅜ teaspoon unbuffered vitamin C crystals if you are using the apple juice OR
    ½ teaspoon unbuffered vitamin C crystals if you are using the stevia and water
2 cups apple juice concentrate OR 1⅜ cups water plus ¾ to 1 teaspoon
    white stevia powder
½ cup oil
1¼ cups milk-free unsweetened carob chips

If you are using the apple juice, boil it down to 1⅜ cups (1¼ cups plus 2 tablespoons) and allow it to cool. In a large bowl, combine the quinoa flour, tapioca flour, baking soda, vitamin C crystals, and stevia, if you are using it. In a separate bowl, stir together the juice or water and the oil, then stir them into the dry ingredients until they are just mixed in. Fold in the carob chips. Drop the dough by tablespoonfuls onto an ungreased baking sheet and flatten them to about ¼ inch thickness with your fingers held together. Bake at 350°F for 10 to 15 minutes, or until the cookies are lightly browned. The stevia-sweetened cookies will not brown, but will feel dry to the touch. Makes about 5 dozen cookies.

Spelt Carob Chip Cookies

You can vary the sweetness of these fruit-sweetened cookies to suit your taste.

2⅓ cups spelt flour
½ teaspoon baking soda
¾ cup apple juice concentrate, thawed, OR 1¼ cups apple juice concentrate,
     depending on the degree of sweetness desired
½ cup oil
¾ cup milk-free unsweetened carob chips (optional)

If you like your cookies fairly sweet, boil 1¼ cup apple juice concentrate down to ¾ cup in volume and allow it to cool. For minimally sweetened cookies, use ¾ cup apple juice concentrate. Stir together the spelt flour and baking soda in a large bowl. Mix the oil and apple juice concentrate and stir them into the flour mixture until they are just mixed in. Fold in the carob chips. Drop the dough by heaping teaspoonfuls onto a lightly oiled baking sheet and bake them at 350°F for 10 to 14 minutes, or until they begin to brown. Makes 3 dozen cookies.

Kamut Carob Chip Cookies

These are a golden take-off on your favorite cookie.

3¼ cups kamut flour
1 teaspoon baking soda
¾ teaspoon unbuffered vitamin C crystals
¾ cup honey
¾ cup water
¼ cup oil
1 cup milk-free unsweetened carob chips (optional)

Stir together the flour, baking soda, and vitamin C crystals in a large bowl. Mix together the honey, water, and oil and stir them into the flour mixture until they are just mixed in. Fold in the carob chips. Drop heaping teaspoonfuls of the dough onto a lightly oiled baking sheet. If you prefer flat rather than domed cookies, flatten them with your hand. Bake them at 350°F for 15 to 20 minutes, or until they begin to brown. Makes about 5 dozen cookies.

Shortbread

These cookies are delicious and very easy to make in several different varieties to fit any day of your rotation diet.

Amaranth:

> 1¼ cups amaranth flour
> 1 cup arrowroot
> ½ teaspoon baking soda
> ⅜ cup (¼ cup plus 2 tablespoons) oil
> ½ cup pineapple juice concentrate, thawed

Date-Oat:

> 2¼ cups oat flour
> ½ cup date sugar, pressed through a strainer to remove any lumps
> ½ teaspoon baking soda
> ⅛ teaspoon unbuffered vitamin C crystals
> ⅜ cup (¼ cup plus 2 tablespoons) oil
> ½ cup water

Spelt:

> 1½ cups spelt flour
> 1 cup arrowroot or tapioca flour
> ½ teaspoon baking soda
> ⅛ teaspoon unbuffered vitamin C crystals (omit if you are using the apple juice)
> ⅜ cup (¼ cup plus 2 tablespoons) oil
> ½ cup water plus ¼ cup cane or beet sugar
>   OR ½ cup apple juice concentrate, thawed

Pineapple- Oat:

   2½ cups oat flour
   ½ teaspoon baking soda
   ⅜ cup (¼ cup plus 2 tablespoons) oil
   ½ cup pineapple juice concentrate, thawed

Barley:

   2 cups barley flour
   ½ teaspoon baking soda
   ⅜ cup (¼ cup plus 2 tablespoons) oil
   ½ cup apple juice concentrate, thawed

Choose one set of ingredients above. Combine the flour(s), baking soda, vitamin C crystals (if the recipe calls for them), and date, cane, or beet sugar (if you are using it) in a large bowl. Stir together the oil and juice or water and add them to the dry ingredients, mixing with a spoon and your hands until the dough sticks together. If necessary, add another 1 to 2 tablespoons of water or juice to help it stick together. Roll the dough out to ¼ inch thickness on an ungreased baking sheet and cut it into 1 by 2 to 3 inch rectangular bars. Bake at 350°F until the cookies begin to brown. This will take about 15 to 20 minutes for the amaranth, oat, and spelt varieties and 20 to 25 minutes for the barley cookies. Makes 2½ to 3 dozen bars.

Pizzelles

These traditional Italian Christmas cookies can be made with or without the anise flavoring.

Make any variety of "Ice Cream Cones," page 175, as directed in the recipe. If you wish to have the traditional flavor, add 1½ teaspoons anise flavoring to the batter before adding the flour. Bake the cookies in a pizzelle iron until they are lightly browned and lay them flat on paper towels to cool. Makes about 2 to 3 dozen 6-inch pizzelles or about 15 pizzelles which are 8-inch circles that break apart into quarter-circles.

Fig Newtons

This old favorite cookie is quite rich even when you make it without the butter.

Filling:

  8 ounces dried figs
  1 cup water
  2 teaspoons corn-free natural vanilla flavoring (optional)

Amaranth dough:

  3 cups amaranth flour
  1 cup arrowroot
  ¾ cup oil
  ⅜ cup (¼ cup plus 2 tablespoons) to ½ cup cold water

Rye dough:

  3 cups rye flour
  1 cup butter, goat butter, or milk-free margarine at room temperature
  ½ cup cold water

Choose one set of dough ingredients, above. Mix together the flour(s) and butter or oil with a pastry cutter until the mixture is crumbly. Gradually add enough of the water to make a soft dough. Divide the dough in half and flatten each half unto a small square. Refrigerate the rye dough for at least an hour. (You do not need to refrigerate the amaranth dough; you can even make it while the fig filling is cooling. See below).

To make the filling, remove the stems from the figs. Combine the figs and water in a saucepan, bring them to a boil, reduce the heat, and simmer them on low heat for 30 minutes. Cool the figs, stir in the optional vanilla, and puree them in a blender or food processor until they are smooth.

Roll one half of the dough out into an 8 by 12 inch rectangle on an ungreased cookie sheet and spread it with the filling. Roll the other half of the dough out into an 8 by 12 inch rectangle on a well-floured pastry cloth or roll it out between two pieces of waxed or parchment paper and peel off the top piece. Invert the pastry cloth or waxed or parchment paper with the dough on it onto the top of the fig filling and dough on the baking sheet. Bake at 400°F for 25 to 30 minutes for the amaranth dough or 30 to 35 minutes for the rye dough, or until it begins to brown. Cool it for 10 minutes, then carefully cut it into 1½ inch squares with a sharp knife. Makes about 3 dozen cookies.

Carob Sandwich Cookies

These are a lot like what the rest of the kids are eating but do not contain any sugar.

1⅔ cups rye flour
⅓ cup carob powder
½ teaspoon baking soda
⅛ teaspoon unbuffered vitamin C crystals
⅔ cup grape juice concentrate, thawed
⅓ cup oil
¾ cup milk-free unsweetened carob chips (optional)

Combine the flour, carob powder, baking soda, and vitamin C crystals in a large bowl. Mix together the juice and oil and stir them into the dry ingredients until they are just mixed in. Drop the dough by heaping teaspoonfuls onto an ungreased baking sheet and flatten them into 2 inch rounds that are about ⅛ to ¼ inch thick with your hand. Bake at 350°F for 7 to 9 minutes, or until the cookies are set and begin to feel dry. Using a spatula, immediately remove the cookies from the baking sheet and allow them to cool completely. Melt the carob chips in a double boiler over water that is just below the boiling point, stirring them frequently. Spread the melted carob chips on the bottoms of half of the cookies. Top each with another cookie to make a "sandwich." Makes about 1½ dozen sandwich cookies. If the carob chips are not used, this recipe makes about 3 dozen single cookies.

Cookie Press Cookies

No one will feel deprived at Christmas time if you have some of these cookies made in the shape of Christmas trees on hand.

Oat:

  2 cups oat flour
  1 cup date sugar
  1 teaspoon baking soda
  ¼ teaspoon unbuffered vitamin C crystals
  ½ cup coconut oil
  ⅝ cup (½ cup plus 2 tablespoons) water
  1 teaspoon corn-free natural vanilla or other flavoring

Spelt:

  2½ cups spelt flour
  1 cup date sugar OR ½ cup beet or cane sugar
  1 teaspoon baking soda
  ¼ teaspoon unbuffered vitamin C crystals
  ½ cup coconut oil
  ¾ cup water with the date sugar OR ½ cup water with the beet or cane sugar
  1 teaspoon corn-free natural vanilla or other flavoring

Barley:

  2½ cups barley flour
  ½ cup beet or cane sugar
  1 teaspoon baking soda
  ½ teaspoon unbuffered vitamin C crystals
  ½ cup coconut oil
  ⅝ cup (½ cup plus 2 tablespoons) water
  1 teaspoon corn-free natural vanilla or other flavoring

Amaranth:

    2 cups amaranth flour
    ½ cup arrowroot
    ½ cup beet or cane sugar
    1 teaspoon baking soda
    ¼ teaspoon unbuffered vitamin C crystals
    ½ cup coconut oil
    ½ cup water
    1 teaspoon corn-free natural vanilla or other flavoring (optional)

Quinoa:

    2 cups quinoa flour
    ½ cup beet or cane sugar (Beet is in the same food family as quinoa).
    1 teaspoon baking soda
    ¼ teaspoon unbuffered vitamin C crystals
    ½ cup coconut oil
    ½ cup water
    1 teaspoon corn-free natural vanilla or other flavoring (optional)

Choose one set of ingredients above. Melt the coconut oil and allow it to cool until it is just very slightly warm. If you are using date sugar, press it through a wire mesh strainer with the back of a spoon to remove any small lumps or they will clog the cookie press. Combine the flour(s), sugar, baking soda, and vitamin C crystals in a large bowl. Mix together the oil, water, and flavoring and stir them into the dry ingredients. Put the dough into a cookie press and press out the cookies onto an ungreased baking sheet. Bake at 375°F until the bottoms of the cookies begin to brown. If you make them as trees, hearts, etc. this takes about 10 to 12 minutes for the oat and amaranth cookies and about 11 to 15 minutes for the spelt, barley, and quinoa cookies. If you make them as spritz strips, which are thinner, reduce the baking time by 2 to 4 minutes for each type of cookie. Remove the cookies from the baking sheet immediately. Makes 4 to 5 dozen cookies.

Gingerbread Men

These are crisp, crunchy, and flavorful.

3 cups spelt flour
¾ teaspoon baking soda
¼ teaspoon unbuffered vitamin C crystals
½ teaspoon ginger
¼ teaspoon nutmeg
¾ cup molasses
½ cup oil
Raisins or dried fruit (optional)

Combine the spelt flour, baking soda, vitamin C crystals, and spices in a large bowl. Stir together the molasses and oil and mix them into the dry ingredients using a spoon and then your hands to make a stiff dough. Roll the dough out to between ⅛ and ¼ inch thickness on a floured board. Cut it into gingerbread men and transfer them to an ungreased baking sheet with a spatula. Decorate them with raisins or small pieces of dried fruit if desired. Bake them at 350°F for 11 to 15 minutes. Makes about 1½ dozen 6 inch tall gingerbread men.

Kamut Gingerbread

These are great Christmas cookie treats.

3 cups kamut flour
1 teaspoon baking soda
¼ teaspoon unbuffered vitamin C crystals
¾ teaspoon ginger
½ teaspoon nutmeg
1 cup molasses
⅜ cup (¼ cup plus 2 tablespoons) oil
Raisins or dried fruit (optional)

Combine the flour, baking soda, vitamin C crystals, and spices in a large bowl. Stir together the molasses and oil and mix them into the dry ingredients using a spoon and then your hands to make a stiff dough. Roll the dough out to between ⅛ and ¼ inch thickness on a floured board. Cut into cookies with cookie cutters and transfer them to an ungreased baking sheet with a spatula. Decorate them with raisins or small pieces of dried fruit if desired. Bake them at 350°F for 11 to 15 minutes. Makes about 14 6 inch tall gingerbread men or 2 dozen 3 inch cookies.

FOS "Sugar" Cookies

These are good for a special occasion treat. Cut them out in holiday shapes for Christmas.

1½ cups barley flour OR 1½ cups plus 1 tablespoon spelt flour
½ cup FOS* (see note below)
¼ teaspoon baking soda
1/16 teaspoon or a "pinch" of unbuffered vitamin C crystals
¼ cup oil
¼ cup water

Combine the flour, FOS, baking soda, and vitamin C crystals in a large bowl. Stir together the water and oil thoroughly and add them to the flour mixture quickly before they have a chance to separate. Mix the dough together with a spoon and then your hands until all of the flour is worked in. Roll the dough out on a well floured board to just under ¼ inch thickness, cut it into shapes, and put the cookies on an oiled baking sheet. Or roll the dough directly on an oiled baking sheet and cut it into squares with a knife. Bake at 350°F for 15 to 20 minutes or until the cookies just begin to brown. Makes 1½ dozen 3 inch cut-out cookies or 3 dozen 1½ inch squares.

Notes: These cookies are minimally sweetened. For a more traditional sugar cookie taste, use ¾ cup FOS and an additional 2 tablespoons flour. When made with this much FOS, the dough is sticky. Flour the rolling pin, surface, and cookie cutters thoroughly when you roll the dough out. Or you may find it easier to roll it directly onto the cookie sheet and cut it into squares.

*See the cautionary note about FOS on page 127.

Sugar Cookies

You can make these light and flaky cookies with a minimal amount of sugar or with stevia. Use the smaller amount of the stevia if you are just getting used to it.

3 cups barley flour or 3⅛ cups (3 cups plus 2 tablespoons) spelt flour
½ cup sugar OR ⅜ to ½ teaspoon white stevia powder
½ teaspoon baking soda
⅛ teaspoon unbuffered vitamin C crystals
½ cup oil
½ cup water

Combine the flour, sugar or stevia, baking soda, and vitamin C crystals in a large bowl. Stir together the water and oil thoroughly and add them to the flour mixture quickly before they have a chance to separate. Mix the dough together with a spoon and then your hands until all of the flour is worked in. If the dough is too stiff, you may add an additional tablespoon or two of water. Roll the dough out on a well floured board to just under ¼ inch thickness. Cut it into shapes and sprinkle the cookies with additional sugar if desired. Bake them at 350°F for 15 to 20 minutes for the barley version or 10 to 15 minutes for the spelt version, or until the cookies begin to brown. The stevia-sweetened cookies will not brown very much, but will feel dry to your touch. Makes 2½ to 3 dozen 3-inch cookies.

Sandwich Cookies

If these cookies are cut out with cookie cutters into creative shapes, they are actually "better" than what the other kids have in their lunch boxes.

1 batch of "Sugar Cookies," above
1 to 1½ cups of milk-free unsweetened carob chips

Melt the carob chips in a double boiler over water that is just under the boiling point, stirring them frequently. When they are just melted, remove the top of the double boiler from the pan. Spread the melted carob on the bottoms of half of the cookies. Immediately after each cookie is spread, top it with another cookie. Cool them completely. Makes 1½ dozen sandwich cookies.

Lemon Crisps

The golden color of kamut matches the lemony flavor of these cookies.

2½ cups kamut flour
½ cup sugar
½ teaspoon baking soda
⅛ teaspoon unbuffered vitamin C crystals
½ cup oil
⅝ cup (½ cup plus 2 tablespoons) water
1½ teaspoons corn-free natural lemon flavoring (optional – Omit or replace with
    vanilla for sugar cookies).

Combine the flour, sugar, baking soda, and vitamin C crystals in a large bowl. Mix together the water, oil, and flavoring and mix them into the dry ingredients with a spoon and your hands. Drop the dough by teaspoonfuls onto an ungreased baking sheet and flatten the cookies to about ¼ inch thickness with your fingers held together. Bake them at 350°F for 20 to 25 minutes, or until they begin to brown. Makes about 2 dozen cookies.

Kamut Sugar Cookies variation: Replace the lemon flavoring above with vanilla.

Gingersnaps

These spicy cookies are delicious and easy to make.

1½ cups barley flour
½ teaspoon baking soda
⅛ teaspoon unbuffered vitamin C crystals
¼ teaspoon ginger
½ cup light molasses
¼ cup oil

Combine the flour, baking soda, vitamin C crystals, and ginger in a large bowl. Mix together the molasses and oil and stir them into the dry ingredients until they are just blended in. Drop the dough by tablespoonfuls onto an ungreased baking sheet and flatten the cookies to about ¼ inch thickness with your fingers held together. Bake them at 350°F for 10 to 15 minutes, or until they begin to brown. Makes 1½ to 2 dozen cookies.

Gingerbread Cutout Cookies

These cookies are strictly grain-free if you make them with the beet sugar and apple juice.

2 cups quinoa flour
⅓ cup cane or beet sugar
1 teaspoon baking soda
¼ teaspoon unbuffered vitamin C crystals
½ teaspoon ginger
½ teaspoon nutmeg
¼ cup oil
¼ cup light molasses plus ¼ cup water OR ½ cup apple juice concentrate, thawed
Raisins or dried fruit (optional)

Mix together the flour, sugar, baking soda, vitamin C crystals, and spices in a large bowl. Combine the oil with the molasses and water or juice, add them to the dry ingredients, and stir until they are just mixed in. Roll the dough out to between ⅛ and ¼ inch thickness on a well-floured pastry cloth, or you can roll the dough out between two pieces of parchment or waxed paper and peel off the top piece. Cut the dough with cookie cutters. Carefully transfer the cookies to an ungreased baking sheet with a spatula. Decorate the cookies with raisins or cut-up dried fruit if desired. Bake them at 350°F for 10 to 12 minutes, or until they begin to brown. Remove them from the cookie sheet immediately with a spatula. Makes about 1½ dozen 6 inch gingerbread men or about 3 dozen 3 inch cookies.

Sugar and Spice Cookies

These grain-free cookies contain foods from just two food families if you make them with beet sugar and avocado oil. If you use beet sugar and a different oil, they contain foods from just three food families.

2 cups quinoa flour
½ cup beet or cane sugar (Beet is in the same food family as quinoa).
1 teaspoon baking soda
¼ teaspoon unbuffered vitamin C crystals
1½ teaspoon cinnamon
¼ cup avocado or other oil (Avocado is in the same family as cinnamon).
⅜ cup plus 1 tablespoon (or ¼ cup plus 3 tablespoons) water

Combine the flour, sugar, baking soda, vitamin C crystals and cinnamon in a large bowl. Mix together the oil and water and stir them into the dry ingredients until they are just mixed in. Form the dough into 1 inch balls and flatten them with your hand to about ¼ inch thickness on a lightly oiled baking sheet. Bake them at 375°F for 10 to 15 minutes, or until they begin to brown. Makes 2 to 2½ dozen cookies.

Cashew Butter Cookies

This is a variation on traditional peanut butter cookies without the peanut butter.

2 cups rye flour
½ teaspoon baking soda
⅛ teaspoon unbuffered vitamin C crystals
⅔ cup cashew butter
¼ cup oil
¾ cup maple syrup

Combine the flour, baking soda, and vitamin C crystals in a large bowl. In a small bowl, thoroughly mix together the cashew butter, oil and maple syrup. Stir this mixture into the dry ingredients. Drop the dough by heaping teaspoonfuls onto an ungreased baking sheet. Use an oiled fork to flatten the balls of dough, making an "X" on the top of them with the fork tines. Bake the cookies at 400°F for 8 to 10 minutes, or until they are golden brown. Makes 3 dozen cookies.

Maple Cookies

These cookies are sturdy enough to take some rough handling of the lunch box.

5 cups rye flour
1¼ teaspoons baking soda
1 teaspoon cream of tartar OR ½ teaspoon unbuffered vitamin C crystals
1½ cup maple syrup
1 cup oil
1½ cups raisins or milk-free unsweetened carob chips (optional)

Combine the flour, baking soda, and cream of tartar or vitamin C crystals in a large bowl. Mix together the maple syrup and oil and stir them into the dry ingredients. Stir in the raisins or carob chips if you are using them. Drop the dough by tablespoonfuls onto a lightly oiled baking sheet and flatten the cookies to ¼ to ⅜ inch thickness with your fingers held together. Bake them at 375°F for 10 to 15 minutes, or until they begin to brown. Makes about 4 dozen cookies.

For easy-to-make diamond-shaped cookies, make the cookie dough as above, but omit the raisins or carob chips. Divide the dough into two parts and roll or pat each half out to ¼ inch thickness on a lightly oiled baking sheet. Cut into 1½ to 2 inch diamonds with a sharp knife. Bake at 350°F for 15 to 20 minutes, or until the cookies begin to brown. Cut them again through the previous cuts. Remove them from the baking sheet. Makes about 5 dozen cookies.

Quinoa Almond Cookies

If you would like to save time on chopping the nuts, almond meal, which is finely chopped almonds, can be used in place of the chopped nuts.

1½ cups quinoa flour
¾ teaspoon baking soda
¼ teaspoon unbuffered vitamin C crystals
½ cup very finely chopped almonds (⅛ inch pieces)
½ cup oil
½ cup honey (for crisp cookies) OR ½ cup honey plus ½ cup water (soft cookies)
    OR 1 cup apple juice concentrate, thawed (for fruit-sweetened soft cookies)

Combine the flour, baking soda, vitamin C crystals, and almonds in a large bowl. Thoroughly mix the oil with the honey, honey and water, or juice in a small bowl, and then immediately pour it into the dry ingredients. Stir the dough until it is just mixed. Drop it by teaspoonfuls onto an ungreased baking sheet and flatten the cookies with an oiled glass bottom or your fingers held together. Bake the cookies at 375°F for 5 to 7 minutes for crisp cookies or for 7 to 9 minutes for soft cookies. Makes about 2 dozen crisp or 3 dozen soft cookies.

Frazelle

This recipe is adapted from an old family recipe that was one of my favorites when my aunt, Louise Giardino, made it when I was a child.

2¾ cups spelt flour OR 2 cups amaranth flour plus 1 cup arrowroot
½ cup beet or cane sugar
¼ teaspoon salt (optional)
½ teaspoon baking soda
¼ teaspoon unbuffered vitamin C crystals
⅓ cup sliced almonds
⅔ cup water
⅓ cup oil
1 teaspoon corn-free natural almond flavor
1 teaspoon corn-free natural vanilla

Stir together the flour(s), sugar, salt, baking soda, vitamin C crystals, and almonds in a large bowl. In a small bowl, mix the water, oil, and flavorings; then stir them into the dry ingredients. Transfer the dough to a generously floured board and knead it about 30 times. On a lightly oiled baking sheet, form the dough into a flat-topped loaf about 14 inches long, 3 inches wide, and 1 inch tall. Bake it at 350°F for 30 to 35 minutes, or until it is set and is barely beginning to brown. Remove it from the oven and, using a serrated knife, cut it down the middle lengthwise and slice it crosswise into ¾ to 1 inch slices. Lay the slices down on their cut sides on the cookie sheet. Bake the slices and additional 20 to 25 minutes, or until they are hard and lightly browned. Makes 2½ dozen cookies.

No-Grain Carob Sandwich Cookies or Carob Wafers

You can put these sandwich cookies together with sugar-free jam or carob chips or eat them plain, as "Carob Wafers," for everyday lunchbox use. For a special occasion, fill them with "White Stuff," below, and they will be just like Oreos™.

1½ cups carob powder
1½ cups tapioca flour
1 teaspoon baking soda
¼ teaspoon unbuffered vitamin C crystals
1 cup apple juice concentrate, thawed OR ¾ teaspoon white stevia powder plus
    1 cup water
½ cup oil
About ⅔ cup all-fruit (sugarless) jam or jelly OR ⅔ cup of "White Stuff," below,
    OR 1 cup milk-free unsweetened carob chips (optional)

Combine the carob powder, tapioca flour, baking soda, and vitamin C crystals in a large bowl. Mix together the juice and oil and stir them into the dry ingredients until they are thoroughly mixed in. Roll the dough into 1 inch balls and place them on an ungreased baking sheet. Flatten each ball to ⅛ to ¼ inch thickness with an oiled glass bottom or your fingers held together. Or, for more perfectly shaped cookies, roll the dough directly onto an ungreased baking sheet to ⅛ to ¼ inch thickness, cut circles with a 2 inch round cookie cutter, and carefully remove the dough between the circles with a fork and your fingers. Bake the cookies at 350°F for 10 to 12 minutes or until they are firm. Remove them from the baking sheet with a spatula and cool them completely. If you are using the carob chips, melt them in the top of a double boiler over water that is just below the boiling point, stirring them frequently. As soon as they are melted, remove the top of the double boiler from the pan. Put the cookies together in pairs, with their bottoms together, using the melted carob chips, jelly or jam, or "White Stuff," below, if desired. Makes about 2 dozen sandwich cookies or 4 dozen plain carob wafers.

WHITE STUFF:

1 cup water
3 cups cane or beet sugar
1/16 teaspoon cream of tartar

Bring the water to a boil in a large saucepan. Remove it from the heat and stir in the sugar until it dissolves. Return it to the heat and bring it to a boil, stirring in the cream of tartar just as it starts boiling. Wash down any crystals from the side of the pan with hot water and a brush. Place a candy thermometer in the boiling liquid, but not touching the bottom of the pan. Cook the solution without stirring it to 238°F at sea level or to 26°F more than the boiling temperature of water in your area. (This difference is because water boils at a lower temperature at high altitudes. See page 212 for more information). When it reaches the right temperature, immediately pour it onto a wet marble slab or wet large stoneware platter. Cool it for a few minutes. Then, using a candy scraper or metal knife-type spatula, lift the edges of the mixture to the center. Continue working it this way until the mixture becomes opaque and creamy. Then knead it with your hands briefly. This white fondant stores well in a covered container at room temperature. Makes about 1½ cups of "White Stuff."

Mix and Match Cookies

These rich cookies can be varied in so many ways that children will not recognize them (or get tired of them) from one batch to the next.

3½ cups oat flour OR 3¼ cups barley flour
1 teaspoon baking soda
¼ teaspoon unbuffered vitamin C crystals
½ teaspoon salt (optional)
1 cup oil
1 cup honey
1 teaspoon corn-free natural vanilla flavoring (optional)
1 to 1½ cups of any combination of raisins, milk-free unsweetened carob chips,
    chopped nuts, chopped dates, or other chopped dried fruit (optional)

Combine the flour, baking soda, vitamin C crystals, and salt in a large bowl. Mix together the oil, honey, and vanilla and stir them into the dry ingredients. Fold in the raisins, carob chips, nuts, or fruit, if desired. Drop the dough by heaping teaspoonfuls at least 2 inches apart on an ungreased baking sheet. Bake at 375°F for 8 to 10 minutes. Cool the cookies for about 5 minutes on the baking sheet before removing them to a dishcloth or paper towel to cool completely. Makes 3½ dozen cookies.

Maple Bars

These easy-to-make cookies are especially chewy when they are fresh.

2⅔ cups rye flour
⅓ cup uncooked rye flakes or cream of rye cereal
½ teaspoon baking soda
¼ teaspoon unbuffered vitamin C crystals
¼ teaspoon salt (optional)
1 teaspoon cinnamon (optional)
1¼ cups maple syrup
⅓ cup oil
1 cup raisins, currants, or milk-free unsweetened carob chips (optional)

Combine the flour, rye flakes, baking soda, vitamin C crystals, salt, and cinnamon in a large bowl. Thoroughly mix together the maple syrup and oil and stir them into the dry ingredients until they are just mixed in. Stir in the raisins, currants, or carob chips. Spread the dough in a oiled and floured 13 by 9 inch baking pan. Bake at 350ºF for 30 to 35 minutes. Immediately it cut into 1½ inch square. Cool the cookies completely before you remove them from the pan. Makes about 3 dozen cookies.

Cakes and Frostings

What is a birthday without a cake? For certain occasions in life, a cake is an integral part of the celebration. Cakes are especially important to children. On their birthdays, they want a cake like the other kids have. If they attend a friend's birthday party, Mom would do well to find out what is going to be served, try to duplicate it as nearly as possible, and send it along to the party.

This chapter provides recipes for cakes rich with fruits and vegetables, spice cakes, gingerbread, carob cakes, and frostings. Most of the cakes are fruit-sweetened. If you want to avoid fruit sweeteners as well as avoiding sugar, there are two recipes in this chapter that are sweetened with stevia, "Stevia Sweetened Spice Cake" and "Stevia Sweetened Carob Cake." There are also some recipes for cakes and frostings minimally sweetened with sugar so mothers can make their allergic children birthday cakes much like what other children have.

Cakes made with alternative flours are not as light or as sturdy as cakes made with refined wheat flour, but what they lack in lightness they make up for in flavor. Try one of these carrot cakes, and you will wonder why you ever liked bakery-type cakes.

There are several ways to cope with the fragility of cakes made with alternative flours. The simplest is to serve the cake from the pan instead of trying to remove it in one piece. If you wish to make a layer cake, you can remove it from the pan more easily if you line the bottom of the pan with waxed or parchment paper. Parchment paper can be purchased at cooking stores, or see "Sources of Special Foods," page 218, for a mail-order source. By using parchment paper you can avoid the chemicals and traces of corn that waxed paper may contain.

To make a cake which is easy to remove from the pan, you must properly prepare the pan before baking the cake. Oil and flour the pan (using the same kind of oil and flour that are in the cake) and then cut a piece of parchment or waxed paper to fit the bottom of the pan. Put the paper in the pan, add the cake batter, and bake the cake. Cool it in the pan for 10 to 15 minutes after removing it from the oven. Run a sharp knife around the sides of the pan. Then place a wire rack on top of the cake, invert it, and lift off the pan. Remove the paper and hold a serving plate or another wire rack against the bottom of the cake and invert it again.

Cool the cake completely before frosting it. When it is time for the party, cut it into pieces and watch everyone enjoy it!

Pineapple Upside-Down Cake

The delicious fruit topping eliminates the need for frosting on this easy-to-make cake.

1 cup pineapple canned in its own juice or fresh pineapple with enough juice
    to cover it
1 cup pineapple juice concentrate, thawed
¼ cup oil
3 cups barley flour
1½ teaspoons baking soda
½ teaspoon unbuffered vitamin C crystals
6 slices of fresh pineapple or pineapple canned in its own juice, drained (about ⅔
    of a 20-ounce can)
A few seedless red grapes or cherries (optional)

Puree the 1 cup pineapple together with its juice in a blender or food processor. Add the pineapple juice concentrate and oil and blend them again briefly. Oil a 9 inch square cake pan. Arrange the pineapple slices in the pan, cutting to fit if needed, and place a grape or pitted cherry in the center of each slice. Combine the flour, baking soda, and vitamin C crystals in a large bowl. Add the pureed pineapple mixture and stir just until the liquid ingredients are mixed into the dry ingredients. Pour the batter into the prepared pan and bake the cake at 375°F for 30 to 40 minutes or until it is golden brown. Cool the cake in the pan for 10 minutes; then run a knife around the edges of the pan and invert it onto a serving dish. Makes one 9 inch square cake, about 9 servings.

Zucchini Cake

The zucchini adds moistness to this cake.

3 cups spelt flour
2 teaspoons baking soda
¼ teaspoon salt (optional)
1 teaspoon cinnamon
¼ teaspoon nutmeg

¼ teaspoon ground cloves
½ cup grated unsweetened coconut
2 cups grated zucchini
1 cup very small pieces of fresh pineapple or pineapple tidbits canned in their
    own juice, drained
1¼ cups pineapple juice concentrate, thawed
½ cup oil

In a large bowl, combine the flour, baking soda, salt, spices, and coconut. In a small bowl, combine the zucchini, pineapple, pineapple juice, and oil. Stir the liquid ingredients into the dry ingredients until they are just mixed in. Pour the batter into an oiled and floured 9 by 13 inch cake pan. Bake at 325°F for 50 to 55 minutes, or until the cake is lightly browned and a toothpick inserted in its center comes out dry. Makes one 9 by 13 inch cake, or about 12 servings.

Banana Carob Chip Cake

This cake is moist and flavorful.

2½ cups kamut flour
1 teaspoon baking soda
¼ teaspoon unbuffered vitamin C crystals
⅓ cup milk-free unsweetened carob chips
1 cup thoroughly mashed or pureed banana
½ cup honey
¼ cup oil

In a large bowl, combine the flour, baking soda, vitamin C crystals, and carob chips. In a small bowl, combine the banana, honey, and oil. Stir the liquid ingredients into the dry ingredients until they are just mixed in. Pour the batter into an oiled and floured 8 by 4 inch or 9 by 5 inch loaf pan. Bake at 350°F for 30 to 45 minutes, or until the cake is lightly browned and a toothpick inserted in its center comes out dry. Frost with ½ batch of "Very Carob Frosting," page 166, if desired. Makes one loaf cake, about 6 to 8 servings.

Date-Nut Bundt Cake

Your non-allergic guests will ask for second helpings when this rich cake is served.

1½ cups quick rolled oats (uncooked)
1½ cups boiling water
¾ cup oil
¾ cup cool water
1½ cups oat flour
1 cup date sugar
1¼ teaspoons baking soda
½ teaspoon unbuffered vitamin C crystals
1 teaspoon salt (optional)
2 teaspoons cinnamon
½ teaspoon ground cloves
1 cup chopped pitted dates
½ cup finely chopped nuts

Combine the oats and boiling water in a large bowl. Allow them to cool for 5 to 10 minutes. Stir in the oil and cool water and beat the mixture until all the lumps are gone. In another bowl, stir together the flour, date sugar, baking soda, vitamin C crystals, salt, spices, dates and nuts. Add them to the oatmeal mixture and stir it until they are just mixed in. Pour the batter into an oiled and floured 12 cup bundt pan or 8 inch square cake pan. Bake it at 375°F for 55 to 60 minutes. Cool the bundt cake in the pan for 30 minutes, then invert it onto a serving dish. The square cake may be served from the pan. If you want to frost this cake, drizzle the tube cake with "Date Glaze," page 165, or frost the square cake with ⅔ of a batch of "Date Frosting," page 164. Makes one bundt or 8 inch square cake, 9 to 12 servings.

Apple Cake

Cakes made with spelt flour tend to become dry quickly. In this recipe, the apple and applesauce add moisture as well as flavor and help the cake keep well.

1⅓ cups apple juice concentrate
3 cups spelt flour
2 teaspoons baking soda
1 teaspoon cinnamon
¼ teaspoon nutmeg
¼ teaspoon cloves
¼ teaspoon salt (optional)
1 cup grated or shredded peeled apple (about 1 medium)
⅔ cup unsweetened applesauce
½ cup oil
1 cup raisins (optional)

Boil the apple juice down to ⅔ cup in volume and allow it to cool. In a large bowl, combine the flour, baking soda, salt, and spices. In a small bowl, combine the grated apple, applesauce, juice, oil, and raisins. Stir the liquid ingredients into the dry ingredients until they are just mixed in. Pour the batter into an oiled and floured 9 by 13 inch cake pan. Bake the cake at 325°F for 40 to 50 minutes, or until it is lightly browned and a toothpick inserted into its center comes out dry. Makes one 9 inch by 13 inch cake.

Spelt Carrot Cake

Although not quite as moist as "Rye Carrot Cake" on the next page, this cake is still delicious.

Prepare the batter for "Apple Cake," above, except substitute 1 cup grated carrots for the grated apple. Bake it as directed above. Makes one 9 by 13 inch cake.

Rye Carrot Cake

This flavorful, moist cake is a favorite at our house.

2½ cups rye flour
2 teaspoons baking soda
½ teaspoon unbuffered vitamin C crystals (Omit if using the pineapple juice).
1½ teaspoons cinnamon
¼ teaspoon cloves
1 cup raisins (optional)
1½ cups shredded carrots
2 cups white grape juice OR 1 cup thawed pineapple juice concentrate
    plus 1 cup water
¼ cup oil

In a large bowl, combine the flour, baking soda, vitamin C crystals (if you are using them), spices, and raisins. In a small bowl, combine the carrots, juice, water (if you are using it), and oil. Stir the liquid ingredients into the dry ingredients until they are just mixed in. Pour the batter into an oiled and floured 9 inch square cake pan. Bake the cake at 350°F for 45 to 55 minutes, or until it is lightly browned and a toothpick inserted into its center comes out dry. Makes one 9 inch square cake, or about 9 servings.

Quinoa Carrot Cake

This carrot cake is both delicious and grain-free.

1 cup grated carrots
1 cup raisins (optional)
1 teaspoon cinnamon
¼ teaspoon nutmeg
¼ teaspoon cloves
1½ cups apple juice concentrate
⅜ cup (¼ cup plus 2 tablespoons) oil
1½ cups quinoa flour
½ cups tapioca flour
1½ teaspoons baking soda

Combine the carrots, raisins, spices, juice and oil in a saucepan. Bring them to a boil and simmer them, covered, for 5 minutes. Allow the mixture to cool to lukewarm or room temperature. In a large bowl, combine the quinoa flour, tapioca flour, and baking soda. Stir the liquid ingredients into the dry ingredients until they are just mixed in. Pour the batter into two oiled and floured 8 by 4 inch loaf pans. Bake the cakes at 325°F for 40 to 50 minutes, or until they are lightly browned and a toothpick inserted into their centers comes out dry. This cake may appear to rise and then fall slightly during baking, but the texture will still be good. Makes two 8 by 4 inch cakes which freeze well.

Spice Cake

This sugar-free cake is moist and tasty. It is good plain or frosted with "Date Frosting," page 164.

4 cups oat, milo, or barley flour
1 cup date sugar, pressed through a strainer to remove lumps
2 teaspoons baking soda
½ teaspoon unbuffered vitamin C crystals
2 teaspoons cinnamon
¾ teaspoon cloves
½ teaspoon allspice
Pureed or thoroughly mashed bananas - 3 cups with oat or milo flour
     OR 4 cups with barley flour
¾ cup oil
1 teaspoon corn-free natural vanilla (optional)

In a large bowl, combine the flour, date sugar, baking soda, vitamin C crystals, and spices. In a small bowl, combine the bananas, oil, and optional vanilla. Stir the liquid ingredients into the dry ingredients until they are just mixed in. Pour the batter into an oiled and floured 9 by 13 inch cake pan, two oiled and floured 8 or 9 inch round cake pans, or 24 to 28 oiled and floured muffin cups. Bake the cake for 25 to 30 minutes or cupcakes for 20 to 25 minutes at 375°F or until lightly browned and a toothpick inserted in the center comes out dry. If you are making a layer cake, cool the layers in the pans for 15 minutes and then remove them carefully because they are very fragile. (See the notes in the introduction to this chapter on lining the pans and removing layer cakes from their pans). Makes one 9 by 13 inch cake, two 8 or 9 inch cake layers, or 24 to 28 cupcakes.

Stevia-Sweetened Spice Cake

This grain-free cake is a real treat for those who must avoid both sugar and fruit sweeteners. If you are just getting used to stevia, use the smaller amount.

2¼ cups amaranth flour
¾ cup arrowroot
2 teaspoons baking soda
½ teaspoon unbuffered vitamin C crystals
1 teaspoon cinnamon
¼ teaspoon cloves
⅛ teaspoon allspice
¼ to ½ teaspoon white stevia powder
1 cup water
¼ cup oil

Combine the amaranth flour, arrowroot, baking soda, vitamin C crystals, spices, and stevia in a large bowl. Mix together the water and oil, and stir them into the dry ingredients until they are just mixed in. (The batter will be stiff). Put the batter into an oiled and floured 8 by 4 inch loaf pan and bake it at 350ºF for 30 to 40 minutes. Cool the cake in the pan for 10 minutes, and then remove it if you wish to. Makes one 8 by 4 inch cake, or about 6 servings.

Shoo Fly Pie Cake

This cake, based on the traditional Pennsylvania Dutch pie, is sweet, spicy, and made with non-grain flours.

2 cups amaranth flour
⅔ cup arrowroot
1 teaspoon baking soda
½ teaspoon unbuffered vitamin C crystals
1½ teaspoons cinnamon
½ teaspoon nutmeg
½ teaspoon cloves

¾ cup molasses
½ cup water
¼ cup oil

Combine the amaranth flour, arrowroot, baking soda, vitamin C crystals, and spices in a large bowl. Mix together the molasses, water, and oil thoroughly and stir them into the dry ingredients until they are just mixed in. Put the batter into an oiled and floured 9 inch square baking pan. Bake the cake at 350°F for 25 to 30 minutes, or until a toothpick inserted in its center comes out dry. Makes one 9 inch cake, or about 9 servings.

Vanilla Cake

This cake is so delicious that when I gave it to a friend, she could not leave it alone until she finished it.

Kamut flour – 2½ cups with the honey or 2¾ cups with the Fruit Sweet™
1 teaspoon baking soda
¼ teaspoon unbuffered vitamin C crystals
¾ cup honey or Fruit Sweet™
¼ cup water
¼ cup oil
1 teaspoon corn-free natural vanilla flavoring (optional)
¼ teaspoon corn-free natural almond flavoring (optional)

In a large bowl, combine the flour, baking soda, and vitamin C crystals. In a small bowl, combine the sweetener, water, oil, and flavorings. Stir the liquid ingredients into the dry ingredients until they are just mixed in. Pour the batter into an oiled and floured 8 by 4 inch or 9 by 5 inch loaf pan. Bake at 350°F for 30 to 45 minutes, or until the cake is lightly browned and a toothpick inserted in its center comes out dry. If you would like to remove the cake from the pan, let it cool on a rack for 10 minutes before doing so. When the cake is completely cool, frost it with a half batch of "Date Frosting," page 164, if desired. Makes one loaf cake, or 6 to 8 servings.

Gingerbread

There are many options for making this gingerbread. Use either a grain or non-grain flour and sweeten it with either molasses or apple juice.

2 cups spelt flour OR 1½ cups amaranth flour plus ½ cup arrowroot
    OR 1¼ cups quinoa flour plus ½ cup tapioca flour
1 teaspoon baking soda
½ teaspoon unbuffered vitamin C crystals if you are using the molasses and water
    OR ¼ teaspoon if you are using the apple juice
¾ teaspoon ginger
1 teaspoon cinnamon
½ cup water plus ½ cup molasses OR 1 cup apple juice concentrate, thawed
¼ cup oil

Combine the flour(s), baking soda, vitamin C crystals, and spices in a large bowl. Mix the molasses and water or the juice with the oil thoroughly and stir them into the dry ingredients until they are just mixed in. Put the batter into an oiled and floured 9 inch square baking pan. Bake the cake at 350ºF for 30 to 35 minutes, or until a toothpick inserted in its center comes out dry. Makes one 9 inch cake, or about 9 servings.

Banana Carob Cake

The bananas make this cake delightfully moist.

3 cups barley flour
1¼ cups carob powder, strained to remove lumps
⅔ cup sugar
2 teaspoons baking soda
½ teaspoon unbuffered vitamin C crystals
3 cups thoroughly mashed or pureed bananas
¾ cup oil
1 teaspoon corn-free natural vanilla (optional)

Combine the flour, carob powder, sugar, baking soda, and vitamin C crystals in a large bowl. Mix together the bananas, oil, and vanilla, and stir them into the dry ingredients until they are just mixed in. Put the batter into two oiled and floured 8 or 9 inch round baking pans and bake the cake at 375°F for 25 to 30 minutes, or until a toothpick inserted into its center comes out dry. Cool the cake in the pans for 10 minutes and then remove it from the pans. This cake may be frosted with "Very Carob Frosting," page 166, or a double batch of "German Chocolate Frosting," page 165, "Coconut Frosting," page 164, or "Party Carob Frosting," page 166. Makes one 2-layer cake, or about 12 servings.

Devil's Food Cake

One of the major challenges that the mother of an allergic child faces is making a cake for a birthday party. This sugar-free cake with "Party Carob Frosting," page 166, will be enjoyed by all of the guests.

2¼ cups rye flour
⅓ cup carob powder, sifted to remove lumps
1½ teaspoons baking soda
1 cup grape juice concentrate, thawed
½ cup oil

Stir together the flour, carob powder, and baking soda in a large bowl. Mix the grape juice and oil and stir them into the dry ingredients until they are just mixed in. Put the batter into an oiled and floured 8 or 9 inch square or round baking pan and bake the cake 350°F for 25 to 30 minutes, or until a toothpick inserted into its center comes out dry. Cool it completely, frost if desired, and serve it from the pan. For a single layer, frost this cake with a half batch of "Very Carob Frosting" or a full batch of "German Chocolate Frosting," page 165, "Coconut Frosting," page 164, or "Party Carob Frosting," page 166. This cake is not as fragile as some, and the cake and frosting recipes may be doubled to make a 2-layer cake. For a layer cake, after baking, cool it in the pans for 10 minutes and then remove it and allow it to cool completely before frosting. Makes one 8 or 9 inch cake, about 9 servings.

Very Carob Cake

This layer cake is great for special occasions.

2¼ cups quinoa flour
¾ cup tapioca flour
1½ cups carob powder, strained to remove lumps
1 tablespoon baking soda
2 cups apple juice concentrate, thawed
1 cup oil

Stir together the quinoa flour, tapioca flour, carob powder, and baking soda in a large bowl. Mix the apple juice and oil and stir them into the dry ingredients until they are just mixed in. Put the batter into two oiled and floured 8 or 9 inch round baking pans and bake the cake at 350ºF for 30 to 35 minutes, or until a toothpick inserted into its center comes out dry. Cool the cake in the pans for 10 minutes and then remove it from the pans. This cake may be frosted with "Very Carob Frosting", page 166 or a double batch of "Coconut Frosting," page 164. Makes one 2-layer cake, or about 12 servings.

Stevia-Sweetened Carob Cake

No one will detect the stevia in this carob treat which contains no sugars of any kind, including fruit sugars.

1½ cups quinoa flour
½ cup tapioca flour
½ cup carob powder which has been pressed through a strainer to remove lumps
2 teaspoons baking soda
½ teaspoon unbuffered vitamin C crystals
¼ to ½ teaspoon white stevia powder, or to taste
1¼ cups water
¼ cup oil

Combine the quinoa flour, tapioca flour, carob powder, baking soda, vitamin C crystals, and stevia in a large bowl. Mix together the water and oil and stir them into the dry ingredients until they are just mixed in. Pour the batter into an oiled and floured 8 by 4 inch loaf pan and bake the cake at 350°F for 25 to 30 minutes. Cool it in the pan for 10 minutes, and then remove it if you wish to. Makes one 8 by 4 inch cake, or about 6 servings.

"German Chocolate" Cake

This cake is lighter than the previous carob cakes in both flavor and color and can be made with either a grain or non-grain flour.

1½ cups quinoa flour plus ¾ cup tapioca flour OR 2¼ cups rye flour
⅓ cup carob powder
1½ teaspoons baking soda
1 cup apple juice concentrate, thawed
½ cup oil

Combine the flour(s), carob powder, and baking soda in a large bowl. Mix the juice and oil and stir them into the dry ingredients until they are just mixed in. Put the batter into an oiled and floured 8 or 9 inch round or square baking pan and bake the cake at 350°F for 25 to 30 minutes, or until a toothpick inserted in its center comes out dry. Cool it in the pan for 10 minutes and then remove it from the pan if you wish to. This cake is not as fragile as some, and the recipe may be doubled to make a 2-layer cake. If you wish to frost this cake use a half batch of "Very Carob Frosting" or a full batch of "German Chocolate Frosting," page 165, "Coconut Frosting," page 164, or "Party Carob Frosting," page 166. Makes one 8 inch or 9 inch cake, about 9 servings.

Coconut Frosting

This frosting can be used on any kind of cake, but it is especially good on carob cakes. It has many sweetener choices so you can match the sweetener in the frosting with the sweetener in the cake recipe you use.

1 cup apple or pineapple juice concentrate OR ¾ cup water plus ½ cup beet or
    cane sugar OR ½ cup water plus ½ cup molasses, honey, or maple syrup
3 tablespoons arrowroot OR 2½ tablespoons tapioca flour
2 cups very finely shredded unsweetened coconut OR 3 cups regular unsweetened
    shredded coconut

Mix the juice or the water and sugar, molasses, honey, or maple syrup with the arrowroot or tapioca flour in a saucepan. Cook the mixture, stirring it frequently, over medium heat until it thickens and boils. Stir in the coconut before it can cool off at all and immediately spread it on the top of the cake. (This frosting is best made with very finely shredded coconut, but if necessary, you can use regular shredded coconut. To obtain very finely shredded coconut, see "Sources of Special Foods," page 216). This recipe makes enough frosting for one 8 or 9 inch cake.

Date Frosting

This is especially good on Vanilla Cake, page 159, "Spice Cake," page 157, or a square "Date-Nut Cake," page 154.

1⅓ cups water
3 tablespoons spelt, rye, milo, kamut, oat, or barley flour
2 cups date sugar

Remove any lumps in the date sugar by pressing it through a wire mesh strainer with the back of a spoon. Mix the water and flour in a small saucepan. Cook the mixture over medium heat until it is thick, smooth, and bubbly, stirring frequently. Remove the pan from the heat, add the date sugar, and beat the frosting until it is smooth. Frost the cake immediately. Makes enough frosting for one 9 by 13 inch cake or two 8 or 9 inch layers.

Date Glaze

Drizzle this on "Date-Nut Bundt Cake," page 154.

⅔ cup water
2 tablespoons oat flour
⅔ cup date sugar

Remove any lumps in the date sugar by pressing it through a wire mesh strainer with the back of a spoon. Mix the flour and water in a small saucepan. Cook the mixture over medium heat until it is thick, smooth, and bubbly, stirring it frequently. Remove it from the heat and add the date sugar. Beat it until it is smooth and drizzle it on the cake.

"German Chocolate" Frosting

This is great on "'German Chocolate' Cake," page 163, but is also good on almost any carob, fruit, carrot, zucchini, or spice cake.

1 cup apple juice concentrate OR ¾ cup maple syrup OR ⅜ cup honey
1 cup finely shredded unsweetened coconut
1 cup finely chopped nuts

Boil the apple juice concentrate or maple syrup down to ⅜ cup volume (it will reach ⅜ cup about the time it starts to foam) or warm the honey. Add the coconut and nuts while it is still hot, mix it well, and spread it on the cake immediately. This frosting tastes tangy and is excellent on fruit cakes if it is made with the apple juice. It tastes more like traditional German chocolate cake frosting if it is made with the maple syrup or honey. This recipe makes enough frosting for one 8 or 9 inch cake and may be doubled for a two-layer cake.

Very Carob Frosting

This not-too-sweet frosting was developed for "Very Carob Cake," page 162, but is good with other carob cakes too.

2 cups thoroughly mashed bananas
¼ cup tapioca flour or arrowroot
1¾ cups carob powder

Beat all of the ingredients together with an electric mixer for about 2 minutes on high speed, or until the frosting is smooth. Frost the cake immediately. This recipe makes enough frosting for the tops and sides of two cake layers.

Party Carob Frosting

This frosting makes a birthday cake special.

1 tablespoon rye or barley flour (Use the same kind of flour as is used in the cake).
⅓ cup water
⅓ cup butter, goat butter, or milk-free margarine
⅓ cup sugar
⅔ cup carob powder that has been pressed through a wire mesh strainer to
    remove all lumps

Mix together the flour and water in a small saucepan and cook them over medium heat, stirring them frequently, until the mixture thickens and boils. Cool it to room temperature, stirring it frequently as it cools. With an electric mixer, cream the butter or margarine and sugar. Beat in about 2 tablespoons of the cooled flour and water mixture, then beat in about ⅓ of the carob powder. Continue adding the flour and water mixture and carob powder alternately until they are used up. Beat the frosting until it is smooth and fluffy. This recipe makes enough frosting for the tops and sides of a 8 or 9 inch cake layer or to thinly frost a 13 by 9 inch cake or pan of "Rye Brownies," page 128. For a special 2-layer birthday cake, double both this recipe and the "Devil's Food Cake" recipe, page 161.

Ice Creams, Sorbets, Cones, and Sauces

Gone are the days when you needed rock salt, crushed ice, and the muscle power for a lot of hand cranking to make ice cream at home. Now you can make delicious ice creams and sorbets that will fit almost any diet with a minimum of effort. Modern ice cream makers feature a built-in freezing unit or a canister which you put into your freezer overnight before using it, thus eliminating the need for salt and ice. You do not have to crank the hand-cranked models continuously for the entire freezing period, and the electric models do all of the work for you. If you do not have an ice cream maker, directions are given in this chapter which allow you to make ice creams and sorbets using your food processor or blender.

This chapter contains recipes for fruit-sweetened ice creams, sorbets, ice cream cones, and sauces for sundaes. There are a few recipes that are sweetened with honey for those who can tolerate it and four ice cream and sorbet recipes that can be sweetened with stevia for those who must avoid even fruit sweeteners. There is also one recipe for FOS sweetened vanilla or carob ice cream. Some of the recipes contain methylcellulose or guar gum as an optional ingredient. The purpose of these fibers is to make the ice cream creamier and to slow down the formation of ice crystals in leftover ice cream stored in the freezer.

MAKING ICE CREAM OR SORBET WITH A FOOD PROCESSOR OR BLENDER

To make ice cream or sorbet using your food processor or blender, you freeze either most of or all of the ice cream or sorbet mixture in ice cube trays. How much of the mixture you freeze depends and whether you use Method I or II, below, depends on the characteristics of the mixture and is specified in each recipe. If you are using a blender rather than a food processor, the ice cream or sorbet may be processed in small batches.

METHOD I:

This method is for sorbets made with stevia and for goat milk ice creams. Prepare the ice cream or sorbet mixture as directed in the recipe. Chill about ¼ of the mixture in the refrigerator and freeze the rest in ice cube trays until it is solid. Remove the cubes from the freezer and let them stand for 5 to 10 minutes at room temperature.

If you plan to serve your ice cream immediately after processing, you may wish to chill you blender while the cubes are standing at room temperature. You can do this by blending about ⅓ of a container of cold water and a few regular ice cubes for one minute. Pour out the water and ice.

Place the chilled mixture from the refrigerator into the blender or processor. Add two of the frozen mixture cubes and blend them until they are smooth. Continue adding cubes two at a time and processing them until they are smooth after each addition until all of the cubes are used up. Place any ice cream or sorbet you do not eat immediately into the freezer.

METHOD II:

This method is for coconut milk ice creams and sorbets made with fruit juice concentrates which do not freeze to rock-like firmness. Prepare the ice cream or sorbet mixture as directed in the recipe. Freeze all of the mixture in ice cube trays until solid. Chill the food processor or blender as in the second paragraph of "Method I" if needed. Remove the cubes from the freezer and immediately process them two at a time as in the third paragraph of "Method I."

Pina Colada "Ice Cream"

This rich and tasty treat is very easy to make because it contains only two ingredients.

1½ cups coconut milk (1 14-ounce can)
½ cup pineapple juice concentrate, thawed

Combine the coconut milk and pineapple juice concentrate. Chill them thoroughly or overnight in the refrigerator and freeze the mixture according to the directions for your ice cream maker. If you do not have an ice cream maker, process this ice cream by "Method II" above. Makes about 1½ pints of ice cream.

Vanilla Ice Cream

You can sweeten this family favorite with honey, Fruit Sweet™, fruit juice, or stevia. The fruit-juice-sweetened version has a delicious tangy twist.

2 cups goat milk plus ¼ cup honey or Fruit Sweet™ OR 1½ cups goat milk
     plus ¾ cup apple or unsweetened white grape juice concentrate, thawed,
      OR 2¼ cups goat milk plus ¼ teaspoon white stevia powder
¾ teaspoon corn-free natural vanilla
Pinch of salt (optional)
1 teaspoon guar gum OR 1 tablespoon methylcellulose (optional)

Combine the sweetener, milk, vanilla, salt, and methylcellulose or guar gum, mixing them until the stevia and fiber are completely mixed in, if you are using them. Chill the mixture thoroughly or overnight in the refrigerator and freeze it according to the directions for your ice cream maker. If you do not have an ice cream maker, process it by "Method I" on page 167. Makes about 1½ pints of ice cream.

Carob Ice Cream

This ice cream is delicious when made with the stevia; the carob masks the stevia taste.

2 cups goat milk plus ¼ cup honey OR 2¼ cups goat milk plus ¼ teaspoon
     white stevia powder
2 tablespoons carob powder
1 teaspoon guar gum OR 1 tablespoon methylcellulose (optional)

Combine the milk, honey or stevia, carob powder, and guar gum, mixing them until the stevia and fiber are completely mixed in, if you are using them. Chill the mixture thoroughly or overnight in the refrigerator and freeze it as directed in the instructions for your ice cream maker. If you do not have an ice cream maker, process it by "Method I" on page 167. Makes about 1½ pints of ice cream.

FOS Vanilla or Carob Ice Cream

This ice cream has the consistency and pure sweetness of sugar-sweetened ice cream.

2 cups goat milk
1 cup FOS*
¾ teaspoon corn-free natural vanilla flavoring OR 2 tablespoons carob powder

Stir the FOS into the milk a few tablespoons at a time, stirring until it is dissolved after each addition. Add the vanilla or carob. Process in your ice cream maker or freeze the mixture in ice cube trays overnight. In the morning, add the cubes to a food processor or blender one or two at a time and process until smooth after each addition before you add more cubes. (Method II, page 168). Makes about 1½ pints of ice cream, or 6 servings.

*Note: This recipe is very high in FOS and may cause diarrhea if large servings are eaten. Please read the cautionary information about FOS on page 127.

Strawberry Ice Cream

This traditional favorite is delicious made with goat milk or coconut milk. The fruit sweetener and strawberries give it a wonderful tangy flavor.

1 cup goat or coconut milk
¾ cup apple, pineapple, or unsweetened white grape juice concentrate, thawed
¾ cup fresh or unsweetened frozen strawberries
½ teaspoon corn-free natural strawberry flavor (optional)

Puree the strawberries. (You should have about ½ cup of puree). Stir in the milk, juice, and optional flavor. Chill the mixture thoroughly or overnight in the refrigerator and freeze it according to the directions for your ice cream maker. If you do not have an ice cream maker, process it by "Method I" on page 167. Makes about 1½ pints of ice cream.

Peach Ice Cream

This is best when you make it with fresh peaches in the summertime, but you can also use frozen or canned peaches.

1 cup goat or coconut milk
¾ cup apple, pineapple, or unsweetened white grape juice concentrate, thawed
¾ cup fresh, unsweetened frozen, or drained water-packed canned peaches

Puree the peaches. (You should have about ½ cup of puree). Stir in the milk and juice. Chill the mixture thoroughly or overnight in the refrigerator and freeze it according to the directions for your ice cream maker. If you do not have an ice cream maker, process it by "Method I" on page 167. Makes about 1½ pints of ice cream.

Orange Ice Cream

This tart and tangy ice cream will remind you of "Creamsicles™."

1½ cups goat milk
¾ cup orange juice concentrate, thawed
½ teaspoon guar gum (optional)

Stir together the milk, orange juice concentrate, and guar gum until the guar gum is completely mixed in. Chill the mixture thoroughly or overnight in the refrigerator and freeze it according to the directions for your ice cream maker. If you do not have an ice cream maker, process it by "Method II" on page 168. Makes about 1½ pints of ice cream.

Choose-Your-Flavor Ice Cream

The Spicery Shoppe™ makes a large variety of flavors to use in this ice cream.

Make "Vanilla Ice Cream" on page 169 or 170, but substitute ¾ teaspoon almond, banana, cinnamon, coffee, maple, or any other corn-free natural flavoring for the vanilla. Makes about 1½ pints of ice cream.

Carob Chip Ice Cream

The carob chips make plain vanilla ice cream special.

Make "Vanilla Ice Cream," page 169, or "FOS Ice Cream," page 170. Stir ¼ cup milk-free unsweetened carob chips into it immediately after freezing it in your ice cream maker or processing it in your blender or food processor. Makes about 1½ pints of ice cream.

Pineapple Sorbet

This is so quick and easy to make with canned pineapple that you may want to keep a can of pineapple in your freezer so you can make it any time.

1 20-ounce can of pineapple packed in its own juice, OR 2½ cups fresh pineapple
  with juice to cover

Freeze the pineapple in its juice overnight. If you are using the canned pineapple, you can freeze it in the can and in the morning run warm water on the can, remove both can ends, and slide the pineapple out. Break the frozen pineapple and juice into chunks and process it in a food processor or in small batches in a blender until it is smooth. Serve it immediately. Makes about 3 cups of sorbet, or 4 to 6 servings.

Banaberry Sorbet

This is simple to make from frozen berries without any advance preparation.

2 ripe bananas
2 tablespoons honey or Fruit Sweet™ (optional)
4 to 6 cups frozen strawberries, blueberries, or raspberries

Puree the bananas and optional sweetener in a food processor or blender until they are smooth. Gradually add the berries, processing after each addition, until the sorbet reaches the desired consistency. Serve it immediately. Makes about 4 cups of sorbet, or 6 to 8 servings.

Apple Sorbet

This tastes like a frozen version of apple pie.

1¼ cups unsweetened applesauce
1 6-ounce can of frozen apple juice concentrate
½ teaspoon cinnamon
¼ teaspoon nutmeg

Freeze the applesauce overnight in an ice cube tray. Remove the apple juice concentrate from the freezer and allow it to stand at room temperature for 10 to 15 minutes. Put the apple juice concentrate and spices in a food processor or blender and turn the machine on. Add the frozen applesauce cubes 2 at a time and process them until the sorbet is smooth after each addition. Serve it immediately. Makes about 2 cups of sorbet, or 4 servings.

Cranberry Sorbet

This tart and tangy dessert is a perfect light ending to a big holiday meal.

12 ounces fresh cranberries (about 4 cups)
1½ cups apple or pineapple juice concentrate, thawed, OR 1½ cups water
    plus ¼ teaspoon white stevia powder

Combine the cranberries with juice or water in a saucepan. Bring the mixture to a boil, reduce the heat, and simmer, stirring occasionally, for about 20 minutes, or until the cranberries have popped and lost their shape. If you are using the stevia, stir it in thoroughly. If you wish to remove the cranberry skins which may be bitter, put the mixture through a food mill or press it through a strainer at this point. Chill the mixture thoroughly and freeze it according to the instructions for your ice cream maker. Or, to make the sorbet with a food processor or blender, if you are using the stevia, use "Method I" on page 167. If you are using the juice, use "Method II" on page 168. Makes about 3½ cups of sorbet, or 6 servings.

Cantaloupe Sorbet

This is delicious in August when the cantaloupes are at their peak.

2 medium-size sweet ripe cantaloupes

Peel the cantaloupes, cut them into chunks, and puree them in a food processor or blender. Chill the puree thoroughly and freeze it according to the directions for your ice cream machine. Or, to make the sorbet with a food processor or blender, measure out 1 cup of the puree and chill it in the refrigerator. Freeze the rest of the puree in ice cube trays overnight or for several hours until the cubes are thoroughly frozen. Put the chilled puree into the food processor and blender and turn the machine on. Add the frozen cubes 2 at a time and process the sorbet until it is smooth after each addition. Serve it immediately. Makes about 4 cups of sorbet, or 6 to 8 servings.

Kiwi Sorbet

This tangy and delicious sorbet can be sweetened with either fruit juice or stevia.

4 to 5 kiwi fruits to make 1½ cups of puree
½ cup apple or pineapple juice concentrate, thawed, OR ½ cup water
    plus $\frac{1}{16}$ teaspoon white stevia powder

Peel the kiwis and cut them into chunks. Puree them in a food processor or blender, and measure out 1½ cups of the puree. To the 1½ cups of puree, add the juice or the water and stevia and blend the mixture again briefly. Chill the mixture thoroughly or overnight and freeze it according to the instructions for your ice cream maker. Or, to make the sorbet with a food processor or blender, if you are using the stevia, use "Method I" on page 167. If you are using the juice, use "Method II" on page 168.. Makes about 2¼ cups of sorbet, or 4 servings.

Ice Cream Cones

You can make ice cream cones with a special ice cream cone iron or with a krum-kake or pizzelle iron. This is one of the rare recipes in which what kind of oil you use makes a difference. The cones are less likely to stick to the iron if you use coconut oil, although you can use other kinds of oil if necessary for any of the cones except the fragile oat cones. If you can tolerate butter or goat butter occasionally, substitute melted butter for the oil, and the cones will be very easy to remove from the iron.

Amaranth Cones:

    1 cup amaranth flour
    1 cup arrowroot
    1 teaspoon baking soda
    ⅛ teaspoon unbuffered vitamin C crystals
    ¼ cup melted coconut oil or other oil
    ¼ cup honey
    ⅝ cup (½ cup plus 2 tablespoons) water

Quinoa Cones:

    1½ cups quinoa flour
    ½ cup tapioca flour
    ½ teaspoon baking soda
    ½ cup melted coconut oil or other oil
    ½ cup apple juice concentrate, thawed

Carob-Quinoa Cones:

    1 cup quinoa flour
    ½ cup carob powder
    ½ cup tapioca flour
    ½ teaspoon baking soda
    ½ cup melted coconut oil or other oil
    1 cup apple juice concentrate, thawed

"Sugar" Cones:

> 2 cups rye flour OR 3 cups spelt flour
> ½ cup melted coconut oil or other oil
> 1¼ cups apple juice concentrate, thawed OR ½ cup water plus ¾ cup apple juice
> concentrate, thawed, depending on the amount of sweetness desired

Carob-Rye Cones:

> 1½ cups rye flour
> ½ cup carob powder
> ½ cup melted coconut oil or other oil
> ¾ cup grape juice concentrate, thawed
> ½ cup water

Oat Cones:

> 1 cup oat flour
> 1 cup arrowroot
> ½ cup melted coconut oil or other oil
> ¾ cup pineapple juice concentrate, thawed

Choose one set of ingredients, above. Begin heating the iron. Combine the flour(s), carob powder (if it is used in the set of ingredients you have chosen), baking soda (if used), and vitamin C crystals (if used) in a large electric mixer bowl. In a small bowl, stir together the oil, juice or honey, and water (if used), and pour them into the dry ingredients. Beat the dough on low speed until the flour is all moistened, then beat it on medium speed for one minute. If you are using a type of oil other than coconut oil, spray or brush both the top and the bottom of the iron with oil before cooking each cone. Put one heaping tablespoon of dough in the iron. (You may need more – this is a starting point as you determine how much dough you should put in to fill the iron when you close it). Cook each cone for 20 to 30 seconds, or until it is golden brown, and remove it from the iron using two forks. (You may have to experiment to determine what cooking time makes the cones easiest to remove). If the cones stick even if you used coconut oil in the batter, brush the iron with melted coconut oil before cooking each cone. Immediately after removing each cone from the iron, roll it into a cone shape. If you wish to have perfectly shaped cones, roll them around metal cone-shaped forms and allow them to cool before removing the forms. Makes 1 to 1½ dozen cones.

Strawberry Sauce

This is delicious served on pancakes and waffles are well as on almost any kind of ice cream or sorbet.

1 pound unsweetened frozen strawberries, thawed (about 3½ cups)
½ cup apple juice concentrate, thawed
2 teaspoons arrowroot or tapioca flour

Stir the arrowroot or tapioca flour into the juice in a saucepan. Add the strawberries and cook the mixture over medium heat, stirring the sauce often and breaking up the strawberries with the spoon a little as you stir. When the sauce thickens and boils, remove it from the heat. Serve it warm or cold. Makes about 2½ cups of sauce.

Pineapple Sauce

This all-fruit sauce is excellent on "Pina Colada Ice Cream," page 168, cake, pancakes, or waffles.

1 8-ounce can crushed pineapple packed in its own juice OR ¾ cup finely chopped
      fresh pineapple
1 cup pineapple juice (Part may be drained from the canned pineapple).
2 teaspoons arrowroot or tapioca starch

If you are using canned pineapple, drain it and reserve the juice to use as part of the 1 cup pineapple juice called for in the ingredient list. In a saucepan, stir the arrowroot or tapioca flour into the juice. Cook the mixture over medium heat, stirring it often, until it thickens and boils. Remove it from the heat and stir in the drained pineapple. Serve it warm or cold. Makes about 1¾ cup of sauce.

Cherry Sauce

This is delicious over ice cream and breakfast foods, as well as on roast duck. See the recipe for "Roast Duck with Cherry Sauce" on page 79.

1 16-ounce can tart cherries, packed in water
1 cup apple juice concentrate
4 teaspoons arrowroot or tapioca flour

Begin preparing this sauce at least ½ hour before you want to serve it or up to two days ahead. Drain the cherries, reserving the liquid. Combine ½ cup of the cherry liquid with the apple juice concentrate and arrowroot or tapioca flour in a saucepan. Cook this mixture over medium heat until it thickens and begins to boil. Stir in the cherries and return it to a boil. Cherry sauce is best made 1 to 2 days ahead so the sweetness of the apple juice can permeate the cherries. You can reheat it right before serving time if you wish to serve it warm. Makes about 2 cups of sauce.

Carob Syrup

Try this on strawberry, peach, or carob ice cream, as well as on vanilla ice cream. My children even like it on oatmeal.

½ cup honey
¼ cup carob powder

Press the carob powder through a wire mesh strainer with the back of a spoon to remove any lumps. Mix the honey and carob powder together thoroughly and serve the sauce. Makes about ⅔ cup of sauce.

Pastry, Fruit Desserts, and Puddings

Pie is one of almost everyone's favorite desserts and is a delicious way to capture the flavor and goodness of fresh summer fruit. However, pies do not have to contain wheat flour, lard, hydrogenated shortening, or sugar to be delicious. This chapter provides recipes for wheat-free and grain-free pie crusts made with oil, fruit-sweetened pie fillings, fruit-sweetened cobblers, other fruit desserts, shortcakes, and puddings.

Pie crusts made with alternative flours and oil tend to break easily when you roll them. You can avoid this problem by pressing the dough into the pie plate and, if you wish to use a top crust, sprinkling crumbs of the dough over the top of the filling. If you want to make a rolled crust, the spelt, rye, kamut, and barley pie crusts can be rolled out, with the spelt and rye dough being the easiest to work with. Roll them on a well-floured pastry cloth using a cloth-covered, floured rolling pin. Then set the pie dish on the edge of the pastry cloth next to the rolled crust, pick up the edge of the cloth farthest away from the dish, and flip the crust and cloth over the pie dish. Peel off the pastry cloth from the crust and patch and trim the crust as needed. If you wish to make a two-crust pie, fill the bottom crust with the filling, repeat the rolling process with the top crust, and flip the crust over the filling. Patch and trim the top crust, prick it gently with a fork, and crimp the edges of the top and bottom crusts together. Then you will have a pie fit for royalty.

Pie Crust

The barley crust is the most like a traditional wheat crust in taste and texture, but all of these crusts are delicious.

Barley:

3 cups barley flour
½ teaspoon salt (optional)
½ cup oil
⅜ cup (¼ cup plus 2 tablespoons) water

Oat:

> 3 cups oat flour
> ½ teaspoon salt (optional)
> ½ cup oil
> ¼ cup water

Rye:

> 2½ cups rye flour
> ½ teaspoon salt (optional)
> ⅔ cup oil
> ¼ cup water

Spelt:

> 3 cups spelt flour
> ½ teaspoon salt (optional)
> ½ cup oil
> ⅓ cup water

Kamut:

> 3 cups kamut flour
> ½ teaspoon salt (optional)
> ⅔ cup oil
> ⅓ cup water

Amaranth:

> 1½ cups amaranth flour
> ¾ cup arrowroot
> ½ teaspoon salt (optional)
> ½ cup oil
> ¼ cup water

Quinoa:

  2 cups quinoa flour
  1 teaspoon baking soda
  ¼ teaspoon unbuffered vitamin C crystals
  ½ teaspoon salt (optional)
  ½ teaspoon cinnamon (optional)
  ½ cup oil
  ¼ to ⅜ cup (¼ cup plus 2 tablespoons) water

Choose one set of ingredients above and on the previous pages. In a large bowl, combine the flour(s) with the salt, or for the quinoa crust, with the salt, baking soda, vitamin C crystals, and cinnamon. Add the oil and blend it in thoroughly with a pastry cutter. Add the water and mix the dough until it begins to stick together, adding an extra 1 to 2 teaspoons of water if necessary. (For the quinoa crust, stir the flour mixture while you are adding the water until you have added enough to make the dough stick together). Divide the dough in half. For one-crust pies, press each half of the dough into a glass pie dish, gently prick it with a fork, and bake it until the bottom of the crust begins to brown. The baking temperatures and times for each kind of crust are as follows:

  Barley: 15 to 18 minutes at 400°F
  Oat: 15 to 20 minutes at 400°F
  Rye: 15 to 20 minutes at 400°F
  Spelt: 18 to 22 minutes at 400°F
  Kamut: 13 to 18 minutes at 400°F
  Amaranth: 15 to 18 minutes at 400°F
  Quinoa: 20 to 25 minutes at 350°F

For a two-crust pie, press half of the dough into the bottom of a glass pie dish, or roll out half of it as described on page 179. Fill the crust with the filling of your choice. To top the pie, either crumble the second half of the dough and sprinkle it over the filling, or roll the second half of the dough out and place it on top of the pie as described on page 179. This recipe makes two single pie crusts or a more than adequate amount of pastry for a two-crust pie.

Coconut Pie Crust

This grain-free pie crust makes a delicious pumpkin or cherry pie. It is best made with very finely shredded coconut.

2 cups very finely shredded or shredded unsweetened coconut (See "Sources,"
    page 216 for very finely shredded coconut).
Melted coconut oil – ⅜ cup (¼ cup plus 2 tablespoons) with very finely shredded
    coconut OR ¼ cup with regular shredded coconut

Thoroughly mix the coconut with the melted coconut oil and press it onto the bottom and sides of a glass pie dish. Bake the crust at 300ºF for 12 to 15 minutes, or until it begins to brown. Cool the crust completely and fill it with "Pumpkin Pie" filling, page 185, "Carob Pudding," page 193, or "Coconut Pudding," page 194. You may also fill this crust with any of the fruit pie fillings, pages 182 to 185, if you cook them until they are thickened and the fruit is tender and allow them to cool slightly before putting them into the crust. Makes one single pie crust.

Apple Pie

You will never miss the sugar in this all-time favorite pie.

⅞ cup (¾ cup plus 2 tablespoons) apple juice concentrate, possibly divided
6 to 7 apples, peeled, cored, and sliced (about 5 cups of slices)
1 teaspoon cinnamon
2 tablespoons tapioca flour OR 3 tablespoons quick-cooking tapioca
1 baked single pie crust OR 1 batch of pastry for a two-crust pie, page 179

If you are using the quick-cooking tapioca, allow it to soak in the ⅞ cup apple juice in a saucepan for 5 minutes. Then add the apples and cinnamon to the pan, bring it to a boil, and simmer until the apples are tender. If you are using the tapioca flour, cook the apples with ⅝ cup of the juice and the cinnamon until tender. Stir the tapioca starch into the remaining ¼ cup of the juice and stir the mixture into the apples. Cook over medium heat until it has thickened. For a one-crust pie, cool the apples for 10 minutes, then pour the filling into a cooled, baked pie crust and refrigerate the pie. For a two-crust pie, you do not need to simmer the apples until they are tender. If you are using the tapioca, just bring the apple-tapioca mixture to a boil and put it into the crust. If you are using the tapioca flour, bring the apples plus ⅝ cup apple juice and cinnamon to a boil, stir in the tapioca flour mixture, and simmer until it is thickened before putting the filling into the crust. Bake a 2-crust pie for 10 minutes in an oven that has been preheated to 400°F, then turn down the oven temperature to 350°F and bake it for 40 to 50 minutes more, or until the bottom crust of the pie begins to brown. Makes 1 pie, or about 6 servings.

Peach Pie

This is delicious made with fresh peaches in the summer, but you can make it year-round using canned or frozen peaches.

⅞ cup (¾ cup plus 2 tablespoons) apple or pineapple juice concentrate, divided
5 cups of peeled, pitted, and sliced fresh peaches OR 5 cups of canned water-
packed peaches, drained, OR 1½ 16-ounce bags of unsweetened frozen peaches
¼ teaspoon cinnamon (optional)
3 tablespoons tapioca flour or arrowroot
1 baked single pie crust OR 1 batch of pastry for a two-crust pie, page 179

If you are using fresh or frozen peaches, simmer the peaches and cinnamon with ⅝ cup of the juice until the peaches are just tender. If you are using canned peaches just combine the peaches and ⅝ cup of juice and bring to a boil. Mix the remaining ¼ cup juice with the tapioca flour or arrowroot, stir it into the peaches, and cook the mixture over medium heat until it has thickened. For a one-crust pie, cool the peaches for 10 minutes, then pour the filling into a cooled, baked pie crust and refrigerate the pie. For a two-crust pie, you do not need to simmer the peaches until they are tender. Just bring the peaches plus ⅝ cup juice to a boil, stir in the tapioca flour or arrowroot mixture, and simmer the mixture until it is thickened before putting the filling into the crust. Bake a 2-crust pie for 10 minutes in an oven that has been preheated to 400°F, then turn down the oven temperature to 350°F and bake it for 40 to 50 minutes more, or until the bottom crust of the pie begins to brown. Makes 1 pie, or about 6 servings.

Blueberry Pie

This pie is scrumptious! and very easy to make using frozen fruit.

¾ cup apple juice concentrate, thawed
2 tablespoons arrowroot or tapioca starch
1 16-ounce package frozen unsweetened blueberries
1 baked single pie crust OR 1 batch of pastry for a two-crust pie, page 179

Stir together the juice and arrowroot or tapioca in a saucepan. Add the blueberries and cook the mixture over medium heat until it thickens and boils, stirring it frequently. For a one-crust pie, cool the filling for 10 minutes, put it into a cooled, baked pie crust, and refrigerate the pie. For a two-crust pie, put the filling into the crusts and bake the pie for 10 minutes in an oven that has been preheated to 400°F, then turn down the oven temperature to 350°F and bake it for about 30 to 40 minutes more or until the bottom crust of the pie begins to brown. Makes 1 pie, or about 6 servings.

Cherry Pie

The flavor of the cherries really shines in this sugar-free pie.

2 16-ounce cans unsweetened tart red pie cherries, drained
1¼ cups apple juice concentrate
¼ cup tapioca
1 baked single pie crust OR 1 batch of pastry for a two-crust pie, page 179

Boil the apple juice concentrate down to ¾ cup in volume. Cool it slightly. Add the drained cherries and tapioca and let the mixture stand for 5 minutes. Then return it to a boil and simmer it for 5 minutes. For a one-crust pie, cool the filling for 10 minutes and put it into a cooled, baked pie crust. If you wish to, sprinkle the top of the filling with crumbs of leftover pie dough that have been baked on a cookie sheet or with coconut if a coconut crust is used. Refrigerate the pie. For a two-crust pie, put the filling into the crusts and bake the pie for 10 minutes in an oven that has been preheated to 400°F, then turn down the oven temperature to 350°F and bake it for about 30 to 40 minutes more or until the bottom crust of the pie begins to brown. Makes 1 pie, or about 6 servings.

Grape Pie

You will be surprised at how flavorful this unusual fruit-sweetened pie is.

4 cups seedless red grapes
⅜ cup unsweetened purple grape juice concentrate, thawed
2½ tablespoons quick-cooking tapioca
1 batch of pastry for a two-crust pie, page 179

Roll out half of the pastry and put it into a glass pie dish as described on page 179 or pat half of it into the dish. Combine the grapes, juice, and tapioca in a saucepan and allow them to stand for 5 minutes. Bring them to a boil and then pour them into the bottom crust. Roll out the top crust and cover the filling with it, or sprinkle the filling with crumbs of the other half of the dough. Bake the pie at 350°F for 50 to 60 minutes, or until the bottom crust begins to brown. Makes 1 pie, or about 6 servings.

Pumpkin Pie

This pie is too delicious to serve only on holidays.

1 envelope unflavored gelatin OR 1 tablespoon coarse agar flakes
    OR 2 teaspoons fine agar powder
1 cup water
1 16-ounce can pumpkin
1 cup date sugar OR ¼ teaspoon white stevia powder
1 teaspoon cinnamon
1 teaspoon nutmeg
¼ teaspoon ground cloves
¼ teaspoon allspice
¼ teaspoon ginger
1 baked pie crust, page 179 or 182

Put the water in a saucepan and sprinkle the gelatin or agar on it. Bring it to a boil and heat it over medium heat until the gelatin or agar is dissolved. Add the pumpkin, date sugar or stevia, and spices and cook the mixture over medium heat, stirring it almost constantly, until it is warmed through. Pour the filling into the cooled baked pie crust and refrigerate the pie. Makes 1 pie, or about 6 servings.

Easy Fruit Crumble

This recipe is as easy as it is delicious.

4 cups fresh blueberries or peeled and sliced apples or peaches OR 4 cups drained
    water-packed canned peaches OR 1 pound frozen blueberries
¾ to 1 cup date sugar, divided
¼ cup arrowroot or tapioca flour
2 to 6 tablespoons water, divided
1 cup oatmeal or millet flakes, uncooked
1 teaspoon cinnamon
¼ cup oil

Taste the fruit you are going to use. If it is sweet, use ¼ cup date sugar with the
fruit. If it is tart, use ½ cup date sugar with the fruit. Combine the ¼ or ½ cup date
sugar and the arrowroot or tapioca flour and stir them into the fruit in an 8 inch square
baking dish. If you are using fresh fruit, sprinkle 4 tablespoons water over the blueberries or apples. Sprinkle 2 tablespoons water over fresh peaches or frozen blueberries.
No water is needed with canned peaches. In a small bowl, combine the cereal, remaining ½ cup date sugar, and cinnamon. Stir in the oil until the mixture is crumbly. Stir in
2 tablespoons of water. Sprinkle the mixture on top of the fruit. Bake it at 325°F for 30
to 40 minutes, or until the topping browns and the fruit is tender when pierced with a
fork. Makes 6 to 8 servings.

Grain and Gluten-Free Easy Fruit Crumble

Of all the recipes new to the revised version of Allergy Cooking with Ease, *this is
my favorite. I'm going to make it for my dessert for Thanksgiving next week. You can
get almond flour at some health food stores or from the King Arthur Flour Baker's
Catalogue. See "Sources," page 217.*

4 cups fresh blueberries or peeled and sliced apples or peaches OR 4 cups drained
    water-packed canned peaches OR 1 pound frozen blueberries
¼ cup arrowroot or tapioca flour
½ to ¾ cup date sugar, divided
Up to 4 tablespoons water

¼ cup almond meal or flour
⅔ cup unsweetened coconut
⅓ cup chopped or sliced almonds
Cinnamon – 1¼ teaspoon with the apples, ¼ teaspoon with the other fruit
¼ cup oil

Preheat your oven to 400°F. Combine the fruit, arrowroot or tapioca flour, 1 teaspoon cinnamon (with the apples only), and ¼ to ½ cup of date sugar (depending on how sweet the fruit is) in a deep 8 or 9 inch square baking dish or 2 to 3-quart casserole dish. Add just enough water to barely moisten the starch and date sugar. The starch-liquid mixture should be like a thick paste. How much water you will need to add will depend on how "juicy" your fruit is; with canned peaches you will not need to add any water.

In a bowl, stir together the remaining ¼ cup date sugar, almond meal, coconut, almonds, and ¼ teaspoon cinnamon. Pour the oil over the mixture and stir until it is evenly distributed. Sprinkle the nut mixture over the fruit in the baking dish. Bake for 10 minutes. Then cover it with foil to prevent excessive browning. Bake for another 30 to 35 minutes or until hot and bubbly. Makes about 6 servings.

Apple Cobbler

This is as delicious and homey as apple pie but not as much work to make.

5 apples, peeled, cored, and sliced to make about 4 cups of slices
½ cup apple juice concentrate, thawed
4 teaspoons arrowroot or tapioca flour OR 2 tablespoons tapioca
½ teaspoon cinnamon
1 batch of any "Cobbler Topping," page 190

Stir the arrowroot, tapioca flour, or tapioca into the juice in a saucepan. If you are using the tapioca, let it stand for 5 minutes. Add the apples and cinnamon and bring the mixture to a boil. If you are using the arrowroot or tapioca flour, simmer it until it is thickened and clear. (You do not have to simmer it if you use the tapioca). Put the apple mixture into a 2½-quart casserole. Make the cobbler topping and put it on top of the fruit. Bake it at 350°F for 25 to 35 minutes or until the topping begins to brown. Makes 6 to 8 servings.

Cherry Cobbler

This easy dessert is one of my favorites.

2 1-pound cans water-packed tart pie cherries, drained, OR 4 cups fresh pitted pie
    cherries
1¼ cups pineapple or apple juice concentrate
4 teaspoons arrowroot or tapioca flour OR 2 tablespoons tapioca
1 batch of any "Cobbler Topping," page 190

Boil down apple juice concentrate to ¾ cup volume and allow it to cool slightly. Stir
in the arrowroot, tapioca flour, or tapioca. If you are using the tapioca, allow the
mixture to stand for 5 minutes. Stir in the cherries, bring the mixture to a boil, and pour
it into a 2½-quart casserole. If you are using the arrowroot or tapioca flour, you do not
have to wait for 5 minutes after combining the ingredients. Simmer the juice, starch,
and cherries until thickened and clear. Put the cherry mixture into a 2½-quart casserole. Make the cobbler topping and put it on top of the fruit. Bake it at 350°F for 25 to
35 minutes, or until the topping begins to brown. Makes 6 to 8 servings.

Blueberry Cobbler

*This delicious cobbler can be made all year 'round using fresh or frozen blueber-
ries.*

4 cups fresh blueberries OR 1 1-pound bag unsweetened frozen blueberries
⅜ cup apple juice concentrate, thawed
4 teaspoons arrowroot or tapioca flour
1 batch of any "Cobbler Topping," page 190

Stir the arrowroot or tapioca flour into the juice in a saucepan. Add the fruit, bring
the mixture to a boil, and simmer it until it is thickened and clear. Put it into a 2½-
quart casserole. Make the cobbler topping and put it on top of the fruit. Bake it at 350°F
for 25 to 35 minutes or until the topping begins to brown. Makes 6 to 8 servings.

Peach Cobbler

This is a delicious and easy way to enjoy fresh peaches in the summertime but can be made with frozen peaches at any time of the year.

4 cups sliced fresh peaches OR 1 1-pound bag unsweetened frozen peaches
½ cup apple or pineapple juice concentrate, thawed
4 teaspoons arrowroot or tapioca flour OR 2 tablespoons tapioca
1 batch of any "Cobbler Topping," page 190

Stir the arrowroot, tapioca flour, or tapioca into the juice in a saucepan. If you are using the tapioca, let it stand for 5 minutes. Add the peaches, bring the mixture to a boil, and pour it into a 2½-quart casserole. If you are using the arrowroot or tapioca flour, you do not have to wait for 5 minutes after combining the ingredients. Simmer the juice, starch, and peaches until thickened and clear. Put the peach mixture into a 2½-quart casserole. Make the cobbler topping and put it on top of the fruit. Bake it at 350°F for 25 to 35 minutes or until the topping begins to brown. Makes 6 to 8 servings.

Rhubarb Cobbler

This is a great way to prepare a rhubarb dessert without using sugar.

3 cups sliced rhubarb
1 cup apple or pineapple juice concentrate
4 teaspoons arrowroot or tapioca flour
1 batch of any "Cobbler Topping," page 190

Boil down the apple or pineapple juice concentrate to ½ cup volume and allow it to cool slightly. Stir in the arrowroot or tapioca flour. Add the rhubarb and bring the mixture to a boil, simmering it until it is thickened and clear. Put it into a 2½-quart casserole. Make the cobbler topping and put it on top of the fruit. Bake it at 350°F for 25 to 35 minutes, or until the topping begins to brown. Makes 6 to 8 servings.

Bing Cherry Cobbler

The sweet fruit makes a pleasing contrast to the topping in this cobbler.

4 cups pitted fresh Bing (dark) cherries OR 1 1-pound bag frozen unsweetened
    Bing cherries
⅜ cup apple juice concentrate, thawed
4 teaspoons arrowroot or tapioca flour
1 batch of any "Cobbler Topping," page 190

Stir the arrowroot or tapioca flour into the juice in a saucepan. Add the fruit, bring
it to a boil, and simmer it until it is thickened and clear. Put it into a 2½-quart casserole. Make the cobbler topping and put it on top of the fruit. Bake it at 350ºF for 25 to
35 minutes or until the topping begins to brown. Makes 6 to 8 servings.

Cobbler Topping

Here is a variety of cobbler toppings to use with whatever fruit filling you choose.

Amaranth:

   ¾ cup amaranth flour
   ¼ cup arrowroot
   ¾ teaspoon baking soda
   ¼ teaspoon unbuffered vitamin C crystals
   ⅜ cup (¼ cup plus 2 tablespoons) apple juice concentrate, thawed
   2 tablespoons oil

Quinoa:

   ⅝ cup quinoa flour
   2 tablespoons tapioca flour
   ¾ teaspoon baking soda
   ⅛ teaspoon unbuffered vitamin C crystals
   ½ cup pineapple juice concentrate, thawed
   1 tablespoon oil

Barley:

   ⅞ cup (¾ cup plus 2 tablespoons) barley flour
   ¾ teaspoon baking soda
   ⅛ teaspoon unbuffered vitamin C crystals
   ⅜ cup (¼ cup plus 2 tablespoons) apple juice concentrate, thawed
   2 tablespoons oil

Rye:

   ¾ cup rye flour
   ¾ teaspoon baking soda
   ⅛ teaspoon unbuffered vitamin C crystals
   ⅜ cup (¼ cup plus 2 tablespoons) apple or pineapple juice concentrate, thawed
   2 tablespoons oil

Spelt:

   ⅞ cup (¾ cup plus 2 tablespoons) spelt flour
   ¾ teaspoon baking soda
   ⅛ teaspoon unbuffered vitamin C crystals
   ⅜ cup (¼ cup plus 2 tablespoons) pineapple juice concentrate, thawed
   2 tablespoons oil

Kamut:

   ¾ cup kamut flour
   ¾ teaspoon baking soda
   ¼ teaspoon unbuffered vitamin C crystals
   ⅜ cup (¼ cup plus 2 tablespoons) apple juice concentrate, thawed
   2 tablespoons oil

Choose one set of ingredients, above. Combine the flour(s), baking soda, and vitamin C crystals in a large bowl. Mix together the juice and oil and stir them into the dry ingredients until they are just mixed in. Put the topping over the fruit mixture in the casserole dish and bake it at 350°F for 25 to 35 minutes, or until the topping is slightly browned. Makes 6 to 8 servings.

Shortcake

This is great with many kinds of fruit.

A double batch of any "Cobbler Topping," page 190
Additional oil and flour for the pan

Oil and flour an 8 inch round or square pan. Make the cobbler topping as directed in the recipe and spread it in the prepared pan. Bake it at 350°F for 25 to 30 minutes or until it is lightly browned. Cool it in the pan for 10 minutes, then remove it and allow it to cool completely on a wire rack. Cut it into wedges or squares. If you wish to, you may split each piece in half horizontally by carefully slicing it with a serrated knife. Serve it with fresh, thawed frozen, or canned fruit. Makes 6 to 9 servings.

Quinoa Pudding

This is a delicious grain-, milk-, and sugar-free takeoff on rice pudding.

1 cup quinoa, thoroughly washed
2 cups water
1 cup apple juice concentrate, thawed, OR ¼ teaspoon white stevia powder plus
    an additional 1 cup water
1 teaspoon cinnamon
½ cup raisins or finely chopped dried pears (optional)

Combine the quinoa and 2 cups water in a saucepan, bring it to a boil, and simmer it for 20 minutes, or until the quinoa is translucent. (If you wish to, you may use 3 cups cooked quinoa instead). Add the apple juice concentrate or the stevia and additional water, the cinnamon, and the dried fruit and simmer the mixture for 10 to 15 minutes more, or until the liquid is absorbed. Or, if you would rather bake the pudding, combine the cooked quinoa, juice or stevia plus water, cinnamon, and fruit in a 1½-quart covered casserole and bake it at 350°F for 20 to 30 minutes, or until the liquid is absorbed. Sprinkle the top of the pudding with cinnamon and serve it warm. Makes 4 to 6 servings.

Apple Tapioca

This sugar-free dessert is delicious when made with fresh Jonathan apples in the fall.

7 cups peeled, cored, and thinly sliced apples (about 10 apples)
1 cup thawed apple juice concentrate, divided
3 tablespoons tapioca
1½ teaspoons cinnamon

Combine the apples, ½ cup of the juice, and the cinnamon in a saucepan, bring the mixture to a boil, and simmer it until the apples are tender, about 15 to 30 minutes, depending on the apples. While the apples are cooking, combine the remaining ½ cup juice and the tapioca and allow them to stand for at least 5 minutes. When the apples are tender, stir the tapioca mixture into the apples, return them to a boil, and simmer for an additional 3 to 5 minutes. Allow the pudding to stand for at least 20 minutes before serving it. Makes about 8 servings.

Carob Pudding

This pudding is delicious sweetened with either honey or stevia.

2 cups goat or coconut milk plus ⅓ cup honey OR 2¼ cups goat or coconut milk
    plus ⅛ teaspoon white stevia powder
5 tablespoons arrowroot
¼ cup carob powder
2 teaspoons corn-free natural vanilla (optional)

Stir together the carob powder, arrowroot, and stevia (if you are using it) in a saucepan. Add ½ cup of the milk and stir the mixture until it is smooth. Add the rest of the milk and the honey (if you are using it), and cook it over medium heat until it thickens and begins to boil. Stir in the vanilla and serve the pudding warm or cold. Makes 4 servings.

Coconut Pudding or Finger Pudding

This is delicious in a "Coconut Pie Crust," page 182, with coconut sprinkled on top.

1 14-ounce can coconut milk (1⅔ cups)
¼ cup honey OR ⅛ teaspoon white stevia powder
¼ cup tapioca flour or arrowroot for a soft pudding or pie filling OR ⅜ cup
    (¼ cup plus 2 tablespoons) water chestnut starch for a finger pudding
Unsweetened grated coconut (optional)

Combine the coconut milk, honey or stevia, and starch in a saucepan and bring the mixture to a boil. Cook it over medium heat, stirring it occasionally at first and then constantly as it begins to thicken, until it is very thick. For the soft pudding, pour it into a bowl or individual dessert glasses, sprinkle it with coconut if you wish, and serve it warm or cold with a spoon. For the finger pudding, pour it into an oiled 8 inch square pan and sprinkle it with grated coconut, if you wish. Refrigerate it until it is very cold, cut it into squares, and serve it on plates. Makes 4 to 6 servings of soft pudding, or 6 to 9 servings of finger pudding.

Tapioca Pudding

This pudding is good if you make it with either the honey or the stevia. For a change from "plain vanilla," try it with The Spicery Shoppe™ alcohol-free, corn-free natural flavorings. It is especially delicious with almond, banana, lemon, orange, or maple flavoring.

2¾ cups goat milk or coconut milk
¼ cup honey OR ⅛ teaspoon white stevia powder
¼ cup quick-cooking tapioca
¼ cup tapioca flour
1 teaspoon corn-free natural vanilla or other flavoring (optional)

Combine the milk, honey or stevia, and tapioca in a saucepan and allow them to stand for at least 5 minutes. Stir in the tapioca flour and cook the mixture over medium heat, stirring it almost constantly, until it comes to a full boil. Stir in the flavoring. Chill it thoroughly before serving it. Makes about 6 servings.

This 'n' That: Beverages, Condiments, Snacks and Tips

This chapter contains recipes for some little things that go along with a meal and make it special. There are recipes for beverages, condiments that will liven up burgers of any kind, cranberry sauce or jelly for the holidays, stevia-sweetened "Mock Maple Syrup" for breakfast, and several types of snacks. Before you make the FOS candy recipes in this chapter, see the information about FOS on pages 127 and 204. This chapter also contains tips about substitutions, altitude, preparing pans for baking, etc.

Hot Carob

This comforting beverage is delicious when you make it with either the honey or the stevia.

1 tablespoon carob powder
2 tablespoons hot water
1 cup goat milk
2 tablespoons honey OR $\frac{1}{16}$ teaspoon white stevia powder OR $\frac{1}{2}$ teaspoon
    stevia working solution, page 207

Combine the carob powder and water in a saucepan and stir them to remove the lumps in the carob. Add the goat milk and sweetener and heat the mixture until it just begins to steam. Makes 1 serving which is just the right size for a 10-ounce mug.

Fruit Shake

Use your imagination as you devise combinations of milks, juices, and fruits to use in this recipe. Some good shakes are made from coconut milk with banana and honey, pineapple juice with banana, and apple juice with kiwi.

$\frac{3}{4}$ cup chilled coconut or goat milk or fruit juice
$\frac{3}{4}$ cup frozen berries or other frozen fruit that has been cut into small pieces
    OR 1 small or $\frac{1}{2}$ large frozen banana, cut into chunks
1 tablespoon honey OR 2 tablespoons frozen fruit juice concentrate (optional)

Puree all the ingredients together in a blender. Makes one large or two small servings.

Carob Soda

This is delicious made with "Carob Ice Cream," "Strawberry Ice Cream," or "Vanilla Ice Cream." See the recipes on pages 169 and 170.

3 tablespoons "Carob Syrup," page 178
¾ cup chilled carbonated water
1 to 2 ice cubes OR one scoop of ice cream

In a glass, mix the carob syrup thoroughly with ¼ cup of the water. Add the rest of the water and the ice, if you are using it. Top it with the ice cream, if you are using it. Makes one serving.

Donna Gates' Lemonade or Cranberry Cooler

Donna Gates, an expert on low-yeast diets, reports that these beverages help her clients satisfy their desire for something sweet without aggravating their yeast problems.

½ cup lemon juice OR ¾ cup pure unsweetened cranberry juice, such as
    Knudsen™ "Just Cranberry" juice OR ⅓ cup cranberry juice concentrate,
    such as Hain™ Cranberry Juice Concentrate
⅛ teaspoon white stevia powder
4 cups cold water or chilled carbonated water

Mix the juice and stevia together until the stevia is completely dissolved. Add the water and serve the drink with ice. Makes about 4 servings.

Grandma's Cranberry Sauce or Jelly

This recipe is adapted from one my mother made for holidays every year.

12 ounces fresh cranberries (about 4 cups)
1½ to 2½ cups (the amount depending on the degree of sweetness desired) apple
   or pineapple juice concentrate, thawed OR ¾ cup water plus ¼ teaspoon white
   stevia powder

If you are using the fruit juice, boil it down to half of its original volume (to ¾ to 1
¼ cups). Combine the water or juice with the cranberries in a saucepan, bring them to
a boil, and simmer them, stirring them often, for 15 to 20 minutes, or until the cranberries have popped. If you are using the stevia, thoroughly stir it into the sauce at this
point. Refrigerate the sauce until serving time. Makes about 2 cups of cranberry sauce.

If you prefer cranberry jelly, after cooking the sauce and adding the stevia (if you
are using it), put the sauce through a food mill or press it through a strainer. Refrigerate the jelly until serving time. (Children tend to prefer the jelly because the cranberry
skins, which may be bitter, have been removed). Makes about 1⅔ cups cranberry jelly.

Mock Maple Syrup

*Here is sweet treat to put on pancakes or waffles for people who must avoid fruit
sugars as well as refined sweeteners.*

1 teaspoon arrowroot OR 1½ teaspoons tapioca flour
1 cup water
⅛ teaspoon white stevia powder
½ teaspoon corn-free natural maple flavoring
½ teaspoon corn-free natural vanilla (optional)

Stir the arrowroot or tapioca flour into the water in a saucepan. Bring it to a boil.
The mixture will thicken slightly and become clear. Stir in the stevia and flavorings
until the stevia is completely dissolved, and serve the syrup. Any leftover syrup may be
refrigerated and, if necessary, reheated to re-dissolve the starch. Makes about 1 cup of
syrup.

Easy Catsup

If you can tolerate canned tomato products, this is a quick and easy way to make something yummy to put on your burgers.

1 6-ounce can tomato paste
½ cup water plus ¼ cup thawed apple or pineapple juice concentrate
    OR ¾ cup water plus ⅛ teaspoon white stevia powder
2 teaspoons finely chopped onion OR ½ teaspoon dry onion flakes (optional)
1 whole clove
½ teaspoon salt
2 teaspoons tart tasting unbuffered vitamin C crystals

Combine the tomato paste, juice or water plus stevia, onion, clove, and salt in a saucepan and bring them to a boil. Simmer them, covered, for 30 to 45 minutes, stirring them at least every 5 to 10 minutes. Remove the clove and stir in the vitamin C crystals. Makes about ¾ to 1 cup catsup.

Fresh Tomato Catsup

This recipe is adapted from the one my mother used to put up tomatoes from her garden.

2 pounds Italian plum or Roma tomatoes
1 teaspoon finely minced onion (optional)
½ teaspoon dry mustard
1 teaspoon salt (optional)
Dash of pepper (optional)
4 slices of pineapple plus ¾ cup pineapple juice OR ⅟₁₆ to ⅛ teaspoon white stevia
    powder OR ½ to 1 teaspoon stevia working solution, page 207
1 teaspoon tart tasting unbuffered vitamin C crystals

Puree the tomatoes in a food processor or blender to yield about 4 cups of puree. If you are using the pineapple, puree it in the pineapple juice. In a saucepan, combine the tomatoes, onion, mustard, salt, pepper, and pineapple or stevia. Bring the mixture to a boil, reduce the heat, and simmer it, stirring it often, for about one hour, or until it is thick. Stir in the vitamin C. Makes 2 cups of catsup.

Cucumber Relish

This recipe developed by Marge Jones is from The Yeast Connection Cookbook. *It is delicious with burgers in place of pickles.*

2 tablespoons water
¼ teaspoon tart tasting unbuffered vitamin C crystals
3 cucumbers
Salt
Freshly ground black pepper to taste (optional)
2 tablespoons fresh dill, finely chopped OR 2 teaspoons dried dill

In a small cup, mix the water and vitamin C crystals; set them aside. Peel the cucumbers and cut them in half lengthwise. Remove the seeds with a spoon or melon ball scoop and discard them. Shred the cucumbers in a food processor or by hand. Salt them lightly and place them in a strainer for 10 to 15 minutes to drain. Press them lightly with your hand, then turn them into a bowl. When the vitamin C crystals dissolve in the water, add the mixture to the cucumbers. Add the dill and mix well. Cover and refrigerate at least 2 hours. Before serving, taste and add salt if needed. Makes about 3 cups of relish.

Mild Mustard

This tastes like ordinary mustard but does not contain vinegar.

2 teaspoons dry mustard
1 cup water
3 teaspoons arrowroot
¼ teaspoon turmeric
½ teaspoon salt (optional)
1 teaspoon tart tasting unbuffered vitamin C crystals

Combine the dry mustard and water in a saucepan and allow them to stand for 10 minutes. Stir in the arrowroot, turmeric, and salt and heat the mixture over medium heat, stirring it often, until it thickens and boils. Stir in the vitamin C crystals and refrigerate the mustard. Makes about 1 cup of mustard.

Hot Mustard

This mustard is for those who like it hot. To purchase dry mild Dijon mustard, see "Sources of Special Foods," page 218.

¼ cup dry mild (Dijon) style mustard
3 tablespoons water

Mix the mustard and water together. Refrigerate the mustard. Makes about ⅓ cup of mustard.

Gorp

This is a great snack to take along on hikes and outings.

2 cups cashew pieces
1½ cups raisins
1 cup milk-free unsweetened carob chips

Mix together the cashew pieces, raisins, and carob chips and enjoy. Try your own combinations of dried fruits and nuts. A rule of thumb is to use smaller amounts of smaller-size ingredients. Makes about 3½ cups of gorp.

Fruit Roll-Ups

Kids love having these for a sugar-free and nutritious snack.

Strawberry, Raspberry, or Cherry:

1 pound of fresh strawberries or raspberries OR a 1-pound bag of frozen
    unsweetened strawberries or Bing cherries
4 cups unsweetened applesauce

Banana:

   About 12 large bananas

Peach:

   4 pounds fresh peaches OR 3 1-pound bags of frozen unsweetened peaches
      OR about 5½ 1-pound cans of water-packed canned peaches, drained

Grape:

   About 4 1-pound cans water-packed canned pears, drained, yielding 4⅔ cups
      pear puree
   1⅓ cups grape juice concentrate, thawed

Apple:

   6 cups unsweetened applesauce
   1½ teaspoons cinnamon

Choose one set of ingredients, above. If you are using fresh fruit, peel or clean it and cut it into chunks. Combine all of the ingredients in a food processor or blender and puree them to yield about 6 cups of pureed fruit. Cover the trays of a food dehydrator or cover cookie sheets, platters, and trays with cellophane or heavy plastic wrap. Put ⅓ cup to ⅜ cup portions of the pureed fruit onto the cellophane or plastic wrap and spread them out into 7 inch circles so that the puree is about ¼ inch thick. Dry them in a dehydrator for about 10 to 12 hours at 135°F or out in the sun, covered with netting, on a hot (90°F), dry day for 10 to 12 hours. You can tell that the fruit leather has dried long enough when it does not have any sticky spots, but also is not so dry that it is brittle. Cut the cellophane or plastic wrap so that the individual circles are separated and roll them up. Makes 14 to 16 fruit roll-ups.

Carob Fudge

This is great for an occasional treat and doesn't last long around our house.

⅝ cup (½ cup plus 2 tablespoons) honey
2 tablespoons oil
½ cup carob powder
¾ cup powdered goat milk
2 tablespoons finely chopped nuts (optional)

Thoroughly mix together the honey and oil. Add the carob powder and powdered milk and beat the fudge until it is smooth. Knead in the nuts, if you wish to use them. Spread the fudge in a lightly oiled pie dish, refrigerate it, and cut it into ¾ inch squares just before serving it. Store the fudge in the pie dish in the refrigerator because it tends to spread. Makes about 50 squares.

Candy Canes

This is a Christmas treat to keep the corn-allergic child from feeling left out.

¾ cup water
3 cups cane or beet sugar
¼ teaspoon cream of tartar
Coconut oil or butter
¼ teaspoon natural spearmint oil

Bring the water to a boil in a saucepan. Add the sugar and cream of tartar and stir the mixture until the sugar dissolves. When the mixture returns to a boil, use a brush and hot water to thoroughly wash down any sugar crystals on the sides of the pan into the sugar solution. Put a candy thermometer into the pan so it is in the solution but not touching the bottom of the pan. Cook the solution without stirring it until the temperature on the thermometer reaches 312ºF at sea level, or 100ºF above the temperature of boiling water in your area. (See "The Effect of Altitude on Candy Making" on page 212). While the sugar solution is boiling, warm the coconut oil until it just begins to melt and use it or butter to thoroughly grease a marble slab or a very large heavy stoneware platter. Watch the candy thermometer continuously as the solution nears its final temperature. When it reaches the right temperature immediately pour it onto the marble slab or platter. As the edges of the candy cool, lift them toward the center with a candy scraper or metal knife-type of spatula. When the candy is partially cooled, sprinkle the spearmint oil over its surface and continue to work it with the scraper or spatula. When it is barely cool enough to handle, form it into a ball and pull it until it takes on a sheen, about 20 pulls. Form it into a rope, cut it into pieces, and form them into cane shapes. Allow the candy canes to harden on the marble slab or platter. Makes 8 to 10 10-inch candy canes.

FOS Candy Canes

These are a good Christmas treat for the child who cannot have the sugar-containing candy canes, above. However eat these just occasionally and in moderate servings. (See the note about FOS below).

2 cups FOS*
⅔ cup FOS* syrup
⅛ teaspoon cream of tartar
Coconut oil or butter
¼ teaspoon spearmint or peppermint flavoring

Combine the FOS, FOS syrup, and cream of tartar in a saucepan and heat, stirring the mixture occasionally, until the FOS dissolves. When the mixture boils, use a brush and hot water to thoroughly wash down any crystals on the sides of the pan into the solution. Put a candy thermometer into the pan so it is in the solution but not touching the bottom of the pan. Cook the solution without stirring it until the temperature on the thermometer reaches 305 to 310°F at sea level, or 93 to 98°F above the temperature of boiling water in your area. (See "The Effect of Altitude on Candy Making" on page 212). While solution is boiling, warm the coconut oil until it just begins to melt and use it or butter to thoroughly grease a marble slab or a very large heavy stoneware platter. Watch the candy thermometer continuously as the solution nears its final temperature. When it reaches the right temperature immediately pour it onto the marble slab or platter. As the edges of the candy cool, lift them toward the center with a candy scraper or metal knife-type of spatula. When the candy is partially cooled, sprinkle the flavoring over its surface and continue to work it with the scraper or spatula. When it is barely cool enough to handle, form it into a ball and pull it until it takes on a sheen, about 20 pulls. Form it into a rope, cut it into pieces, and form them into cane shapes. Allow the candy canes to harden on the marble slab or platter. Makes 10 to 12 10-inch candy canes.

*Note: Before you use FOS, you should be aware that it will support the growth of a few of the unfriendly bacteria which can cause dysbiosis. Be sure that FOS-containing treats will not be eaten by anyone who has problems with these organisms. If you do not have these "unfriendly" bacteria, FOS may be better for you than sugar, but should be used with caution. Even healthy people will get diarrhea from FOS if they eat it in very large amounts because it is not absorbed. Indulge in FOS-containing candies in small amounts only. To obtain FOS and FOS syrup, see "Sources of Special Foods," page 219.

FOS Taffy

These are a nice birthday party treat – but don't eat too many FOS candies at one time.

2 cups FOS*
2 cups FOS* syrup
1½ teaspoons salt
½ teaspoon corn-free natural flavoring of your choice
Coconut oil or butter

Combine the FOS, FOS syrup, and salt in a saucepan and heat over medium heat without stirring until the mixture comes to a boil. Use a brush and hot water to thoroughly wash down any crystals on the sides of the pan into the solution. Put a candy thermometer into the pan so it is in the solution but not touching the bottom of the pan. Cook the solution without stirring it until the temperature on the thermometer reaches the hard ball stage, 265-270°F at sea level or 53-58°F above the boiling temperature of water in your area. While solution is boiling, warm the coconut oil until it just begins to melt and use it or butter to thoroughly grease a marble slab or a very large heavy stoneware platter. Also grease a cookie sheet. Watch the candy thermometer continuously as the solution nears its final temperature. When it reaches the right temperature immediately pour it onto the marble slab or platter. As the edges of the candy cool, lift them toward the center with a candy scraper or metal knife-type of spatula. When the candy is partially cooled, sprinkle the flavoring over its surface and continue to work it with the scraper or spatula. When it is barely cool enough to handle, form it into a ball and pull it. Pick up the candy, and pull and fold it repeatedly it until it becomes opaque and shiny and is almost completely cooled, about 20 minutes. Pull it into a rope and place it on the prepared cookie sheet. Cut it into pieces with a greased pair of kitchen shears. Store it uncovered on the cookie sheet for several hours or overnight. Then store it in a metal tin. Makes about 2 pounds of taffy.

 * See the note about FOS on page 204 at the end of the previous recipe.

FOS Suckers

These are great for Halloween.

2 cups FOS*
1⅛ cups (1 cup plus 2 tablespoons) FOS* syrup
½ teaspoon corn-free natural flavoring
Coconut oil or butter
About 20 sucker sticks

Combine the FOS and FOS syrup in a saucepan and heat over medium heat without stirring until the mixture comes to a boil. Use a brush and hot water to thoroughly wash down any crystals on the sides of the pan into the solution. Put a candy thermometer into the pan so it is in the solution but not touching the bottom of the pan. Cook the solution without stirring it until the temperature on the thermometer reaches the hard crack stage, 305 to 310°F at sea level or 93 to 98°F above the boiling temperature of water in your area. While solution is boiling, warm the coconut oil until it just begins to melt and use it or butter to thoroughly grease a cookie sheet. Lay the sticks on it about 4 inches apart. When the syrup reaches the right temperature, stir in the flavoring. Drop large spoonfuls of the candy over the sticks on the prepared sheet. Let the suckers cool completely and wrap them with plastic wrap or cellophane. Makes about 20 3 to 4 inch suckers.

 *See the note about FOS on page 204 at the end of the "FOS Candy Canes" recipe on page 204.

Milk-free Carob or Chocolate Chips

Milk-free carob chips are getting harder to find for purchase and often contain grain sweeteners or other sweeteners. If you can't find any you can tolerate, here is recipe for homemade carob or chocolate chunks to use in your cookies.

Unsweetened carob chips:

    1 cup carob powder, sieved
    ⅝ cup melted coconut oil

Sugar alcohol sweetened carob chips

    ¾ cup carob powder, sieved
    ⅜ cup sorbitol, xylitol, or erythritol
    ½ cup plus 1 tablespoon melted coconut oil

Sugar alcohol sweetened chocolate chips

    8 ounces unsweetened baking chocolate
    1½ cups sorbitol, xylitol, or erythritol
    3 tablespoons oil

Chose one set of ingredients, above. If you are making carob chips, press the carob powder through a wire mesh strainer with the back of a spoon to break up all lumps. Then measure the sieved powder. Melt the coconut oil in your microwave oven or over low heat a saucepan and measure out the required amount. Stir together the carob powder, coconut oil, and sugar alcohol if you are using it. The mixture should be a very thick paste. Because of the variations in carob powder, the amount needed may vary and you may need to add a little more melted coconut oil or carob powder to achieve the desired consistency.

To make the chocolate chips, melt the chocolate over boiling water in the top of a double boiler. Add half of the sugar alcohol and stir it in thoroughly. Add the oil and stir. Then stir in the rest of the sugar alcohol.

Generously grease a baking sheet with butter or melted coconut oil. Spread the carob or chocolate mixture on the sheet to a thickness of between ⅛ and ¼ inch. Chill in the refrigerator for at least 30 minutes or until it is hard. Remove the baking sheet from the refrigerator. Use a long knife, such as a butcher or chef's knife, to cut the carob or chocolate into strips about ¼ inch wide. Then cut the carob or chocolate strips in a direction perpendicular to the first cut to form ¼ inch squares. Remove the squares from the baking sheet with a spatula and store them in a glass jar or plastic bag in the refrigerator.

Makes about 2 cups unsweetened carob chips, 1⅔ cups sweetened carob chips, or 3½ cups chocolate chips.

Stevia Working Solution

This solution allows you to add to recipes amounts of stevia too small to be measured as a powder.

1 teaspoon white stevia powder
2 tablespoons plus 2 teaspoons water

Put the stevia powder into the water and stir it until it is completely dissolved. Any solution that you do not use immediately should be refrigerated or frozen for future use. Making this solution makes it easier to measure extremely small amounts of stevia accurately. For example:

2 teaspoons solution = ¼ teaspoon white powder
1 teaspoon solution = ⅛ teaspoon white powder
½ teaspoon solution = $\frac{1}{16}$ teaspoon white powder
¼ teaspoon solution = $\frac{1}{32}$ teaspoon white powder.

Allergy Cooking Tips

SUBSTITUTIONS: In allergy cooking, some substitutions work and some do not. You may have seen tables of how much barley, rye, oat, rice or "whatever" flour to substitute for a cup of wheat flour. The only thing wrong with these tables is that the substitutions don't work predictably! Each type of flour behaves very differently in baking, and the differences extend far beyond how much liquid they take up. Gluten content is especially important. Also, each kind of flour varies in how it behaves for different types of recipes. For example, barley flour behaves much like wheat in pie crust but nothing like wheat in yeast bread. So for baking with non-wheat flour, the easiest and best thing to do is to use a recipe specially developed for the specific kind of flour you want to use, such as the recipes in this book.

Non-wheat flours also do not substitute predictably for each other either. People call me and say, "I've got your recipe made with spelt flour and I want to make it with oat flour. How can I do this?" I usually can't give them a definite answer, although I try to make suggestions that may or may not work. There is no "rule" or conversion factor for substitutions between any two types of non-wheat flour, just as is the case between wheat and non-wheat flour.

The "bottom line" on flour substitutions is this: be prepared to "tweak" a recipe made with a substitute flour several times before it is right or even to never have it work. If there is not a recipe for something you want in this book, see The *Ultimate Food Allergy Cookbook and Survival Guide* as described on the last pages of this book. Because that book is designed to be the "ultimate" help for people whose diets may be extremely limited, I attempted to make each type of flour (including rarely eaten foods such as tuber flours, chestnut flour, starch flours, and non-gluten grain flours) into as many types of recipes as possible and only omitted a certain recipe if it really was not possible. For example, the only reason the book does not contain a recipe for milo yeast bread is because I was unable, after many tries, to make a loaf that did not collapse. However, it does have a milo non-yeast bread recipe made with eggs to help hold it together. (This is one of the very few egg-containing recipes in the book). There are also recipes for fruited milo non-yeast bread (where the fiber in the fruit keeps it together), milo muffins in which either fruit or sweet potatoes is a binder, and crackers, tortillas, pancakes, cake, and cookies made with milo flour.

Unlike wheat flour, milk is an ingredient where substitutions in "normal" recipes usually work. In most recipes, you can replace the milk called for with an equal amount of water. Sometimes you can replace milk with fruit juice, but the acidity of the juice can affect the leavening process and result in a collapse of your baked product.

Eggs can usually be replaced with an equal volume of water (1 extra-large egg = ¼ cup water) if the recipe is not depending on the egg for structure. However, in a recipe made with a gluten-free or low gluten flour, the egg is probably serving to replace some of the structure normally provided by gluten, and replacing the egg with water may lead to a collapse.

In this book, many ingredient combinations occur together repeatedly (apple with quinoa, grape with rye, and so on) because I used them together on the same day of my family's rotation schedule at the time I was developing the recipes. To fit your family's rotation schedule, you can usually substitute an equal volume of any fruit juice, fruit juice concentrate, or fruit puree (such as applesauce) for another fruit juice, concentrate or puree of about the same consistency. For instance, you can substitute apple juice for grape juice or pureed peaches for applesauce. Pureed bananas, however, are much thicker than applesauce, so this substitution will now work as expected. Pineapple is more acidic than the other fruits so substituting pineapple juice concentrate for another juice concentrate often requires adjustments in the leavening, such as leaving out or decreasing the amount of the vitamin C the recipe calls for. Pureed pineapple, however, *sometimes* may substitute without leavening changes because it is less concentrated and therefore less acidic. Again, it depends on the recipe, and the only way to know if it will work is to try it.

Refined starches can also usually be substituted for each in the same amounts. You can use arrowroot and tapioca flour interchangeably in baking. Water chestnut starch and cornstarch also will usually substitute for other starches in baking. However, the starches behave differently when used to thicken sauces, so you might need more or less than you expect to get the desired result. But don't hesitate to try this substitution. Making a sauce is not like baking where there is nothing you can do by the time you see your bread collapsing in the oven! If the sauce you are making seems too thick, just add more water, and if it seems too thin, add more starch.

Home ground flour may also behave differently than commercially ground flour, and it can vary from batch to batch of the grain that you grind. If you use very finely milled flour or a coarsely milled or blender-ground flour you will have to change the amount of liquid used in the recipe. The best use of home-ground flour is in yeast breads where you routinely compensate for differences in the flour by adding flour until the dough "feels right." For more about judging the consistency of yeast bread dough and compensating for variations, see *Easy Breadmaking for Special Diets* as described on the last pages of this book.

FLOURING BAKING PANS and PASTRY CLOTHS: Always use the same kind of flour used in the recipe to flour your baking pans or pastry cloth. Also, use the same oil as you are using in the recipe to prepare the pans.

MEASURING ACCURATELY may not be essential if you are making a roast or a casserole, but it is critical to your success in allergy baking. Since allergy baking is more exacting than "normal" cooking, you will see less-commonly used amounts of ingredients in this book, such as ⅝ cup, ⅛ teaspoon, etc. If your recipe calls for ⅝ cup of flour, you need to measure ½ cup plus ⅛ cup (or 2 tablespoons if you do not have a ⅛ cup flour measuring cup). The "Table of Measurements" on page 215 gives conversions for all the measurements you will see in this book.

Although the previous paragraph and the Table of Measurements say that ⅛ cup = 2 tablespoons, in my experience, measuring tablespoons are all a little scanty of ¹⁄₁₆ cup, so 2 tablespoons is a little short of ⅛ cup. Therefore, if you need to measure, for example, ⅜ cup of liquid, it will probably be more accurate to "eyeball" an amount halfway between ¼ cup and ½ cup than to use ¼ cup plus two tablespoons. The best way to measure ⅜ cup of liquid is to fill your measuring cup to the third ⅛-cup line if it is marked in ⅛-cup intervals or to the 3 ounce line if it is marked in ounces. To measure ⅛ cup of a dry ingredient, a ⅛ cup flour measuring cup is ideal. Sometimes you can find an inexpensive ⅛ cup measuring cup sold separately (not as part of a measuring cup set) as a coffee measure.

It is important to use the right kind of measuring cups for the type of ingredient you are measuring. Measure liquids in a glass or see-through plastic measuring cup designed for measuring liquids. On such cups, the top measurement line will be a little below the top of the cup. These cups usually have a spout for pouring liquids. Buy a cup that has ⅛-cup markings; two-cup capacity is most useful. To read the amount of liquid in a measuring cup, have your eyes down at the level of the cup. Fill the cup until the bottom of the meniscus (the curve that the surface of the liquid makes in the cup) lines up with the measurement you want to use. If you want fewer dirty dishes to wash, you can measure several liquid ingredients in the measuring cup at one time and then mix them together in the cup. For example, if your recipe calls for ½ cup water and ¼ cup oil, fill the cup with water to the ½ cup line. Then add oil until the level of the liquids reaches ¾ cup.

To measure dry ingredients such as flour, use a set of nested plastic or metal measuring cups. On these cups, the maximum capacity measurement is at the very top edge of the cup. Use the cup of the capacity that your recipe calls for. You may have to use more than one cup. If, for example, your recipe calls for ¾ cup of flour, measure ½ cup of flour and add it to your mixing bowl, and then measure ¼ cup of flour and add it to the bowl. You do not need to sift flour before you measure it for the recipes in this book. Instead, get a large spoon, stir the flour to fluff it up, lightly spoon it into a measuring cup for dry ingredients, and then level it off with a straight-edged knife. Do not tap the cup or pack the flour into it.

Measuring spoons are used for both liquid and dry ingredients. It is helpful to have a set which includes a ⅛ teaspoon. To measure liquids, fill the spoon with the liquid, making sure that it does not round up over the top of the spoon. To measure dry ingredients, stir up the ingredient with the spoon to fluff it up, dip the spoon in, and level it off with a straight-edged knife. When measuring spices from a metal canister, you can level off the spoon against the straight edge of the opening in the top of the canister.

MEASURING EXTREMELY SMALL AMOUNTS, SUCH AS LESS THAN ¼ TEASPOON OF STEVIA OR OTHER INGREDIENTS: Fill the ¼ teaspoon measuring spoon with stevia or the ingredient to be measured, level it off with a knife, and then, using a dinner knife with a rounded end, cut the powder in the spoon in half and scrape half of it out of the spoon and back into its container to measure ⅛ teaspoon. If ¹⁄₁₆ teaspoon is required, cut the remaining ⅛ teaspoon in half again and scrape half of it out. Use what remains in the spoon. Or, use "Stevia Working Solution," page 207, to measure very small amounts of stevia.

The most accurate way to measure ⅛ teaspoon is to purchase a set of measuring spoons with a ⅛ teaspoon measure. Some sets even have a ¹⁄₁₆ teaspoon measure. Such sets may be found at cooking or department stores, or see "Sources," page 218 to order such a set from the King Arthur Flour Baker's Catalogue.

STIRRING TECHNIQUE and SPEED OF GETTING THINGS IN THE OVEN are also important in allergy baking. To make the quick breads, muffins, cakes, and cookies in this book successfully, there are a few things you must do correctly. Preheat your oven and prepare your baking pans before you do anything else. Mix the dry ingredients in a large bowl. Mix the liquids in a small bowl or measuring cup. Stir the liquid ingredients into the dry ingredients using folding as well as stirring motions to reach all parts of the bowl, but don't over-mix. It is all right to have a few small dry spots in your batter; stop while you're ahead. If you over-mix, the chemical reaction that makes gas which causes the dough rise will happen in the bowl instead of happening in the oven, and you will end up with very dense baked goods. After mixing, quickly put the batter into the pans and pop them into the oven.

THE EFFECT OF ALTITUDE ON BAKING: All of the recipes in this cookbook were developed at an altitude of about 5,000 feet but they have been used at lower altitudes without difficulty. Since they are not for delicate baked products, such as angel food cake, there is little chance of difficulty at lower altitudes. However, if you do encounter difficulty at a lower altitude, the following changes may be made in the recipe:

1. Increase the amount of baking soda and vitamin C crystals by ¼ of the amount called for in the recipe.

2. Decrease the amount of liquid by 2 to 3 tablespoons per cup of liquid called for.

3. Decrease the baking temperature by 25°F.

THE EFFECT OF ALTITUDE ON CANDY MAKING: When making candy at any altitude except sea level, you should check the boiling temperature of water in your area before starting. Bring a pan of water to a boil with a candy thermometer in the water but not touching the bottom of the pan. Let it boil for a few minutes; then read the temperature on the thermometer. Subtract this temperature from 212°F, then subtract this difference from the temperature your recipe says to cook the candy to at sea level.

References

Crook, William G. M.D., *Detecting Your Hidden Allergies*, Professional Books, Inc., Box 3246, Jackson, TN 38303, 1988.

Crook, William G., M.D., *The Yeast Connection*. Professional Books, Jackson, Tennessee, 38303, 1983. (Dr. Crook wrote a series of "Yeast Connection" books such as *The Yeast Connection and the Woman,* all of which are very useful books).

Crook, William G., M.D. and Marjorie Hurt Jones, R.N. *The Yeast Connection Cookbook*. Professional Books, Jackson, Tennessee, 38303, 1989.

Dumke, Nicolette M. *Easy Breadmaking for Special Diets*. Adapt Books, Allergy Adapt, Inc., 1877 Polk Avenue, Louisville, CO 80027, 1995; Revised edition, 2007.

Dumke, Nicolette M. *Easy Cooking for Special Diets: How to Cook for Weight Loss/Blood Sugar Control, Food Allergy, Heart Healthy, Diabetic and "Just Healthy" Diets – Even if You've Never Cooked Before*. Adapt Books, Allergy Adapt, Inc., 1877 Polk Avenue, Louisville, CO 80027, 2007.

Dumke, Nicolette M. *The Low Dose Immunotherapy Handbook: Recipes and Lifestyle Advice for Patients on LDA and EPD Treatment*. Adapt Books, Allergy Adapt, Inc., 1877 Polk Avenue, Louisville, CO 80027, 2003.

Dumke, Nicolette M. *The Ultimate Food Allergy Cookbook and Survival Guide*. Adapt Books, Allergy Adapt, Inc., 1877 Polk Avenue, Louisville, CO 80027, 2007.

Jones, Marjorie Hurt, R.N. *The Allergy Self-Help Cookbook*. Rodale Press, Emmaus, Pennsylvania, 1984, Revised edition, 2001.

Lewis, Sondra K. with Lonette Dietrich Blakely. *Allergy and Candida Cooking: Understanding and Implementing Plans for Healing*. Canary Connect Publications, 605 Holiday Road, Coralville, IA 52241-1016, 2006.

Randolph, Theron G., M.D. and Ralph W. Moss, Ph.D. *An Alternative Approach to Allergies*. Bantam Books, New York, 1980.

Appendix A: The Spelt-Wheat "Debate"

A great deal of confusion has risen concerning spelt recently. The United States Government is now requiring that foods be labeled to indicate whether they contain any of eight food allergens. As part of the implementation of this law, the FDA has declared that spelt is wheat. Although spelt and wheat are indeed closely related, they are two different species in the same genus. Spelt is *Triticum spelta* and wheat is *Triticum aestivum*. When asked why they had decided that spelt is wheat, an FDA official said that it was because spelt contains gluten. (They had no answer to the question of whether rye would also be considered wheat because it contains gluten, and indeed, bags of rye flour in the health food store are still labeled "wheat-free"). Spelt does indeed contain gluten and should not be eaten by anyone who is gluten-sensitive or has celiac disease, but the presence of gluten does not make spelt wheat.

The gluten in spelt behaves differently than the gluten in wheat in cooking. It is extremely difficult to make seitan from spelt. When making it from wheat, a process of soaking in hot water is used to remove the starch from the protein. If the same process is followed with spelt, the protein structure also dissolves in the hot water. Spelt seitan must be washed by hand very carefully under running cold water.

Because the gluten in spelt is more soluble than wheat gluten, making yeast bread with spelt is also different than making it with wheat. The individual gluten molecules join up more readily to form long chains and sheets that trap the gas produced by yeast. This means that it is possible to over-knead spelt bread. There are some bread machines that work quite well for wheat and even other allergy breads but are unacceptable for spelt bread because they knead so vigorously that they over-develop the gluten. See pages 32 to 33 of *Easy Breadmaking for Special Diets* (described on page 234) for recommendations about bread machines to use for making spelt bread.

It is possible that the greater solubility of spelt protein makes it easier to digest than wheat. Undoubtedly, most people have had much less prior exposure to spelt than to wheat resulting in less opportunity to become allergic to spelt. Whatever the reason, there are many people who suffer allergic reactions after eating wheat but do not react to spelt. (I have talked to hundreds of them). Restricting one's diet unnecessarily, as the new law will undoubtedly lead people to do, is counterproductive to good nutrition. Consult your doctor about your own food allergy test results and follow the diet recommended for you, but do not unnecessarily restrict spelt consumption based on the faulty logic behind the new government labeling requirements.

Appendix B: Table of Measurements

You may occasionally need to measure "unusual" amounts like ⅜ cup or ⅛ teaspoon. The easiest and most accurate way to do this is to have a liquid measuring cup with ⅛ cup markings, a set of dry measuring cups that contains a ⅛ cup measure, and a set of measuring spoons that has a ⅛ teaspoon. You can order such kitchen equipment from the King Arthur Flour Baker's Catalogue (See "Sources," page 218) but in the meantime, use this table to make your recipes work.

⅛ teaspoon	= ½ of your ¼ teaspoon measure	
⅜ teaspoon	= ¼ teaspoon + ⅛ teaspoon	
⅝ teaspoon	= ½ teaspoon + ⅛ teaspoon	
¾ teaspoon	= ½ teaspoon + ¼ teaspoon	
⅞ teaspoon	= ½ teaspoon + ¼ teaspoon + ⅛ teaspoon	
1 teaspoon	= ⅓ tablespoon	= ⅙ fluid ounce
1½ teaspoons	= ½ tablespoon	= ¼ fluid ounce
3 teaspoons	= 1 tablespoon	= ½ fluid ounce
½ tablespoon	= 1½ teaspoons	= ¼ fluid ounce
1 tablespoon	= 3 teaspoons	= ½ fluid ounce
2 tablespoons*	= ⅛ cup	= 1 fluid ounce
4 tablespoons	= ¼ cup	= 2 fluid ounces
5⅓ tablespoons	= ⅓ cup	= 2⅔ fluid ounces
8 tablespoons	= ½ cup	= 4 fluid ounces
16 tablespoons	= 1 cup	= 8 fluid ounces
⅛ cup	= 2 tablespoons*	= 1 fluid ounce
¼ cup	= 4 tablespoons	= 2 fluid ounces
⅜ cup	= ¼ cup + 2 tablespoons*	= 3 fluid ounces
⅝ cup	= ½ cup + 2 tablespoons*	= 5 fluid ounces
¾ cup	= ½ cup + ¼ cup	= 6 fluid ounces
⅞ cup	= ¾ cup + 2 tablespoons*	= 7 fluid ounces
	OR ½ cup + ¼ cup + 2 tablespoons*	
1 cup	= ½ pint	= 8 fluid ounces
1 pint	= 2 cups	= 16 fluid ounces
1 quart	= 4 cups OR 2 pints	= 32 fluid ounces
1 gallon	= 4 quarts	= 128 fluid ounces

*Note: In my experience, measuring tablespoons are all a little scanty of ¹⁄₁₆ cup, so 2 tablespoons is a little short of ⅛ cup. Therefore, if you need to measure, for example, ⅜ cup of liquid, it will probably be more accurate to "eyeball" an amount halfway between ¼ cup and ½ cup than to use ¼ cup plus two tablespoons.

Sources of Special Foods and Products

This is a listing of the manufacturers of many of the special foods and products used in the recipes in this book. It includes mail-order and Internet sources of these products. Your health food store can order foods from these sources, or your can order directly from many of them yourself. Sources are not listed for all of the special foods used in this book because many of them are available at most health food stores.

BUFFALO AND GAME MEATS:

Game Sales International, Inc.
P.O. Box 5314
2456 E. 13th Street
Loveland, CO 80537
(303) 667-4090 or (800) 729-2090

CAROB CHIPS, UNSWEETENED:

NOW Natural Foods *(order from them through your health food store)*
395 S. Glen Ellyn Road
Bloomingdale, IL 60108
(800) 283-3500
www.nowfoods.com

(It has become more difficult to find milk-free carob chips recently, but you can make your own. See the recipe on page 206).

COCONUT, FINELY SHREDDED UNSWEETENED:

Jerry's Nut House, Inc.
2101 Humboldt Street
Denver, CO 80205
(303) 861-2262

COCONUT MILK, UNSWEETENED:

Asian Food Grocer
131 West Harris Avenue
San Francisco, CA 94080
(888) 482-2742 or (650) 873-7600
www.asianfoodgrocer.com

DAIRY PRODUCTS (ALTERNATIVE):

Goat Cheese
Mt. Sterling Cheese Corporation
P.O. Box 103
Mt. Sterling, WI 54645
(608) 734-3151
http://grantcounty.org/visitor/farm.html

Goat Milk
Meyenberg Goat Milk
Jackson-Mitchell
P.O. Box 934
Turlock, CA 95381
(800) 891-GOAT
www.meyenberg.com

Sheep Cheese and Yogurt
Hollow Road Farms
Old Chatham Sheepherding Co.
155 Shaker Museum Road
Old Chatham, NY 12136
(518) 794-7333
(888) SHEEP60
www.blacksheepcheese.com

FLAVORINGS, NATURAL, CORN- AND ALCOHOL-FREE:

The Spicery Shoppe
1525 Brook Drive
Downers Grove, IL 60515
(630) 932-8100 or (800) 323-1301

FLOUR and GRAIN PRODUCTS:

MANY TYPES OF FLOUR – RYE,
BUCKWHEAT, WHITE RICE, BROWN
RICE, KAMUT, ETC.

Arrowhead Mills
The Hain Celestial Group, Inc.
4600 Sleepytime Drive
Boulder, CO 80301
(800) 434-4246
www.hain-celestial.com

MANY TYPES OF FLOUR – POTATO
FLOUR, TAPIOCA, ARROWROOT,
TEFF, ETC.

Bob's Red Mill
Natural Foods, Inc.
5209 S.E. International Way
Milwaukie, OR 97222
(503) 654-3215
(800) 349-2173
www.bobsredmill.com

ALMOND FLOUR OR MEAL:

The King Arthur Flour Baker's Catalogue
P.O. Box 876
Norwich, Vermont 05055
(800) 827-6836
www.kingarthurflour.com

AMARANTH FLOUR, WHOLE GRAIN,
OR PUFFED CEREAL:

Nu-World Amaranth, Inc.
P.O. Box 2202
Naperville, IL 60567
(630) 369-6819
www.nuworldfoods.com

CASSAVA MEAL (ALSO CALLED
MANIOC FLOUR):

Sundial Herbal Products
3609 Boston Post Road
Bronx, NY 10466
(718) 798-3962
www.sundialherbs.com/html
     /other_products.html

CHESTNUT FLOUR:

**Gold Mine Natural Food
  Company**
7805 Arjons Drive
San Diego, CA 92126
(800) 475-FOOD
www.goldminenaturalfood.com

MILO AND MILLET FLOUR:

Purcell Mountain Farms
HCR 62 Box 284
Moyie Springs, ID 83845
866-440-2326
www.purcellmountainfarms.com

QUINOA FLOUR:

The Quinoa Corporation
Post Office Box 279
Gardena, CA. 90248
(310) 217-8125
www.quinoa.net

SPELT FLOUR (PURITY FOODS
WHOLE AND WHITE SPELT):

Purity Foods, Inc.
2871 W. Jolly Road
Okemos, Michigan 48864
(517) 351-0231
www.purityfoods.com

TUBER FLOURS (sweet potato, cassava,
malanga, true yam, water chestnut, etc.):

Special Foods
9207 Shotgun Court
Springfield, VA 22153
(703) 644-0991
www.specialfoods.com
(Water chestnut flour may also be found
at Oriental grocery stores).

MUSTARD, MILD DRY:

Penzeys Spices
P.O. Box 933
Muskego, WI 53150
(800) 741-7787
www.penzeys.com

PARCHMENT PAPER, MEASURING SPOONS, ETC:

**The King Arthur Flour Baker's
  Catalogue**
P.O. Box 876
Norwich, Vermont 05055
(800) 827-6836
www.kingarthurflour.com

PASTA

**Bean or buckwheat pasta
Eden Foods, Inc.**
701 Tecumseh Road
Clinton, MI 49236
(517) 456-7424
(888) 424-EDEN (3336)
www.edenfoods.com

Quinoa pasta
The Quinoa Corporation
Post Office Box 279
Gardena, CA. 90248
(310) 217-8125
www.quinoa.net

Rice pasta
Ener-G Foods, Inc.
P. O. Box 84487
Seattle, WA 98124
(206) 767-6660
(800) 331-5222
www.ener-g.com

Spelt pasta
Purity Foods, Inc.
2871 W. Jolly Road
Okemos, MI 48864
(517) 351-9231
www.purityfoods.com

Uncommon pastas (amaranth, barley, lentil, millet, milo, oat, quinoa, rye, sweet potato, cassava, malanga, yam)
Special Foods
9207 Shotgun Court
Springfield, VA 22153
(703) 644-0991
www.specialfoods.com

SWEETENERS

Date Sugar
NOW Natural Foods *(order through your health food store)*
395 S. Glen Ellyn Road
Bloomingdale, IL 60108
(800) 283-3500
www.nowfoods.com

FOS
Flora Inc.
P.O. Box 73
805 E. Badger Road
Lynden, WA 98264
www.florahealth.com
(Visit this website to find a health food store where you can get FOS).

Fruit Sweet™, Grape Sweet™, Pear Sweet™
Wax Orchards, Inc.
22744 Wax Orchards Road S.W.
Vashon Island, WA 98070
(800) 634-6132
www.waxorchards.com

Stevia
NOW Natural Foods *(order through your health food store)*
395 S. Glen Ellyn Road
Bloomingdale, IL 60108
(800) 283-3500
www.nowfoods.com

Sugar Alcohols (Xylitol, Sorbitol, Erythritol)
NOW Natural Foods *(order through your health food store)*
395 S. Glen Ellyn Road
Bloomingdale, IL 60108
(800) 283-3500
www.nowfoods.com

THICKENERS:

Guar Gum
Bob's Red Mill
Natural Foods, Inc.
5209 S.E. International Way
Milwaukie, OR 97222
(503) 654-3215
(800) 349-2173
www.bobsredmill.com

Methylcellulose
Ener-G Foods, Inc.
P. O. Box 84487
Seattle, WA 98124
(206) 767-6660
(800) 325-9788
www.ener-g.com

TORTILLAS, SPELT OR WHOLE SPELT:

Rudi's Organic Bakery
3300 Walnut, Unit C
Boulder, CO 80301
(303) 447-0495
(877) 293-0876
www.rudisbakery.com

VITAMIN C CRYSTALS, UNBUFFERED, CORN-FREE, FOR BAKING AND SALADS:

N.E.E.D.S
6666 Manlius Center Road
East Syracuse, NY 13057
1-800-634-1380
www.needs.com

YEAST, regular and quick-rise, corn, gluten- and preservative-free:

Red Star Yeast and SAF Yeast
Universal Foods Corporation
Consumer Service Center
433 E. Michigan Street
Milwaukee, WI 53202
(414) 271-6755
www.redstaryeast.com

The Red Star Yeast company is a great information source but does not sell direct to consumers. To purchase Red Star™ or SAF™ yeast (including SAF Gold™), contact:

The King Arthur Flour Baker's Catalogue
P.O. Box 876
Norwich, Vermont 05055
(800) 827-6836
www.kingarthurflour.com

Index of the Recipes by Major Grain or Grain Alternative Used

"It's barley day. What can I eat?" This index will give you an easy way to answer a question that occurs commonly on a rotation diet by listing the recipes in this book according to the major grain or grain alternative that they contain. The recipes that do not contain a grain or grain alternative, such as those for most of the main dishes, vegetables, ice cream, etc., are not listed in this index but can be found by name in the "General Index," page 226. Arrowroot, tapioca flour, and water chestnut flour are used as binders or thickeners in many recipes in this book. They are included in the listing below only when they are the main flour-type ingredient in a recipe and could be rotated separately.

General Index

Informational sections appear in italics.
Recipes appear in standard type.

Books to Help You with Your Special Diet

***Allergy Cooking With Ease* (Revised Edition).** This classic all-purpose allergy cookbook was out of print and now is making a comeback in a revised edition. It includes all the old favorite recipes of the first edition plus many new recipes and new foods. It contains over 300 recipes for baked goods, main dishes, soups, salads, vegetables, ethnic dishes, desserts, and more. Informational sections of the book are also totally updated, including the extensive "Sources" section.

ISBN 1-887624-10-4 or 978-1-887624-10-7 . . . . $19.95

The Ultimate Food Allergy Cookbook and Survival Guide: How to Cook with Ease for Food Allergies and Recover Good Health gives you everything you need to survive and recover from food allergies. It contains medical information about the diagnosis of food allergies, health problems that can be caused by food allergies, and your options for treatment. The book includes a rotation diet that is free from common food allergens such as wheat, milk, eggs, corn, soy, yeast, beef, legumes, citrus fruits, potatoes, tomatoes, and more. Instructions are given on how to personalize the standard rotation diet to meet your individual needs and fit your food preferences. It contains 500 recipes that can be used with (or without) the diet. Extensive reference sections include a listing of commercially prepared foods for allergy diets and sources for special foods, services, and products.

ISBN 1-887624-08-2 or 978-1-887624-08-4 . . . . $24.95

Easy Breadmaking for Special Diets contains over 200 recipes for allergy, heart healthy, low fat, low sodium, yeast-free, controlled carbohydrate, diabetic, celiac, and low calorie diets. It includes recipes for breads of all kinds, bread and tortilla based main dishes, and desserts. Use your bread machine, food processor, mixer, or electric tortilla maker to make the bread YOU need quickly and easily.

Revised Edition – ISBN 1-887624-11-2 or 978-1-887624-11-4 . . . .$19.95

Original Edition – ISBN 1-887624-02-3 . . . . $14.95

Easy Cooking for Special Diets: How to Cook for Weight Loss/Blood Sugar Control, Food Allergy, Heart Healthy, Diabetic and "Just Healthy" Diets – Even if You've Never Cooked Before. This book contains everything you need to know to stay on your diet plus 265 recipes complete with nutritional analyses and diabetic exchanges. It also includes basics such as how to grocery shop, equip your kitchen, handle food safely, time management, information on nutrition, and sources of special foods.

ISBN 1-887624-09-0 or 978-1-887624-09-1 . . . . $24.95

The Low Dose Immunotherapy Handbook: Recipes and Lifestyle Tips for Patients on LDA and EPD Treatment gives 80 recipes for patients on low dose immunotherapy treatment for their food allergies. It also includes organizational information to help you get ready for your shots.

ISBN: 1-887624-07-4 or 978-1-887624-07-7 . . . . $9.95

How to Cope With Food Allergies When You're Short on Time is a booklet of time saving tips and recipes to help you stick to your allergy diet with the least amount of time and effort.

$4.95 or FREE with the order of two other books on these pages

You can order these books on-line by going to www.food-allergy.org or by mail using the order form on the page 236 or 238.

Mail your order form to:

Allergy Adapt, Inc.
1877 Polk Avenue
Louisville, CO 80027

Online orders can also be placed with Amazon.com at www.amazon.com.

Order Form

Ship to:

Name:

Street address:

City, State, ZIP code:

Phone number (for questions about order):

Item	Quantity	Price	Total
*Allergy Cooking with Ease**		$19.95	
*The Ultimate Food Allergy Cookbook & Survival Guide**		$24.95	
*Easy Breadmaking for Special Diets** – Original Edition		$14.95	
Revised Edition		$19.95	
*Easy Cooking for Special Diets**		$24.95	
The Low Dose Immunotherapy Handbook		$9.95	
How to Cope with Food Allergies When You're Short on Time		$4.95 or **FREE**	
Order any TWO of the first five books above and get *How to Cope* **FREE!**	Subtotal		
	Shipping – See chart below		
	Colorado residents add 4.1% sales tax		
	Total		

Shipping:

    IF YOU ARE ORDERING JUST ONE BOOK, FOR SHIPPING ADD:

        $4.00 for any one of the first four (starred*) books above.

        $2.00 for either of the last two (non-starred) books above.

    TO ORDER MORE THAN ONE BOOK, FOR SHIPPING ADD:

        $6.00 for up to three starred* and two non-starred books

        $9.00 for four starred* and up to two non-starred books

Call 303-666-8253 if you have questions about shipping calculations or large quantity orders. Mail this order form and your check to the address on the previous page. Thanks for your order!

On the opposite side of this page
is extra mail-order form
to tear out and
give to a friend or use yourself.

Mail your order form to:

Allergy Adapt, Inc.
1877 Polk Avenue
Louisville, CO 80027

For more information or
to order eBooks or
BARGAIN editions of
these books, go to:

www.food-allergy.org.

Online orders can also be placed with
Amazon.com at
www.amazon.com.

Order Form

Ship to:

Name: _____

Street address: _____

City, State, ZIP code: _____

Phone number (for questions about order): _____

Item	Quantity	Price	Total
*Allergy Cooking with Ease**		$19.95	
*The Ultimate Food Allergy Cookbook & Survival Guide**		$24.95	
*Easy Breadmaking for Special Diets** – Original Edition		$14.95	
Revised Edition		$19.95	
*Easy Cooking for Special Diets**		$24.95	
The Low Dose Immunotherapy Handbook		$9.95	
How to Cope with Food Allergies When You're Short on Time		$4.95 or **FREE**	
Order any TWO of the first five books above and get *How to Cope* **FREE!**	Subtotal		
	Shipping – See chart below		
	Colorado residents add 4.1% sales tax		
	Total		

Shipping:

    IF YOU ARE ORDERING JUST ONE BOOK, FOR SHIPPING ADD:

        $4.00 for any one of the first four (starred*) books above.

        $2.00 for either of the last two (non-starred) books above.

    TO ORDER MORE THAN ONE BOOK, FOR SHIPPING ADD:

        $6.00 for up to three starred* and two non-starred books

        $9.00 for four starred* and up to two non-starred books

Call 303-666-8253 if you have questions about shipping calculations or large quantity orders.
Mail this order form and your check to the address on the previous page. Thanks for your order!